George Eliot and the Politics of National Inheritance

George Eliot and the Politics of National Inheritance

Bernard Semmel

New York   Oxford
OXFORD UNIVERSITY PRESS
1994

To Stuart

Oxford University Press

Oxford   New York   Toronto
Delhi   Bombay   Calcutta   Madras   Karachi
Kuala Lumpur   Singapore   Hong Kong   Tokyo
Nairobi   Dar es Salaam   Cape Town
Melbourne   Auckland   Madrid

and associated companies in
Berlin   Ibadan

Published by Oxford University Press, Inc.,
200 Madison Avenue, New York, New York 10016

Oxford is a registered trademark of Oxford University Press

Library of Congress Cataloging-in-Publication Data
Semmel, Bernard.
George Eliot and the politics of national inheritance / Bernard Semmel.
p. cm.   Includes bibliographical references and index.
ISBN 0–19–508567–1
ISBN 0–19–508657–0 (pbk.)
1. Eliot, George, 1819–1880—Political and social views.
2. Politics and literature—Great Britain—History—19th century.
3. Political fiction, English—History and criticism.
4. National characteristics, English, in literature.
I. Title. PR4692.P64 1994   823'.8—dc20
93–13641

1 3 5 7 9 8 6 4 2

Printed in the United States of America
on acid-free paper

Preface

Readers today, like those over a century ago, have had quite different opinions concerning the complicated politics of George Eliot. Eliot certainly cannot be placed mechanically in one or another of the usual political camps. Her tangled relationship to the ideas of Auguste Comte and the Positivists has long been a subject of controversy. It seemed to me that the meanings Eliot gave to the idea of inheritance—a frequent subject of her fiction and of her intellectual journalism and correspondence—might prove useful in understanding her outlook.

Intermittently, over a number of years, I have tried to work out the implications of these ideas, a pursuit that added to my pleasure in reading and rereading Eliot's writings. I have received useful suggestions from a number of people, among them a former colleague, Richard A. Levine. My most considerable debt is to Robert K. Webb, whose wide knowledge of history and literature and perceptive editorial judgment have saved me from a number of errors.

I should also like to thank Nancy Lane and Henry Krawitz, and Philip G. Halthaus of Oxford University Press, for their assistance in preparing this volume for publication.

My wife Maxine's enthusiasm for George Eliot's fiction first led me beyond Eliot's better known novels. I am grateful for her loving help and encouragement at every stage. To my son, Stuart, my obligation is both professional and personal, benefiting as I have from his grasp of the subject, his sense of style, and his sustaining friendship. The book is dedicated to him.

Stony Brook, N.Y.   Bernard Semmel
May 1993

Contents

George Eliot and the Politics
of National Inheritance

Prologue

At the time of her death at age sixty-one in 1880, George Eliot was mourned by her admirers, who compared her accomplishments to those of Sophocles, Dante, and Goethe. Justin McCarthy, a contemporary Irish journalist, described the veneration of Eliot by much of the liberal reading public as "a kind of cult, a kind of worship."[1] Lord Acton, one of the most respected historians of the period, pronounced her "the greatest genius among women known to history."[2] In his classic portrait of Victorian England, written more than a half century later, the historian G. M. Young observed that in carrying to an agnostic age "the Evangelical faith in duty and renunciation," George Eliot had fixed her place "in the history of ideas." Young added that she had been chief among those who "transposed [ethics] from a Christian to a Stoic key" and had thereby almost single-handedly "saved us from the moral catastrophe which might have been expected to follow upon the waning of religious conviction."[3]

The reverence for Eliot as a writer spanned nearly a generation during her lifetime. Very soon after her death, however, her literary reputation went into rapid decline. In the past thirty years the critical view of her works has once again become favorable—almost worshipful in some quarters—in part because of the women's movement, which applauded Eliot's achievement and her defiance of sexual conventions while regretting her failure to take a more feminist position.[4] Even when the judgment of her talents was at a low ebb, certain of her works—*Silas Marner, The Mill on the Floss,* and *Adam Bede*—were required reading in American and

British secondary schools. This reading-list status had the consequence of further diminishing the appreciation of her work both by the unwilling students and by serious critics (some of whom had been reluctant adolescent readers in their earlier years) who saw her writings as redolent of Victorian sentimentality, dated in style, and outmoded in opinions. Although Eliot's *Middlemarch* continued to be cited as one of the more estimable novels of the century, it was, like Tolstoy's *War and Peace,* more praised than read, often set aside to be taken up at some indefinite time in the future. Critics who valued *Middlemarch* considered Eliot's last novel, *Daniel Deronda,* a failure and wondered why she had troubled to write so inartistic a novel as *Romola,* a historical romance set in Renaissance Florence. Her epic drama of fifteenth-century Spain, *The Spanish Gypsy,* had experienced a brief period of celebrity at the time of its publication but was no longer read.

Yet all her fiction had been widely welcomed and appreciated by her contemporaries. Eliot had aimed not only to satisfy her own aspirations as an artist but to suit the popular taste. She began her career as a translator of scholarly and philosophical works, an editor, and a writer for intellectual quarterlies. She turned to writing novels when nearly forty, on the advice of her lover, the playwright, critic, and philosopher George Henry Lewes, with whom she enjoyed a close intellectual companionship. Lewes saw her novelistic talent as a means of supporting their household, given his much less remunerative pursuits, as well as providing for the unfaithful wife he was unable to divorce and for the children of that marriage. Needing to earn money, Eliot chose to write romances—mostly historical romances— which Victorian readers were eager to buy. The novels of the founder of the genre, Sir Walter Scott, and those of his successor, Edward Bulwer-Lytton, had proved immensely popular. Eliot herself was among Scott's admirers. She wrote a friend that "I worship Scott so devoutly,"[5] and Lewes declared that "Scott is to her an almost sacred name."[6]

Sir Walter Scott's tales of eighteenth-century Scotland chronicled the great transformation—one common to all of western Europe—from a traditional to a modern society. One usually thinks of historical romance as set in the distant past, like Scott's crusader tales, of which *Ivanhoe* is the best known, Bulwer-Lytton's *Last Days of Pompei* or *Rienzi,* or Eliot's own *Romola.* But Scott's first historical novel, *Waverley,* and such successors as *Guy Mannering* and *The Antiquary,* described events no more distant from the time of their writing than those in *Adam Bede* or *Silas Marner* were when Eliot wrote these works. All of Eliot's novels but one—*Daniel Deronda,* with its setting in the 1860s—were historical romances set at least a generation earlier.

Eliot, like Scott, was acutely aware of the great changes in society, with the preindustrial era giving way to the modern era, as were the leading nineteenth-century social theorists. The French philosopher to whom Lewes believed himself most indebted, the Positivist Auguste Comte, considered the most profound transformation to be an intellectual evolution from the theological and metaphysical stages to a scientific one. The sociologist and philosopher Herbert Spencer, Eliot's closest male friend after Lewes, saw it as a passage from a feudal and militant society to a peaceful, industrial society. The legal historian Sir Henry Maine pictured the coming of the modern as a movement from the traditional "status" of a hierarchical society, where every man and woman occupied a position established at birth, to the "contract" of modern society, where privileges and obligations were determined by individual worth and freely constructed arrangements. A later German sociologist, Ferdinand Tönnies, spoke of the traditional order as a collective community, or *Gemeinschaft,* and the modern as an individualistic, commercial society, or *Gesellschaft.* We shall see that Eliot, like Scott before her, at times had some difficulty choosing between the two.[7] A nostalgic feeling for a lost heritage pervaded the views of a great many of those who, on the whole, welcomed the modern world—and this sentiment may well have contributed to the popularity of Eliot's fiction.

In introducing *Ivanhoe* in 1817, Scott wrote that he himself had experienced "the very recent existence of that state of society" which echoed the medieval setting of his novel. But in a generation "an infinite change" had come upon the country, and Scotland had left behind much of its traditional, quasi-medieval institutions and manners to adopt those of England's commercial society. A contemporary Englishman, Scott wrote, could no longer imagine that "the complete influence of feudal tyranny once extended over the neighbouring village, where the attorney is now a man of more importance than the lord of the manor" ("Dedicatory Epistle"). Yet for inhabitants of English country towns and villages (the traditional patriarchal communities in which lords of the manor exercised a predominant and pervasive influence though no longer a "feudal tyranny"), the old ways were very much alive before the 1830s, and Eliot would focus her attention upon the final decades of this change.

The necessary movement from the traditional community to modern society became a tenet of the liberal faith. Such a change reassured the nineteenth-century middle classes that their social order would supplant the aristocracy and gentry as the preeminent force influencing the nation's policymakers. Bourgeois values would overwhelm feudal values, and merchants, industrialists, and professional men would claim the power traditionally held by landholders, the military, and the clergy. The "intellectual classes," as the representatives of the modern constellation were described by the Victorian historian H. T. Buckle, would supplant the feudalists, who sat on inherited acres and sought to perpetuate wars and superstition from which they alone profited.[8] In modern society achievement and individual merit would triumph over the false values an unscientific era had attached to birth. This message underlay the plots of a number of Eliot's novels and helped to make them so attractive to liberal Victorians. Yet we shall see that there was another, essentially contradictory, message in her novels, one more usually associated with the conventional themes of romance.

The theme of inheritance played an important part in Eliot's novels, as it did in so many of the conventional plots of Victorian fiction. Her novels discussed inheritance in two principal forms. The first addressed the common meaning of the term, the passing on of goods and property to heirs, which she saw as emblematic of family affections and obligations, a tie binding parents and children. Especially in her later writings she stressed the second, more metaphoric form, namely, the inheritance of the nation's culture and historical traditions. We shall see that in virtually every part of Eliot's thinking and writing, both before and after she turned to fiction in the late 1850s, the idea of inheritance is prominent as naked fact or metaphor, or both.

She wrestled with these two different views of inheritance, each governed by its distinctive moral system. In what was for her time a modern, individualistic argument concerning generational rebellion, she declared that while a parent was obliged to will his goods to his children, a child, as an independent, self-directed being, was free to reject such a bequest and the duties accompanying it. In *Silas Marner* and *Felix Holt* Eliot examined the circumstances that would permit, even morally compel, an heir to reject a legacy, thereby disinheriting herself or himself. This position contended with the more traditional, *Gemeinschaft* view that it was morally necessary not only for a parent to bequeath but for an heir to accept a legacy and the obligations it incurred. (The latter, of course, was the more usual attitude of the conventional nineteenth-century British romance.) In Eliot's later works—in *The Spanish Gypsy* and *Daniel Deronda,* for example—we shall see Eliot's insistence on the national inheritance, its distinctive ethos and network of traditions, as an heirloom that could not be forsaken by a person of principle.

In her mature thinking, this second, metaphoric form was joined to elements of the first. Eliot had become convinced that the *Gesellschaft* values of individualism and cosmopolitanism that prevailed in British liberal circles would impair both family affection and social cohesion. Only a nation, a society that she saw as based on filial sentiment, perceived national kinship, and common historical traditions—one that linked past and future in the same way in which the transmission of property from parents to children linked the generations—could provide a realistic foundation for communal solidarity. These ties would make it possible for an individual to transcend selfish egoism and to feel a deep sympathetic concern, first toward his kin and then toward the extended family of the nation. Any more ambitious ascent from egoism to harmonious identification with all of mankind, she came to believe, could not be managed until a very long time in the future.

The leading social and political creeds of the nineteenth century were antinational in their thrust. These doctrines frequently proclaimed abstract, uniform laws derived from a deterministic social science that ignored, along with individual differences, what Eliot saw as important variations in national character. In her youth Eliot had felt drawn to such ideological thinking, but she was eventually persuaded that attempts to realize these abstract systems would be dangerous to liberty and threatened to impose a repressive authoritarian state. Against the ideological models erected by liberal intellectuals, she posed what I will call an almost Burkean "politics of national inheritance."

This study will attempt to uncover Eliot's politics of inheritance, and, in so far as possible, connect these views with the events of her own life. It will examine her position on philosophical/theological questions (notably, free will and determinism), linked as these ideas were with the politics of inheritance, and attempt to put Eliot in the context of the nineteenth-century school of German philosophers like Strauss and Feuerbach as well as that of the leading English conservative writers, whose views were much like her own. And it will explore her relationship to Auguste Comte's Positivist system, with which she is frequently identified, and which, despite its many curious beliefs and practices, played a considerable part in nineteenth-century English and continental thinking and culture.

Some of the leading thinkers of Eliot's time—Comte among them—constructed social and political ideologies that aimed at achieving on earth what the religions of earlier centuries had postponed for heaven. Indeed, a number of observers have called the nineteenth century an age of ideology. Intellectuals, particularly those of the younger generation, were (as they still are) most frequently the chief targets and carriers of ideologies. Enthusiasts, in revolt against the established order, these intellectuals saw themselves as the harbingers of a new polity and a new morality that would sweep centuries of corruption into the dustbin of history. Their doctrines usually provided an interpretation of the historical process that seemed not merely to make sense of a complex past, but dared to predict the future, frequently portrayed as the final state at whose threshold the present generation stood; and though the culmination of the process was certain, these ideologues called upon those to whom history had assigned the role of the elite to contribute their efforts to produce the inevitable outcome. This elite would lead the spiritually and materially oppressed to the promised land. The warming bonds of sympathy and community which modern commercial society had worn away would then be restored. The function of these secular religions was to portray this mission and its paradisiacal goal, both sanctified by history and certain of fulfillment.[9]

The nineteenth-century utopias took different forms, but for many of their prophets the communities established by such religious enthusiasts as the fifteenth-century Italian reformer Savonarola, the sixteenth-century Protestant rebel Calvin, and the regicide seventeenth-century English Puritan Cromwell became models. All had attempted to create republics of virtue. This had been Robespierre's grand purpose during the French Revolution and became that of the leading shapers of ideologies—Saint-Simonians, Comtists, and Marxists—of the following century. Some of these ideologues, in translating theological into political doctrine, formulated intellectual systems as obscurantist and narrow in conception, and often as perilous to society, as the dogmas of the age of religion during the worst periods of sectarian persecution.

Comte's doctrines greatly influenced the ideas of the social and intellectual circle in which Eliot and Lewes moved. Comte and his followers saw their ideological rivals as utopians who failed to appreciate how much the past had molded the present. (Engels, similarly, distinguished in this way between his and Marx's "scientific socialism" and the "utopian socialism" of the followers of Robert Owen, Saint-Simon, and Fourier.) While these visionaries had rejected the inheritance of the past, believing all of it to be bad, Comte proclaimed that he treasured it, and insisted on its continuing influence. He declared not only that "the dead rule the living," but, following the conservative French political theorist de Maistre, also argued that earlier centuries, particularly those of Europe's medieval period, had much to teach the society of the future. In reality, however, Comte's detailed construction of the future Positivist state, and creation of a Positivist religion replete with its peculiar liturgies and rituals, also broke most links with what had preceded. For the Comtists, a knowledge of the laws of a scientific sociology, which Comte believed himself to have uncovered, would enable all men and women to free themselves from the theological and metaphysical (and, implicitly, historical) burdens of the past.

What helped to attract George Eliot to Comte was his often repeated conviction of the importance of history, the heritage of the past. Eliot was drawn at first to what she saw as this antiutopian posture. But she later came to recognize that Comte was, nonetheless, a utopian. And she knew she could not share the ideal of the authoritarian society that Comte and his followers proposed—for her a dystopia, as we shall see her fiction would make clear.

For over a century there has been contention among commentators concerning the significance of Eliot's attraction to Comtism—indeed, to what extent she may be called a Comtist at all. Eliot's 1851 article in the *Westminster Review,* "The Progress of the Intellect," certainly bore all the marks of what may be called the modish Comtism of that quarterly,[10] but many of these ideas were the commonplaces of contemporary discourse among liberal intellectuals. (A biographer of Harriet Martineau has noted that Martineau, who abridged and translated Comte's *Cours de philosophie positive* for an English audience, and consequently was erroneously regarded as a Comtist, had already expressed many of Comte's leading ideas in the 1830s, before her supposed master had published his work.[11]) Eliot's biographer G. S. Haight has doubted any real doctrinal connection between her and the Comtists, noting the remark of a leader of the London Positivists, Richard Congreve, that "she is not nor ever has been more than by her acceptance of the general idea of Humanity a Positivist."[12] A student of European positivism has seen Lewes, though not Eliot, as a virtually complete disciple of Comte; but Lewes saw himself as joining the philosopher and political theorist John Stuart Mill in accepting Comte's philosophy and his philosophy of history but not the politics and religious system outlined in Comte's later works.[13] A historian of literature has identified Eliot's "'conservative-reforming' impulse" with that of Comte, but stressed that this attempt at reconciling order and progress was characteristic of many thinkers of the century, not merely of the Comtists.[14]

Many of Eliot's contemporaries were quite uncertain concerning her relationship to Comte's system. In his *Recollections,* the journalist, essayist, and Liberal statesman John Morley, who, like Mill, praised the philosophical and historical ideas of Comte's *Cours de philosophie positive* but not the politics or religion of Comte's later volumes of the *Système de politique positive,* saw Eliot and Lewes as accepting Positivist doctrines without being formal members of the group.[15] The journalist Justin McCarthy described Eliot's and Lewes's attachment to the Positivist circle, but noted that thousands of Englishmen were, like Mill, adherents of Comte's philosophy of history as a "grand, scientific, inexorable truth," but were not prepared to take on the Comtian religion.[16] The American Hegelian Josiah Royce, an admirer of Eliot, writing in 1881 after Eliot's death, saw her as owing more to Strauss and Feuerbach (and to the seventeenth-century Dutch-Jewish philosopher Spinoza) than to Comte, seeing Comte as having contributed only the theory of the three historical stages to Eliot's thinking; Royce found no evidence in her writings of any sympathy with "the rituals and the observances, the fanatical solemnity, and the pharasaical vanity of that sect."[17]

On the other hand, Lord Acton, most curiously, insisted that Eliot, unlike Lewes, revered not so much the philosophical Comte but the "dogmatising and emotional" Comte of the *Politique,* and that this attachment was a "yoke" that she never shook off. On what seems quite insubstantial evidence—Eliot's, like Comte's, love of Thomas à Kempis's *Imitation of Christ* and her having gone to hear Cardinal Manning preach—the Catholic Acton imputed to Eliot a strong attraction to the Catholic church, thus in circular fashion explaining Eliot's supposed love of Comte's pseudo-Catholic rituals and liturgy.[18] Acton also noted the emotional and intellectual sacrifices Eliot had been prepared to make for a Comtian Lewes because they did not appear "too high a price for the happiness of a home." He described Lewes as "a boisterous iconoclast," of the kind represented in John Chapman's free thinking *Westminster Review* (which Eliot helped to edit) and in the Voltairean writings of the historians H. T. Buckle and W. E. H. Lecky, with which Eliot would express little sympathy. Eliot held her own against Lewes on the values of the religious life, Acton concluded, but yielded to him on other issues: "She became indulgent towards sentiments she disapproved and appreciated the reason and strength of opinions repugnant to her."[19]

Herbert Spencer believed that Eliot was especially attached to Comte's religion of humanity, but he seems to have meant by the term those hopes for the sympathetic bonding of all men that were equally the aspirations of Feuerbach's religion of humanity, of which she proclaimed herself an admirer, and not Comte's ritualistic sect.[20] And Benjamin Jowett, the Oxford classicist, reported that Eliot had told him "that she was never a Comtist, but as they were a poor and unfortunate sect, she would never renounce them."[21] What bound her to them, she seemed to be saying, was friendship, not ideological commitment.

The future Fabian socialist Beatrice Webb may have consciously pictured herself as the Dorothea of *Middlemarch,* as a nineteenth-century Saint Theresa, when she observed that during the middle decades of that century, "in England, the impulse of self-subordinating service was transferred, consciously and overtly, from God to man." She traced this conception of moral duty to Comte, who dominated "the particular social and intellectual environment in which I lived." She read the works of Comte, Lewes, Mill, and "above all, the novels of George Eliot," which were "eagerly read and discussed in the family circle"—a circle which both the Comtian barrister and man of letters Frederic Harrison and the anti-Comtian Herbert Spencer regularly visited. Webb especially valued Eliot's novels for their depiction of a woman's need for "emotive thought," and not merely "one side of our nature, the purely rational."[22]

George Eliot's relationship to Positivist doctrines was complex. Eliot was torn between an attraction to certain Comtian views, which she shared with both Lewes and members of the London Positivist circle, notably Maria Congreve, the wife of the Positivist leader, for whom she had warm feelings, and her determined resistance to Comte's authoritarianism and to the ideological formulas to which Comtists like Frederic Harrison wished to subject her. She displayed marks of friendship with members of the Positivist circle, which led to her being identified as a Positivist by much of the British public, but kept her distance, which was understood by the Positivists themselves as an indication that, although sympathetic, she was not of their number.[23]

There was, we see, both attraction and repulsion. Eliot certainly approved Comte's stress on a sense of moral duty based on feelings of sympathetic altruism. Her dictum that feeling was more important than thought appeared as almost a restatement of what Comte called his "fundamental doctrine," a political as well as a philosophical one, namely "that the Heart preponderates over the Head," and moreover that it ought to. In a Positivist society, Comte declared, the chief focus would be on man's moral, not his intellectual, nature.[24] She welcomed Comte's often proclaimed appreciation of the important role played by the nation-state and the historical past, but she distrusted Comtian sociology, with its contradictory depiction of a mankind whose uniform nature transcended national boundaries and culture. Similarly, Comte's cosmopolitan religion of humanity, she believed, could not compare with national feeling in creating the sympathetic bonds essential to social stability. In *Romola,* she rejected the authoritarianism of Comte's own projected utopia, itself a break with past history. She studiously avoided the even greater disassociation with the past envisioned by many of her friends among Comte's English followers who in the 1860s and 1870s advocated a revolutionary, class-warfare doctrine. In *Middlemarch* she defended England's policy of compromise, an essential principle of the national political tradition.

Finally, in her later works—*The Spanish Gypsy* and *Daniel Deronda*—she wrote of the central importance of nation or race, and the national inheritance one was morally obligated not to reject but to take up and fulfill. (The Jews, at least as represented by such opponents of assimilation as Mordecai and Daniel Deronda in her last novel, became for her a model to counter the cosmopolitanism of liberal Englishmen.) This program, one may argue, constituted still another ideology.

By the time she wrote her novels, Eliot saw herself as an opponent of ideological thinking, while continuing to be aware of the seductive charms of doctrinal creeds for vulnerable intellectuals. In her novella *Janet's Repentance,* in a possible reference to Plato's Allegory of the Cave, Eliot remarked that "ideas are often poor ghosts. Our sun-filled eyes cannot discern them; they pass athwart us in thin vapor, and cannot make themselves felt." But sometimes these ideas "are made flesh." "They breathe upon us with warm breath" and "touch us with soft, responsive hands" and "speak to us in appealing tones." When thus "clothed in a living human soul, with all its conflicts, its faith, and its love," then "their presence is a power; then they shade us like a passion, and we are drawn after them with a gentle compulsion" (chap. 19). This was the effect, as she observed in her fiction, that Tryan had upon Janet, Savonarola upon Romola, and Mordecai upon Daniel. The Evangelical clergyman, the Florentine preacher, and the Jewish enthusiast provided ideals and ideologies for Eliot's protagonists to follow. This had perhaps been the early sheltering effect of ideological systems upon Eliot herself. By the middle 1850s, when nearly forty, she had learned better.

Yet the attraction of ideology remained great, and, one may argue, she fell captive to an ideology that masked itself in her mind as an anti-ideology. In an ideological age, intellectuals—perhaps all who see themselves as intellectuals—have an inclination to ideological thinking, but there are some who are more prone to fall into such snares than others. George Eliot was such a person. She moved from a rigid Calvinism to an equally doctrinaire free thought (a position she upheld as unbendingly as if it were religious doctrine), to a species of positivism, primarily in the early 1850s, the period when she was virtual editor of the *Westminster Review,* and, finally, to what she probably saw as the nonideological position of the politics of national inheritance. In her youth she shared the intellectual and emotional ideological experiences of her generation, and her novels displayed her sympathy with those who, for the most praiseworthy motives, had followed false prophets.

What virtually all these ideologies had in common, not the least being that of the politics of national inheritance, was a call for the renewal of community in a time of alienation. Eliot experienced again and again this longing for sympathetic association. Feeling, sympathetic feeling, was better than thought—this sentiment was an oft-repeated incantation in her fiction. Of course, Comte was hardly the exclusive source of this principle, for sympathy had become a critical concept in the liberal thinking of Eliot's time. The free-market economist Adam Smith, in his *Theory of Moral Sentiments* (1759), had written of the need to cultivate sympathy—to check the selfish and encourage the benevolent parts of our character—as a means of achieving the perfection of human nature.[25] Yet the sacrifice of private to the public interest was not to be expected at all times. Indeed, in the marketplace, as Smith's *Wealth of Nations* (1776) argued, self-sacrificing behavior might prove opposed to the general interest. (Eliot, and Dorothea Brooke in *Middlemarch,* confronted this issue and solved it by seemingly subordinating sympathy to political economy.) Nonetheless, liberals were convinced that future moral progress depended on extending the bonds of sympathy, and Comte (with his insistence on altruism) would agree that the widening and strengthening of these bonds was crucial to moral improvement.

Even such a doctrinaire individualist as Eliot's friend Herbert Spencer, in his 1879 *Data of Ethics* (which Eliot prized), although stressing that modern society no longer required the wholesale sacrifice of private to social needs and praising the uses of egoism, saw social altruism as essential to human development. Spencer called for a "compromise" between egoism and altruism, and argued that the future gave promise of the growing importance of the latter. In modern society, Spencer argued, for the first time in human history, sources of pleasure were becoming much greater than those of pain and suffering, and thus an obstacle to the growth of sympathy with those in pain had been removed. Indeed, egoism itself was promoting sympathy, and altruism in its "ultimate form" would be "gratification through sympathy with . . . [the] gratifications of others." The opposition between egoism and altruism would in this way disappear and the demand for genuine self-sacrifice would become "rare and much prized." Even at the present time, Spencer declared, such a state of affairs existed in "the highest natures."[26] (One recent writer has stressed Spencer's insistence that the confrontation between egoism and altruism would have to be decided on a case-by-case basis, adding that Eliot elaborated this idea in her novels.[27])

In an early essay on the eighteenth-century poet Edward Young's *Night Thoughts.* Eliot described the higher nature to which Spencer would later allude. She dismissed Young's setting of rewards and punishments in an afterlife as the most substantial basis for virtue. What was wanted was "a delicate sense of our neighbour's rights, an active participation in the joys and sorrows of our fellowmen, a magnanimous acceptance of privation or suffering for ourselves when it is a condition of good to others, in a word the extension and intensification of our sympathetic nature."[28] All of Eliot's most-admired moral philosophers—Feuerbach, Comte, and

Spencer—were in general agreement on this issue. In his view of Eliot's life, her husband J. W. Cross, whom she married after Lewes's death, noted that her "great hope, for the future" was in "the gradual development of the affections and the sympathetic emotions," rather than in "legislative enactments" and "party measures."[29]

For Eliot the idea of sympathy became increasingly identified with a sharing of the inheritance of the past, and more specifically with the sharing of one's national past with others belonging to the national community. For in contrast to cosmopolitan liberals, Positivists, socialists, and, indeed, most of the "advanced" thinkers of the time, she did not doubt the underlying reality and power of national feelings and national differences. The life of the individual could not be separated from that of the nation, whose past had shaped him and to whose traditions he was the heir, regardless of his own wishes. Duties replace rights in Eliot's vision, and those duties find their place primarily in the family and in the national community as an extended family. Parents had the duty not only to pass on their goods to their children but also to nurture their offspring; and children had filial obligations to nurturing parents. The nation—with its rich traditions and culture—was such a nurturing parent. Eliot employed the metaphor of national inheritance as an instrument against ideology, which in her day as in ours was so often directed against institutional links with the past. But in doing this, she ran the danger of succumbing to the ideology of nationalism. (In just this way, it may be argued, a once-liberal Burke, in excoriating the doctrine of the Enlightenment and the French Revolution, created a counterrevolutionary conservative ideology.[30])

The issue was somewhat confused. As we shall see, Eliot believed herself to be a supporter of cultural pluralism—as was the eighteenth-century German historian whom she referred to as "the great Herder."[31] J. G. von Herder was among the earliest writers to put forward the concept of the organic development of the nationality, sui generis, peculiar to itself. He was first of all a cultural nationalist and a pluralist who delighted in the interplay of environment, historical period, and national character that produced the poetry, the music, the art, the politics, and the society that were inherent in the nature and development of the profoundly different national organisms. He placed this vision in opposition to the utopian views of the French philosophes, and the men of the French Revolution, who in a cosmopolitan spirit insisted that all men were alike and that all could be subjected to the same plan of government and society. (Burke and Coleridge later wrote in terms similar to those employed by Herder.) Herder believed feeling to be much more valuable than the reason of the philosophes. For Herder, no national culture was superior to another; and no nation had the right to impose itself or its culture on another. Although convinced that an individual was too much a part of his national culture to express himself in cosmopolitan terms, he nonetheless aspired beyond *Volk* to *Humanität*.[32] Unfortunately, Herder's many, mostly German, successors, most prominently the *völkisch* populist writers of the Blut und Boden (blood and soil) school, insisted on the superiority of their own *Volk* and its right to impose its culture on "inferior" breeds.

It is of some interest to note, in this study of Eliot in which Jews play a considerable role, that Herder urged Jews, in consideration of their national honor, not to continue as "parasitical plants on the trunks of other nations" but to find a country of their own.[33] Almost from her earliest days, the "Jewish Question"—as it came to be called by continental (usually anti-Semitic) writers—occupied Eliot's attention. At first she appeared unsympathetic to Jews; but by the end of her life she became their most enthusiastic champion among English writers. She wrote about Jewish life in London in perceptive sections of *Daniel Deronda,* but there, as elsewhere, her views were colored by her use of Jews as a metaphor, one, we shall see, interacting with her stress upon the idea and metaphor of inheritance. For her, Jews would become a central feature in her treatment of the nationality question.

We must distinguish between the idea of nationality, as presented by Herder, and what must be called the ideology of nationalism—and at times it proves difficult to see to which Eliot's views were closer. But in the end, it seems clear that she followed Herder and anticipated such twentieth-century writers as the socialist-liberal George Orwell in clinging to the national tradition without descending into jingoism or xenophobia. She certainly would not have approved the aggressive cultural nationalism of the *völkisch* writers, then so common in Germany, who later dominated so much of German thinking. Among these was the historian W. H. Riehl. Yet in the mid-1850s she wrote an admiring review of Riehl's "natural history" of Germany, apparently unconcerned about, or oblivious to, the more pernicious of Riehl's opinions, among them an anti-Semitism that Eliot later made one of her prime targets.

Our century's experience with the German Third Reich of the 1930s and 1940s necessarily colors our view of even Herder's pluralistic cultural nationalism which we fear may end in a miscreant like Hitler. And admirers of Eliot cannot avoid some feelings of distress when they find such sentiments in her writings. (Such an unhappy response may be seen in remarks of a present-day student of Eliot.[34]) I will argue that Eliot's embrace of Herder's position on the national inheritance represented a protest against what she as a liberal—favoring individual freedom and happiness along with communal sympathy and cultural diversity—saw as the despotic and alienating uniformity advocated by modern secular faiths.

England, with its expanding industry, seemed to be eliminating the satisfying, traditional society Eliot had known as a child in the rural Midlands. Britain's new world status not only as the leading industrial but also as the leading commercial and financial power was turning the liberal middle classes from an insular patriotism and a naive pride in the national character to what was for Eliot a bloodless cosmopolitanism. The forces of modernity appeared to be robbing Britain of its national inheritance. And in her personal life, Eliot felt herself dispossessed of the loving security of her early years as her evolving religious opinions and flouting of social conventions alienated her father and brother whom she loved. On all sides, she was experiencing what was for her a trauma of disinheritance.

1

The Myth of the Disinherited One

In late December 1869 George Eliot expressed the wish that a friend's Christmas would be "very happy among the dear Kith and Kin." "I cling strongly to Kith and Kin," she added, "even though they reject *me*."[1] Marian Evans, (her name from birth—she adopted her nom de plume in 1857) was twice rejected by her family, first by her father, in 1842, after she had fallen away from her religious beliefs; and then by her brother Isaac a dozen years later, in 1854, when, though unmarried, she began to live with G. H. Lewes. Both rejections were painful. She suffered no actual disinheritance, though occasionally her brother had to be reminded after their father's death to send her payments of the small income due her. Isaac declined to have any social contact with his sister until 1880, when after Lewes's death she married J. W. Cross, and could be properly addressed as a respectable matron.

Eliot had been hurt by her father's hostility to her new views on religion. Disabused of her severe Calvinist Evangelical faith, she became a doctrinaire freethinker. She made her conversion a more serious occasion than it need have been by refusing to accompany her father to church, an act she was later to regret. Mr. Evans at this point instructed an agent to lease the house he shared with Eliot, intending to live with a married daughter and her husband. Feeling abandoned, Eliot decided to find lodgings of her own and to support herself by teaching. After several months of distress the breach was healed, and Eliot continued to live with her father until his death in 1849.

At this period in her life Eliot was self-righteously determined to disseminate her newfound convictions. She wished to devote herself to the freeing of truth from a "usurped domination." "I cannot rank among my principles of action," she wrote a correspondent in January 1842, "a fear of vengeance eternal, gratitude for predestined salvation, or a revelation of future glories as a reward."[2] Her Calvinism had departed. Her soul felt "liberated from the wretched giant's bed of dogmas on which it has been racked and stretched ever since it began to think," she noted nearly two years after her break with Calvinism. She breathed the "bracing air of independence," and set out to make converts for the truth within her.[3] During this period she rarely resisted an opportunity to argue her views.

In time, however, Eliot became ashamed of the disputatious temper that had so alienated her family. This searing event convinced her that it was unproductive to argue with believers of any kind. Ideas, she now felt, were so entrenched in individuals that they could not be removed "without destroying vitality." It was her opinion that "speculative truth begins to appear but a shadow of individual minds," for "agreement between intellects seems unattainable, and we turn to the *truth of feeling* as the only universal bond of union." She now described as the "quackery of infidelity" the view that freethinking would be a welcome restorative. She was anxious not to separate herself from those with whom she sympathized, and sought to bring her feelings into harmony with believers, "often richer in the fruits of faith though not in reasons."[4] That feelings were more important than thoughts became a key theme of her writings. She saw the French philosophe Rousseau and the woman novelist George Sand as her mentors in this matter.

An even greater influence, though, were the novels of Sir Walter Scott, and what was perhaps the leading theme of his plots. Eliot told one of her admirers that Scott's works had provided her with many joyous hours of reading during her childhood. As an adult she continued to venerate his work. She read the Waverley novels aloud to her father as well as to Lewes, whom she converted to a love of their author. "No other writer would serve as a substitute," she declared. It was "a personal grief" and "a heart-wound" when she heard "a depreciating or slighting word" about him.[5] We may see in her own stories an absorption with one of Scott's often-repeated motifs—one common to romance—that of inheritance, and of disinheritance. Eliot employed the metaphor of inheritance in several different but related ways. It is my belief that her uses of the concept clarify her philosophical and theological ideas as well as her political posture. What I will call "the myth of the disinherited one" informed the ways in which she understood the metaphor, and suggest the power it possessed for her.[6]

The critic Northrop Frye has argued that myth is an essential structural element in all forms of literature. In its Aristotelian sense, the mythos is the narrative or plot. While the archetypal, primal form of a myth may be presented without embellishment, there are a wide range of what Frye has called "displacements," which to a greater or lesser degree disguise the myth so as to make it appear more realistic, and thus more acceptable both logically and morally to readers. The recognition of the relationship of the myth to its displacement may in some cases be almost immediate, but at times these plots so elaborate the myth as to make it difficult to discover. The leading plots of Romance, according to Frye, are archetypal myths that involve a minimum of displacement.[7]

One writer, in a similar vein, has suggested that Sir Walter Scott's novels created an "archetypal, not historical" past.[8] In his *Essay on Chivalry,* perhaps anticipating such a charge, Scott noted that the fairy-tale adventures of Don Quixote portrayed the essential life of the feudal past more accurately than could a history that relied on facts alone. "In the more ancient times, the wandering knight could not go far without finding some gentleman oppressed by a powerful neighbour, some captive immured in a feudal dungeon, some orphan deprived of his heritage," Scott observed.[9] In Scott's tales of medieval feudalism or of quasi-feudal late-seventeenth- and eighteenth-century Scotland, where so much depended on inherited claims of social position and wealth, it was not surprising that disinheritance, by force or fraud, should seem to be one of the most heinous of injustices.

Was the bourgeois nineteenth century, where gentlemanly status continued to depend on a leisured existence, very different in this matter from its quasi-feudal predecessor? Frye has described how dependent novelists of the period were on "the motif of mysterious birth," a myth found both in the Bible and in classical mythology.[10] Scott, Dickens, and Trollope, among others, also made good use of the chivalric and quixotic plot of "some orphan deprived of his heritage," in Scott's phrase. Often the two plots were joined, as they were in a number of Scott's novels. Frye has noted the popularity of Trollope's novel *Doctor Thorne,* in which the heroine, though apparently Thorne's daughter, is actually the child and heiress of a considerably wealthier man, a circumstance which, once it becomes known, makes it possible for her to marry the hero. Frye's conclusion is that "after a glance at Scott and Dickens, we may say that what *Doctor Thorne* had was not *a* good plot but *the* good plot."[11]

If we generalize "*the* good plot" to be the myth of the disinherited one, then we can say that five of George Eliot's seven novels, as well as her epic drama *The Spanish Gypsy,* embody that myth, with significant variations, and different degrees of displacement. It has long been accepted that Eliot's earlier novels were romances. We shall see that even *Middlemarch* and *Daniel Deronda,* her most realistic efforts, were akin to romances in which the themes of inheritance and disinheritance played an important part.[12] In *Daniel Deronda,* the myth emerges clearly. The novel's plot includes a romantic search for a father, an identity, and a mission, the kind of chivalric quest a hero might have undertaken in earlier times but which seemed unsuited to the nineteenth century. Eliot perceives Deronda as a "romantic." He is one of those individuals whose "young energy and spirit of adventure" had "helped to create the world-wide legends of youthful heroes going to seek the hidden token of their birth and its inheritance of tasks" (chap. 41). Here is Eliot's romance of the disinherited one set in mid-Victorian England.

To expect to use this myth as the key to understanding all of Eliot's writing would be as vain and foolish as Casaubon's search in *Middlemarch* for the key to all mythologies. That the disinheritance myth was central to so many of her plots might suggest little more than Eliot's recognition of the theme's popularity, and of her need to sell books. But there is evidence of what may be called a consistent pattern of intention, intellectual and moral. In the ways she chose to vary the myth of the disinherited one, Eliot transcended what might have been mere formula romance, making her stories into vehicles for thought, metaphors for her outlook on the social transformation of which I have spoken. Her methods enable us to understand better, as she intended we should, the complexities and ambivalences of her religious and political opinions, while disguising what the circumstances of her life obliged her not to say.

In this study I am concerned with Eliot's political imagination—with her politics of inheritance—which, I will argue, was an aspect of what may be called her moral imagination. Eliot's efforts to convert Scott's romances to her own purposes led her to conclusions concerning society, religion, and politics not too different from Scott's liberal-conservative compromise, at bottom a decision not to discard the inherited good of the national past while attempting to shed its clinging evil. In such a compromise lay difficulties from which she could never entirely extricate herself.

An understanding of the myth of the disinherited one, whose various meanings Eliot explored, includes its common form, where the issue concerns family property, as well as its more metaphoric meanings. Without descending into a simplistic reductionism, we might ask whether the myth may have been congenial—if not compelling for Eliot—because of the difficulties of her personal situation, as the autobiographical *The Mill on the Floss* might suggest.

One of Eliot's friends described a conversation with Eliot in the summer of 1869 concerning *The Mill on the Floss,* published nine years earlier. Eliot at this time claimed her "sole purpose" in writing the book had been "to show the conflict which is going on everywhere when the younger generation with its higher culture comes into collision with the older, and in which, she said, so many young hearts make shipwreck far worse than Maggie." She described her own experience as a worse one, and regretted that she could not write an autobiography in which she would show "how wrong *she* was." "She spoke of having come into collision with her father and being on the brink of being turned out of his house. And she dwelt a little on how much fault there is on the side of the young in such cases, of their ignorance of life, and the narrowness of their intellectual superiority."[13] The fault so often lies, as was observed again and again in *The Mill on the Floss,* in the failure of the young to value sufficiently the bonds that join them to their parents, and in their desire to cut their links with the past.

The Mill on the Floss, then, concerned the generational conflict between the "sense of oppressive narrowness" of the world of the Dodsons and Tullivers and its effects on the lives of the Tulliver children, Tom and Maggie. Such a conflict, Eliot wrote in the novel, was always present, given "the onward tendency of human things" to rise "above the mental level of the generation before them," a generation "to which they have been nevertheless tied by the strongest fibres of their hearts." This conflict which brought "suffering, whether of martyr or victim," belonged "to every historical advance of mankind" and was "represented . . . in every town and by hundreds of obscure hearths" (bk. IV, chap. 1). Doctor Kenn, the parish clergyman in the novel, bemoans that "at present everything seems to be tending towards the relaxation of ties—towards the substitution of wayward choice for the adherence to obligation which has its roots in the past" (VII, 2). In real life, Marian Evans was the martyr, sacrificing the love of her father while in pursuit of rational truth rather than feelings. In the novel, as we shall see, Maggie is undone in good part by her decision *not* to sacrifice obligation to what might seem a more rational "wayward choice."

But first we must consider the question of inheritance, in its most prosaic aspect, which appears many times in the course of *The Mill on the Floss.* The family obligation of the testator is set against a capricious choice of heir, and duty properly triumphs. The sisters of Maggie's mother, *née* Dodson, have married well, and are continually deliberating on wills and the legacies they intend to leave their nephews and nieces. By this means, as "people of independent fortune," they exercise power within the family (I, 9)—even though, as Mr. Tulliver knows, they will not so favor one over the others as to "make the country cry shame on 'em when they are dead" (I, 6). One sister, Mrs. Glegg, boasts "that no Dodson had ever been 'cut off with a shilling' and no cousin of the Dodsons disowned" (I, 12). Even after Mr. Tulliver has offended her, the childless Mrs. Glegg continues in her intention to divide her money with "perfect fairness among her own kin," for "in the matter of wills personal qualities were subordinate to the great fundamental fact of blood"; one's legacies must be determined by "a direct ratio to degrees of kinship" and not by a "caprice." According to the narrator, this was "one form of that sense of honour and rectitude which was a proud tradition in such families—a tradition which has been the salt of our provincial society" (I, 13).

"The religion of the Dodsons," the narrator notes later in the volume, "consisted in revering whatever was customary and respectable," and this included the leaving of "an unimpeachable will." You "sank in the opinion" of your fellows by "leaving your money in a capricious manner without strict regard to degrees of kin." One might not deprive one's kin of "the smallest rightful share" of the family estate (IV, 1). Even after Maggie's disgrace, Mrs. Glegg continues in her testamentary faith: "Lightly to admit conduct in one of your own family that would force you to alter your will, had never been the way of the Dodsons." The "hereditary rectitude" of the Dodsons, like that of other middle-class provincial families of the time, joins their "fundamental ideas of clanship" and of "equity in money matters" (VII, 3). To a friend, Eliot would later defend the Dodsons "for keeping up the sense of respectability"—"the only religion possible to the mass of English people." Neither the narrator nor any of the novel's characters expresses a contrary view.[14]

The Mill on the Floss, which appeared in 1860, may be seen as a fictionalized treatment of George Eliot's childhood and of her trauma of abandonment. The heroine Maggie Tulliver is the loving daughter (and the pride) of a miller who lives and works beside the River Floss. Before he dies, Maggie's father, somewhat anxious about her future, entrusts her welfare to her brother Tom, her idol and early playmate. Maggie, grown to be an attractive young woman, is forced by circumstances to stay overnight in a neighboring town with Stephen Guest, the fiancé of her beautiful cousin Lucy Deane. Stephen expresses his love for Maggie, and she admits her affection for him, but she is virtuously unwilling to spoil her cousin's engagement. Lovesick, Stephen leaves his betrothed, and exiles himself from the vicinity—actions that only serve to make the gossip worse. Although entirely innocent of an affair she is widely believed to have initiated, a miserable Maggie is compelled by the hostility of her brother Tom, whom she has loved above all others, to leave her home, and to find other lodgings. In time, Lucy, whom Maggie has inadvertently injured, recognizes that Maggie is innocent of wrongdoing, but Tom, a prisoner of convention, remains unforgiving. The river on which the town is situated overflows after a torrential storm, and Maggie heroically rows a boat through a maelstrom of rushing waters past the roofs of the flooded town to save Tom. She succeeds in finding her brother, who is deeply moved by her act, and regrets his harsh treatment of her. A moment later their boat is submerged in the torrent, and they drown in each other's arms.

If the older generation that disposed of legacies accepted a duty to their rightful heirs, these heirs, or at least those like the conscientious Maggie, were prepared to undertake a reciprocal obligation. When presented with Stephen's suggestion that they run off to marry, Maggie does not consider a utilitarian "balancing of consequences." She cannot betray the family's trust. In the "shifting relation between passion and duty," "conscience . . . was a safer guide." To act otherwise would make Maggie "feel like a lonely wanderer—cut off from the past" (VII, 2). "If the past is not to bind us," she says earlier, "where can duty lie? We should have no law but the inclination of the moment." She cannot be "false to that debt," for that would be "a warrant for all treachery and cruelty" and would "justify . . . breaking the most sacred ties that can ever be formed on earth." If she cannot cling to "all that my past life has made dear and holy to me," she declares, "I shall feel as if there were nothing firm beneath my feet" (VI, 14).

But if Maggie accepts the moral obligations of the past, she refuses to accept its immoral prejudices. Tom is determined to wreak vengeance on the crippled Philip Wakem, Maggie's persistent suitor, for an offense Philip's father committed against Mr. Tulliver. Tulliver before his death had commanded his children to be unforgiving to Wakem and his family. Tom, the narrator tells us, belongs to a class of persons marked by the rigid and narrow mental qualities that "create severity." "Let a prejudice be bequeathed" to such persons, then "these minds will give it a habitation." For such persons "can get no sustenance out of that complex, fragmentary, doubt-provoking knowledge which we call truth" (VI, 12). If she marries Philip, Tom warns Maggie, she must give up Tom. Maggie has loved Tom "better than any one else in the world" (V, 2). After her unhappy and misunderstood encounter with Stephen, she turns to Tom for comfort and "for refuge." He replies, "You have disgraced us all—you have disgraced my father's name." In a rage he tells her, "You will find no home with me. . . . I wash my hands of you for ever. You don't belong to me" (VII, 1). Maggie calls Tom "nothing but a Pharisee" (V, 5). Like Saint Paul, one of Eliot's models, Maggie elevates love above a legalistic severity, but she is cast aside and disowned.

George Eliot, in her early correspondence, saw the personal difficulties she had experienced as an epitome of what was happening in the greater world. One member of a family foregoes an observance—such as Eliot's refusal to accompany her father to church—which the others see as essential; not understanding his motives, they regard his behavior as morally destructive. "The rest are infected with the disease they imagine in him; all the screws by which order was maintained are loosened, and in more than one case a person's happiness may be ruined by the confusion of ideas which took the form of principles." Man is alienated from man, and society becomes unhinged. Then should nothing be done to propagate true opinions and thus contribute to human development? With both individuals and nations, Eliot answered, "the only safe revolution is one arising out of the wants which their *own progress* has generated." The seed must be planted in ground prepared to receive it or the wheat will be uprooted with the tares. Eliot cited Saint Paul's reasoning concerning the duties of the strong toward the weak, and noted his cautions against "doubtful disputations" that could only inhibit the conversion of the Gentiles.[15]

Both Eliot and Lewes were admirers of the seventeenth-century Dutch-Jewish philosopher Spinoza—Eliot even translated Spinoza's *Ethics,* though through a mischance the translation has remained unpublished—and discovered that his view of inheritance was similar to Eliot's own. In an adulatory essay by Lewes on Spinoza, Lewes noted that when Spinoza's father died, his two sisters attempted to withhold his inheritance from him, possibly believing, Lewes suggested, that an excommunicated heretic had relinquished any claim. Spinoza asserted his claim in a court of law, not out of greed but in pursuit of justice. Having won his case, he bestowed his inheritance on his sisters, in Lewes's words, "saving his sisters from fraud and himself from an indignity." In the last years of his life, having previously rejected a gift of one thousand florins from his pupil Simon de Vries, Spinoza heard that de Vries had willed his entire property to him, disinheriting de Vries's own brother. Spinoza set off for Amsterdam to persuade Simon to rectify this injury to his brother and succeeded in accomplishing this charitable act. The heir, in gratitude, and after some effort, persuaded Spinoza to accept a small sum in recompense for his unselfish conduct.[16]

In *The Mill on the Floss* Eliot seemed to have no doubts that parents had the duty to endow their children, and that children owed them a reciprocal obligation, although she had little use for Tom's insistence on a hereditary vengeance. She saw, then, a distinction between a duty to the past, and a wish to shed its ignoble prejudices. In the historical romances *Silas Marner* and *Felix Holt* Eliot took up what was apparently a modern heresy, that of the obligation of parents and the freedom of heirs. This was also to be her position in her later novel *Middlemarch,* or at least this was to be Dorothea Brooke's philosophy of inheritance, as we shall see. In these novels, however, the heirs achieve this freedom because of a failure on the part of parents—either one of moral character, as in *Silas Marner* and *Middlemarch,* or one of circumstances, as in *Felix Holt*—to fulfill their duties. In both the earlier novels the heroines respond to a sense of greater moral obligation.

The plot of *Silas Marner,* published in 1861, a year after *The Mill on the Floss,* is well known to generations of schoolchildren. In the country village of Raveloe, Godfrey Cass, the squire's eldest son, has contracted an unfortunate marriage but has managed to keep from his father the secret of his wife and two-year-old daughter, who live in a town some miles away. Should his secret become known, Godfrey would be disinherited by Squire Cass, and he would lose the affection of his longtime love, Nancy Lammeter, the daughter of a neighboring landowner.

Silas Marner, a linen-weaver from a town in the north, settles in Raveloe after being unjustly expelled from his Nonconformist sect. He works diligently, indeed obsessively, at his trade, and accumulates a small fortune in gold. Robbed of this treasure on a night when he failed to secure his door, the weaver is distraught. On New Year's Eve, Godfrey's wife (with her young daughter) treks from the neighboring town to make herself known to Squire Cass, fulfilling a long-standing threat. Dazed by alcohol and laudanum, the woman stumbles to her death along the way, and her daughter crawls into Marner's nearby cabin. Marner warms the little girl by the fire and feeds her. The weaver decides to raise the two year old, whom he names Eppie. He dearly loves her and comes to believe that she is Providence's recompense for the loss of his gold. Marner sheds his reclusive habits and becomes part of the village community.

Years elapse. Eppie dotes on Marner. She has grown into an attractive woman and has fallen in love with a young gardener who wishes to marry her. Meanwhile, Godfrey Cass has married Nancy and succeeded to the estate. Though Godfrey knows he is Eppie's father, he says nothing. He is happy with his wife, but they have had no children, which Godfrey feels is retribution for his desertion of Eppie. He confesses the story of his earlier marriage to Nancy and tells her that Eppie, now sixteen, is his daughter. On hearing this news, Nancy agrees to his plan that they adopt Eppie. Both the Casses know that an injury has been done to Eppie, and they determine now to rectify it.

The Casses also have a sense of title, of paternal possession. They go to Marner's cottage and tell their story. "But I have a claim on you, Eppie—the strongest of all claims," Godfrey assures his daughter. He informs Silas, "It is my duty, Marner, to own Eppie as my child, and provide for her. She is my own child—her mother was my wife. I have a natural claim on her that must stand before every other." But Silas Marner sets this argument aside. Why had not Cass spoken out earlier before the weaver had come to love Eppie? Godfrey had turned his back on his child, and now has no right to her. Cass points to the advantages he can offer Eppie, and demands to be allowed "to do my duty." Even Nancy, more sensitive to the feelings of affection that have grown between Silas and Eppie, has no doubt as to the justice of her husband's position: "Her code allowed no question that a father by blood must have a claim above that of any foster-father" (chap. 19). (Blood is a most potent force in romantic novels, as Northrop Frye has told us.[17]) Nancy believes that Eppie, "in being restored to her birthright, was entering on a too-long withheld but unquestionable good." But Eppie's "feelings" for Silas overcome mere "thoughts," or rational arguments. "He's took care of me and loved me from the first, and I'll cleave to him as long as he lives," she tells the Casses. When Nancy reminds her of "a duty you owe to your lawful father," Eppie replies that "I can't feel as I've got any father but one" (chap. 19).

Silas Marner is a fable about a society in a time of change. In the traditional tale—as in the case of the heroine of *Doctor Thorne*—the princess raised as a shepherdess never hesitates to take her proper place. She is pleased to be restored to the rank to which blood assigned her, though she will no doubt reward the old shepherd who raised her so devotedly. Eppie, however, rejects the traditional code of blood in favor of a modern one of deed. She turns aside Godfrey's natural claim to her by virtue of birth in favor of Marner's earned merit as a loving father. Cass has an obligation toward Eppie, as a daughter, for whose existence he is responsible, but Eppie owes none to him merely because of blood relationship. Her moral obligation, founded upon feeling, not "lawful" right, is to Silas (chap. 19). She marries the young gardener who has long loved her, rejecting the possibility of a husband more suited to the status she might now enjoy.

George Eliot located her tale quite explicitly in the context of the social transformation from the traditional, aristocratic society to the modern one. Her first two chapters picture the traditional community of Raveloe in the last years of the Napoleonic Wars, perhaps between 1813 and 1815, when high wartime agricultural prices had made the district prosperous, and thereby supported the patriarchal predominance of the local landowners like Squire Cass. With the end of the war and the decline in agricultural prices, accompanied by continued improvements in transportation, the patriarchal authority of the landed gentry declined, and middle-class public opinion began to prevail. Godfrey and Nancy have become merely "Mr. and Mrs. Cass"—"any higher title has died away" (chap. 16). When Silas takes Eppie on a visit to the northern town from which he had journeyed some thirty years earlier, he discovers that it has become a factory town, with its former artisans replaced by an industrial proletariat. The decline of the traditional community, Eliot appears to suggest, has made possible Eppie's spirited choice of merit over blood. To employ the language of present-day social theorists, the modern criterion of "achievement" has overwhelmed the unearned feudal "ascription" of birth.

Blood itself plays an ambiguous role in this novel, as it does in other works of Eliot. Nancy's father, whose own father had come to Raveloe from somewhere in the north, is quite different in appearance from the general run of Midlands farmers. He finds this distinction "in accordance with a favorite saying of his own, that 'breed was stronger than pasture'" (chap. 11) Victorian liberals, in contrast, were apt to stress pasture over breed, environment rather than heredity. We know that the philosopher and economist John Stuart Mill and his father agreed that John Stuart's remarkable intellectual development was a product of parental education, not native ability; of achievement, not birth. This was the new society's reply to the conservative insistence, like that of the conventional romantic novel, that blood would tell. Yet the narrator pictures Eppie as startlingly different from the peasant girls of the village, for she is a lady in appearance and manner. The narrator describes Eppie's "delicate prettiness," while Silas tells her, "You're dillicate made, my dear" and notes that she needs to have somebody to work for her (chap. 16). Later, Godfrey reminds Marner that Eppie was "not fit for any hardships: she doesn't look like a strapping girl come of working parents" (chap. 19), and tells Nancy that there was not "such a pretty little girl any where else in the parish, or one fitter for the station we could give her" (chap. 17). Of course, romantic convention also played a part in Eliot's decision to portray Eppie as delicately pretty.

Silas Marner embodies an interesting departure from Eliot's championing of the modern ethos: her elevation of feeling over reason. Social theorists have written of the move from "affectivity" to "affective neutrality," the quintessentially modern effort to keep emotion in check, to strive for control.[18] In *A Christmas Carol* Dickens had parodied through Scrooge the calculating rationality of the new middle-class society, and contrasted it with the overflowing feelings of the traditional England of the past; in *Hard Times* he contrasted the self-interested, rational bourgeois

Bitzer with the loving feeling of Sissy Jupe. Similarly, in *Silas Marner,* Eppie's feelings concerning her foster father overwhelm whatever practical reasons might attract her to consider Godfrey's offer.

Despite her adoption of elements of the modern, Eliot stressed the virtues of tradition. She pictured Marner as loving "the old brick hearth as he had loved his own brown pot": "The gods of the hearth exist for us still," she declared; "and let all new faith be tolerant of that fetichism, lest it bruise its own roots." Marner tries to secure "a consciousness of unity between his past and present" (chap. 16), and Eliot made a similar effort. Eliot joined Scott and Dickens in rejecting the prosaic, commonsensical aspirations of a commercial society, with its separation of individuals from traditional communal ties. The love of Eppie replaces Marner's preoccupation with accumulation and restores him to the fellowship of *Gemeinschaft.*

The myth of the disinherited one pervades *Silas Marner.* Marner himself has been dispossessed: expelled from his sect and from his hope of salvation, he becomes a bereft wanderer, journeying with his pack from his familiar country into a strange land. Godfrey Cass lives in fear of his father's anger and rejection if his low marriage becomes known. Godfrey's long refusal to acknowledge her has disinherited Eppie. Yet when Godfrey attempts to restore to Eppie the inheritance he long denied her, she rejects his offer and yields the privileges she might enjoy because of her love for Marner, valuing the merit of both Marner and her gardener suitor. Love has led her to disinherit herself, which Eliot's philosophy of inheritance acknowledges as her right. This is the moral fable of *Silas Marner.* With small variations, it is also the fable of *Felix Holt.*

Like *Silas Marner,* the story of *Felix Holt, the Radical,* published in 1866, bears the aspect of romantic melodrama, though with a more realistic cast. *Felix Holt* is set in a society in which commerce plays a greater role. In this work Eliot sees the coming of Catholic Emancipation in 1829, the spread of railways, and the passage of the Reform Bill of 1832 (which extended the franchise) as momentous events that divided traditional from modern England. It is the time of which Scott had written, "[T]he attorney is now a man of more importance than the lord of the manor," though in *Felix Holt* Eliot presents a more ambiguous view of the relationship of lawyers to gentlemen. Following Scott, Eliot reminds her readers that "there is no private life which has not been determined by a wider public life" (Chap. 3).

The Transomes are a gentry family of dwindling means. The simple-minded father has for some time been incapable of managing his estate, and Mrs. Transome, a more considerable personality, has entrusted the family's business to a local attorney, Jermyn. The elder Transome son, like his father an incompetent, has died, and the younger son, Harold, the favorite of his mother and the one she has always hoped would somehow become the Transome heir, has recently returned from the East, where he has made his fortune. Mrs. Transome soon discovers she has lost all authority over this son. Harold is determined, much to his mother's displeasure, to stand for the House of Commons as a Liberal rather than a Tory, and, furthermore, much against his mother's wishes, he seeks a showdown with the lawyer Jermyn, whom he correctly suspects of having embezzled money from the estate.

If the Transomes are in some sense the Casses of the earlier novel, the Lyon family, a Nonconformist minister and his daughter Esther, re-enact the roles of Silas and Eppie. Esther is not Rufus Lyon's daughter by blood, but rather the daughter of a French woman whom the Baptist minister had come to love and whom he had married before her death. Esther's true father—and legal spouse of her mother—was an English gentleman, now also dead. Lyon has been afraid to tell Esther the truth of her birth for fear of losing her affection. Esther, a graceful beauty of aristocratic appearance and demeanor—breed rather than pasture again telling—appears, and is, out of sympathy with her surroundings. Educated beyond her lower-middle-class status, she reads Byron, speaks French, and has served as a governess. Very much the lady, she is secretly persuaded that she was meant to fill a grander position. But Esther meets and falls in love with Felix Holt, once a medical student, now a simple artisan watchmaker who has undertaken a mission to the poor. No demagogue, Felix seeks to persuade the working classes to improve themselves if they wish to better their condition. Although she finds Felix "very coarse and rude," Esther is nonetheless taken with him (chap. 5); equally smitten, Felix is convinced that Esther is too much the lady to live among the proletariat.

The facts of Esther's birth become known. Esther, through her natural father, is the true heir to the Transome estate. Harold Transome admires Esther, and sees their marriage as the solution to the inheritance tangle. Such a marriage would fulfill Esther's long-fantasied desire for social eleva-tion; she has moreover become convinced of Harold's sincere regard for her, nor is she indifferent to him. Yet her love for Felix (and his for her) makes a match with Harold impossible. She knows, moreover, that Felix would never agree to marry an heiress. Nor does she wish to injure the bonds of love between herself and her adoptive father, bonds that the new revelations have strengthened rather than weakened. She rejects Harold's proposal and makes over her rights to the estate to the Transomes. She marries Felix, joining him in his mission.

Thus once again an heiress to gentry status and fortune rejects her inheritance, preferring a merited love to a comfortable birthright. While Eppie never dreamed of a social ascent, Esther has prepared for it, and seems to have been awaiting it. "It's a case of fitness," Felix tells her after the truth has emerged: "The first time I saw you your birth was an im-mense puzzle to me. However, the appropriate conditions are come at last" (chap. 45). Yet Esther remains loyal to her adoptive father, and permits herself to be declassed. Indeed, she is declassed twice. She rejects her inherited position at the Transomes' manor, after living there experimen-tally, and apparently satisfactorily, for some months. Then she rejects even the lower-middle-class life of minister Lyon to follow Felix, who has similarly declassed himself, on his mission to serve the industrial proletariat. Because of her love and respect for Felix, she chooses to identify herself with the most despised class in society. Feeling has again vanquished reason.

Clearly, in both *Felix Holt* and *Silas Marner* Eliot took the elements of the romantic novel and turned them on their head. While the influence of blood is far from slighted in these tales, at the moment of choice the heroines reject rightful inheritances—impermissible in the standard romances—in favor of merit and moral obligation. (Scott's novels would not usually have admitted a serious difference between the two.) In two of her later works Eliot, apparently more conventionally, accepted the predominance of the blood tie. But we shall see that these are also far from conventional romances, though romances they are. Their plots, indeed, are, in varying degress, inversions of two of Scott's novels. They were designed to demonstrate, in the traditional rather than the modern manner, that there are some inheritances an heir is morally obliged to accept. But I shall discuss this question in a later chapter.

Having sufficiently, for the moment, demonstrated the role of the myth of the disinherited one in three of Eliot's novels—we shall see that it appears in others as well—I must delve more deeply into George Eliot's intellectual development. For before turning to fiction, and incorporating her convictions into her stories, poetry, and novels, Eliot had thought through virtually all the chief positions with which she would later identify herself.[19]

What for her would become a dominating theme, very closely related to the questions with which we are concerned, including that of inheritance, was the hoary problem of free will and determinism.[20] Eliot's attempts to sort out the question of inheritance, with parents *bound* to pass on legacies to their children and children *free* (in some cases) to reject them, reflected the efforts of a number of liberal writers of the time to offer a satisfactory solution to an ultimately unsolvable dilemma. These writers wished to avoid a necessity, seemingly dictated by a deterministic science, that would make of men and women what the German philosopher Kant had called "living machines." (Kant, for whom Eliot had a high regard, preserved the free will of individuals while stressing a providential necessity as the law for collectivities such as mankind.) Sensitive men and women in the nineteenth century wished to make some room for metaphysical liberty even as they recognized the force of scientific necessity. Eliot's contemporary John Stuart Mill, for example, in his *System of Logic* (1843), which she had read, had viewed the individual as freely able to add his own willed contribution to the combination of external forces shaping his existence.[21]

Born over a decade before Eliot, Mill described the "mental crisis" of his twenties as a consequence of the deterministic doctrine that decreed him to be "the helpless slave of antecedent circumstances." Mill's demanding and unaffectionate father, the historian and philosopher James Mill, believed that his son's genius was the product of his long and patient teaching, owing nothing either to a heavenly Father (in whom James, a former Calvinist, no longer believed), or to any thing individual in his son. John Stuart himself had long accepted this view, repressing his antagonistic feelings toward his father. What rescued Mill from his emotional depression was a new appreciation of what he called the "really inspiriting and ennobling" doctrine of free will, "the conviction that we have real power over the formation of our character." This realization followed Mill's reading of a passage from Marmontel that told of the death of the hero's father and the son's sudden realization that he could fill his father's place in his family's affection.[22] A different yet somewhat analogous situation may be seen in the life of the philosophical (and theological) New England writer, Henry James, Sr., the novelist's father, who also struggled to achieve a measure of free will in a deterministic universe.[23]

That the issues of free will and of inheritance were linked in Eliot's thinking we shall see more clearly in the following chapter. Her solution to what was a not uncommon Victorian religious and intellectual dilemma was similar to that advanced by Mill. Like Mill, Eliot fought to overcome residues of a Calvinist determinism and achieve a measure of freedom. Eliot's liberal view of inheritance placed the necessitarian duty of bequest on parents but left the child free to choose. Yet Eliot also accepted the obligations of the younger generation to the older and the duties that the past imposed on the present. In *The Mill on the Floss,* Maggie willingly behaves in keeping with a code of family duty, a code whose violation would be dishonorable. In her later works, Eliot argued that a freely willed acceptance, bordering on a necessary duty, of the national inheritance, was as strong as obligations to family.

In all this, we may better understand why the metaphor of inheritance was so important to Eliot and, in varying forms, to other nineteenth-century intellectuals for whom the traditional injunctions of obedience to fathers and to God remained deeply felt even as confidence in the plausibility of a hierarchical society or faith in the reality of the God of Revelation were fading.

2

Free Will and the
Politics of Inheritance

To understand how Eliot perceived both the idea and the metaphor of
inheritance, and how her use of the inheritance metaphor was related to
her views on religion, philosophy, and politics, we must place Eliot in the
context of others who wrote about these questions. We know from Eliot's
correspondence that she read the writings of the foremost contributors to
the British discussion of the politics of inheritance: Burke, Coleridge, and
Disraeli. She studied (and wrote about) the works of the French Positivist
Comte and the German *völkisch* historian W. H. Riehl, both of whom had
pursued their own inquiries regarding national inheritance. But the politics of inheritance, particularly as Eliot conceived them, were also connected with certain theological and philosophical matters, notably, the
conflict between free will and necessity. Therefore we must first examine
Eliot's views on this issue and compare them with the opinions of those
thinkers, on both sides of the controversy, whom she most admired—
among them her religious (and philosophical) mentors Saint Paul and
Calvin, the German nineteenth-century writers D. F. Strauss and Ludwig
Feuerbach, and both Comte and Charles Bray, her friend and a member of
the Coventry circle of freethinkers with whom she was associated as a
young woman.

Over a century ago the French historian Hippolyte Taine noted the importance of religion in nineteenth-century Britain. Protestantism gave Englishmen guidance in the formulation of an inner moral code that revealed
to them their duties, he wrote; it attempted to bring about "a voluntary

reformation, . . . the habit of self restraint, and a kind of modern stoicism, almost as noble as the ancient." In Protestant England "the God of conscience reigns alone," and most English writers, he concluded, were "not artists, but moralists." Taine saw as an example of this phenomenon "chiefly those [novels] of George Eliot."[1] Lord Acton agreed: for Eliot, he wrote, "If the doctrine, separate from the art, had no vitality, the art without the doctrine had no significance."[2] Nearly fifty years ago the Cambridge critic F. R. Leavis described Eliot as belonging to "the great tradition" of the English novel (a moral tradition encompassing Jane Austen, Henry James, Joseph Conrad, and D. H. Lawrence), one that did not hesitate to advocate proper conduct.[3] More recently a historian of ideas has identified Eliot (as well as Mill and the Victorian Liberal prime minister William Gladstone) as a "public moralist."[4]

For a few years during her youth George Eliot was a stern Evangelical, a Calvinist and a determinist; the effect upon her later life of this earlier persuasion was considerable, at times as a positive factor, but more often as one against which she would react severely. For her, determinism was also associated with the crude materialism of a friend of her youth, Charles Bray, and with the constraints of ideological systems (such as Calvinism and Comtian positivism), while free will was a weapon with which to oppose such rigid doctrines. Without the existence of free will, in a sufficiently potent form, a moral teacher would be addressing herself to an audience that might hear her words but would be incapable of responding to them in meaningful terms.[5]

What had helped bring Eliot to this position was her study of the writings of the biblical scholar D. F. Strauss and the materialist philosopher Ludwig Feuerbach. In reaction against the excessive scientism of the Enlightenment, both Strauss and Feuerbach stressed the role of free will. These German writers, following paths charted by Spinoza and Hegel, philosophized Christianity to make it more acceptable to a scientific age, and called for a religion of humanity.

The French philosopher Auguste Comte, whose books Eliot admired, also preached a religion of humanity. Comte was a materialist and, in the mode of the physical sciences, a determinist for whom the future Positivist society was an inevitable stage in mankind's development. As philosophical necessitarians, the Comtists had abandoned the absolute separation of body and soul demanded by Christianity. They embraced phrenology to demonstrate their convictions that matter (the convolutions of the brain, revealed by bumps on the cranium) shaped spirit, and that a person inherited his aptitudes and dispositions, and could not alter them.

As has already been noted, liberals felt two ways about the grand philosophical question of free will and determinism. Liberals saw a rational and deterministic science as an ally in the war against an obscurantist religion that accepted providential intervention in human affairs. Science viewed both nature and society (as depicted by men like the philosopher Herbert Spencer and the historian H. T. Buckle) as under the aegis of law.

But if all things were determined by natural or social law, and if, as advanced liberals believed, even the behavior of individuals, at first blank slates, was under the control of past associations, what room was left for liberty? As we have seen, J. S. Mill adopted a compromise that permitted him to accept a good measure of free will. This widely debated issue was for many, ultimately, a theological question, and it may be that Eliot first grappled with it in theological terms.

The reformed theology of Luther and Calvin—the deterministic Evangelical theology to which George Eliot gave credence in her youth—rested firmly on the doctrine of justification by faith alone. First Paul and then Augustine had set down this principle and elaborated its implications. For the Protestant reformers, the theology of the sixteenth-century papacy seemed virtually that of the heretic Pelagius. The early reformers refuted the idea that man might earn salvation by his own efforts, either by his own good works, or by securing a share of the merits of the saints through the purchase of indulgences. Instead, they held that natural man was wholly depraved and therefore incapable of doing good without the saving power of God's grace. By his own efforts, man could never be reconciled with God or earn redemption from the sinfulness of his corrupt nature; such reconciliation and redemption were obtainable by faith alone, and could only be bestowed as a free gift by God.

All this had been set down by Saint Paul, particularly in his Epistle to the Romans. In the ninth chapter of this work, Paul elaborated these convictions in the peculiar form they were to have in the history of Christian thought. Paul identified salvation by faith with determinism, and salvation by works with free will. Both faith and determinism were held to be proved by God's preference for Isaac's second son, Jacob, even before his birth, over the true possessor of the birthright, the firstborn Esau. Esau's disqualifications for the birthright, like Jacob's merit, then, had been implanted in the womb. They had been part of God's great design. And how could a creature have any ground for complaint on this score against his creator? Paul employed this instance of God's apparently unmotivated choice of Jacob as a precedent for arguing that he had now passed over the firstborn chosen people of Israel, "the children of the flesh," since they had failed to accept Jesus as their Messiah, in favor of the newly chosen Christian church, "the children of the promise." (A recent social theorist has written of "the Jacobic myth of the elect," which in various forms has played a role in the making of modern ideologies, offering intellectuals like Jacob—who feel cheated of the authority to which they believe their intelligence and moral superiority entitle them—the birthright assigned to the firstborn Esaus, the men of physical prowess.[6]) The terms employed in the King James version of Paul's Epistle, like those in the original, were words associated with mundane matters of inheritance and disinheritance, and the message was clear: God could do what he wished with his own. Christians saw in the despised position held by the Jews the fulfillment of the biblical prophecy that those who rejected Christ would themselves be rejected.

In Eliot's view, after her lapse from Evangelical faith, the Jews had been deceived into expecting a temporal rather than a spiritual savior. She discussed this question with a believer, her friend and a member of the Coventry circle that Eliot joined in the early 1840s, the Independent minister John Sibree. (Sibree's translation of Hegel's *Philosophy of History*, one may note, remains the standard one.) In a conversation, recollected by Sibree's daughter, Mrs. Cash, which took place during the period when Eliot was estranged from her father and felt ill-treated and misunderstood, Eliot suggested that God ought not to have so deluded his chosen people. Sibree countered, following Paul, "But we have no claim upon God," to which Eliot indignantly replied, "No claim upon God! We have the strongest possible claim upon Him."[7] On another occasion—again Mrs. Cash is our source—Eliot spoke of the claim a child had upon a parent: "There may be conduct on the part of a parent which would exonerate his child from further obligation to him; but there cannot be action conceivable which should absolve the parent from obligation to serve his child, seeing that for that child's existence he is himself responsible." Mrs. Cash readily connected this position on the question of inheritance with Eliot's earlier view of mankind's claim on God.[8] Here we have an early statement of Eliot's view of inheritance expressed in theological as well as worldly terms.

When George Eliot moved to Coventry in 1841 she became acquainted with the Brays and the Hennells, families originally of dissenting and Unitarian backgrounds, who had become freethinkers. The Brays and Hennells formed an intellectual circle which Eliot, after her fervent Evangelicalism had passed, joined. Charles Bray—who married Caroline Hennell—was the son of a well-to-do Methodist ribbon manufacturer. Bray read the works of the eighteenth-century American Calvinist Jonathan Edwards and the utilitarian philosopher Jeremy Bentham, and distilled from their writings a determinist position of his own. In *The Philosophy of Necessity* (1841) Bray presented his philosophical opinions, among them an adherence to phrenology. Such a view, the proponents of phrenology insisted, was essential to bridging the gap between what the religious saw as the entirely separate entities of spirit and matter. This union of mind and body would provide, they argued, a "physiological basis" for a genuine "social science."

The subject of a determinist phrenology divided advanced liberals in England. Both Eliot and Lewes shied away from accepting the contention that cranial bumps revealed unalterable aptitudes and dispositions. In 1855 Bray accused both of having abandoned a scientific "physiological basis." Eliot insisted that she held to the physiological basis, and appreciated all that "phrenology has rendered to the science of man." She simply could not accept all the views of "organology and psychology" of phrenologists, observing that many able men could not.[9] She may have had in mind not only Lewes but J. S. Mill, whose close relationship with Auguste Comte in the 1840s had deteriorated, in part because Mill would not accept Comte's phrenological determinism. Mill's hostility to phrenology had exasperated the French doctrinaire who believed, as did both the Brays and the Hennells, that the acceptance of phrenology (whether its details proved true or not) was the essential basis for a new scientific faith.[10]

When Eliot rejected their specifically phrenological opinions, the Brays and the Hennells feared that she was retreating from adherence to their broader philosophical basis as well. In 1857, in a letter to Sara Hennell, Mrs. Bray's sister, Eliot attempted to allay her friend's fears. There was too much "sectarian feeling" on the subject of phrenology, she wrote. "The last refuge of intolerance is in not tolerating the intolerant," she remarked, and then confessed, "I am often in danger of secreting that sort of venom."[11] Her jibe at sectarianism was resented. In a subsequent letter to Bray, Eliot retreated and blamed a bad headache for what she had written. She had intended no attack on Bray, though she suggested that he too shared the rigidity of many phrenologists who seemed moved by "the same sort of spirit as that of religious dogmatists"—"that in proportion as a man approximates to their opinions without identifying himself with them, they think him obnoxious and contemptible." She concluded by wishing her friends all happiness ("all sorts of love and good feeling") which was the "best result that can ever come out of science."[12]

The portions of Eliot's letter that dealt with the philosophical basis for Bray's book were more penitent but not entirely reassuring:

> In the fundamental doctrine of your book—that mind presents itself under the same condition invariableness of antecedent and consequent as all other phenomena (the only difference being that the true antecedent and consequent are proportionately difficult to discover as the phenomena are more complex)—I think you know that I agree. And every one who knows what science means must also agree with you that there can be no Social Science without the admission of that doctrine.

(But Eliot's last sentence was certainly ambiguous since in the previous year, as we shall see, in an article on Riehl, Eliot had expressed considerable doubts as to the possibility of such a deterministic universal social science.) What had particularly offended Eliot, her letter to Bray continued, was Bray's having described, in Eliot's words, "the disregard of individuals as a lofty condition of mind." This view, she wrote, "I dislike extremely." She was increasingly convinced that "our moral progress may be measured by the degree in which we sympathize with individual suffering and individual joy."[13] Clearly, Eliot had set herself in opposition to doctrinal systems that prided themselves on subordinating individuals to the supposed interest of the community.

Eliot, along with other advanced liberals, was wrestling with the problem of free will and determinism. The Brays and Hennells, as has already been noted, were following the dominant deterministic traditions of Bentham's utilitarianism and Priestley's Unitarianism, with which movements they had strong personal associations. But even among Unitarians and utilitarians a new spirit was arising that demanded a place for free will. James Martineau, the most able and articulate leader of British Unitarianism, with whom Eliot became acquainted in the 1840s and whose writings for the *Westminster Review* she admired, moved decisively toward this position.[14] Similarly, John Stuart Mill, as we have seen, overcame his hereditary link to Benthamism to champion a decisive place for free will in his *System of Logic,* which Eliot read and valued.[15] Eliot, then, first rejected Calvinist determinism and next rejected the liberal, scientific determinism of her Coventry friends, to embrace what both Martineau and Mill described as a joyful liberation from the moral and psychological burdens of necessity.

After Caroline Hennell, whose family tradition had been Unitarian, married Charles Bray in 1836, she became worried about her husband's freethinking rationalism, and appealed to her brother Charles for support in her Christian faith. Charles Hennell's careful re-examination of the New Testament, undertaken to refute Bray's views, convinced him that Bray was on sound ground. Hennell's *An Inquiry into the Origins of Christianity* was published in 1838. Quite independently, it would seem, without having read Strauss's *Life of Jesus,* which had appeared in 1835, or any of the writings of German higher criticism, Hennell had come to many of their conclusions. Strauss later commended Hennell for having avoided the polemical tone of "ridicule and scorn which characterize his countrymen of the Deistical school." Hennell had written in the spirit of contemporary German philosophy, Eliot observed some years later, not "deriving religion from priestcraft, but from the tendencies and wants of human nature."[16]

In 1846 the publisher John Chapman published Eliot's translation of Strauss's *Life of Jesus* in three large volumes. Caroline Hennell—by now won over to her husband's and her brother's opinions—had begun the work of translation, but it had proved too difficult for her, and Eliot assumed the task. This had been a considerable undertaking, requiring a good knowledge of ancient and modern languages and biblical scholarship of a high order. The publication of the translation gave Eliot a considerable reputation in English freethinking circles.

In his *Life of Jesus* Strauss had sought a new way of understanding the life of Jesus, "the mythical." The orthodox treatment of these events had long since ceased to convince, and now the rational, historical view of the Gospels was in doubt. Strauss's method was to present the mythical view by refuting both "supernaturalistic and rationalistic opinions."[17] These New Testament myths were not inventions by an individual, he argued, but had been fashioned gradually.[18] The long expectation of a Messiah among the Jews would alone make mythic infiltration into the

Gospels' story probable, nor would there have been any reluctance to allegorize and introduce outright fiction into such accounts, particularly if this were to the interest of a patriotic or religious party. If widely accepted, Strauss suggested, even such individual inventions would prove agreeable to popular sentiment and partake of the character of myth.[19]

Strauss saw himself as "intrinsically a believer," neither an eighteenth-century Deist nor a freethinker, but rather, in the modern spirit, as one moved by a "veneration for every religion, and especially for the substance of the sublimest of all religions, the Christian, which he perceives to be identical with the deepest philosophical truth."[20] Strauss turned to Saint Paul's Epistle to the Romans for evidences of this truth. In becoming human, as Paul had made clear, Jesus had recognized all men as his brothers, equally the children of God. The "servile relation of man to God" had ceased as love took the place of law and dread of punishment. A sinful man no longer needed to struggle to conform to a law that no human could possibly fulfill.[21] Finding difficulties in all previous Christology, Strauss urged as the solution to the theological question that humanity be substituted for the historical Christ. "Is not the idea of the unity of the divine and human natures a real one in a far higher sense, when I regard the whole race of mankind as its realization, than when I single out one man . . . ?" For Strauss this substitution was "the key" to Christology. "And shall we interest ourselves more in the cure of some sick people in Galilee," Strauss inquired, "than in the miracles of intellectual and moral life belonging to the history of the world—in the increasing, the almost incredible dominion of man over nature—in the irresistible force of ideas."[22]

The church had understood the Gospels as history: Strauss's critical theology saw them as myth. Ludwig Feuerbach wrote along similar lines in *The Essence of Christianity* (1841), a translation of which George Eliot published in 1854. Writing to Sara Hennell as she was completing her translation, Eliot declared that "with the ideas of Feuerbach I everywhere agree."[23]

In her Evangelical years Eliot's model had been Saint Paul. Years after falling away from her Evangelical beliefs, Eliot could still ask, as she had in 1849, "When shall I attain to the true spirit of love which Paul has taught for all the ages?"[24] When she encountered Feuerbach's views in 1851, she was prepared, thanks to Hennell and Strauss, to enter sympathetically into his humanistic approach, particularly because of the German philosopher's insistence on love as the central term of his philosophy.

For Christians, Feuerbach argued, God was a "morally perfect being," the projection of man's idealized image of his own moral nature. This idea was at the heart of Feuerbach's anthropology. But an immense chasm stood between man and this conception of God, Feuerbach observed, and alienated man was dispirited by his consciousness of how far he stood from this moral ideal. Man's incapacity as a sensual being to follow the law made him conscious of his being a worthless sinner. For Feuerbach as for Paul, love constituted the means of reconciling a sinful man with a perfect God.

For Paul, however, this reconciliation was only possible through the freely given grace of God, for man was incapable of securing such redemption by his own self-righteousness, or even, on his own, by praying for the necessary grace. All was in the power of a predestinating deity. For Feuerbach, on the other hand, love and sympathy were natural to all men and not dependent on the grace bestowed on a few. For him, sympathetic love was a further and necessary step in the continuing progress of civilization. "Love is God himself, and apart from it there is no God," Feuerbach declared. "Love makes man God and God man"; it was "the true unity of God and man, of spirit and nature." Love "idealises matter and materialises spirit."[25] Here was a union of matter and spirit that did not require a belief in phrenology.

Feuerbach's love, moreover, was a "sensuous," a "flesh and blood" love: "Love is materialism; immaterial love is a chimera," he proclaimed. Feeling was more important than ideas, just as love and mercy were more important than the rectitude of the law.[26] Saint Paul's derogation of the natural life, particularly the sexual life, was for Feuerbach the insidious result of a supernatural religion.[27] Pauline Christianity not only venerated virginity, but considered marriage a sinful indulgence to the weakness of the flesh, and unlike the Old Testament eschewed divorce.[28] The Christian wanted to be perfect and was ashamed of his sexual instinct. Feuerbach saw man and woman together as "the true man."[29] For him, love, particularly sexual love, "works wonders." Through such love, man transcended his individuality and proceeded to love of the species.[30]

Feuerbach rejected the narrow and exclusive view of faith and the faithful preached by Saint Paul. The Pauline conception isolated God, alienated man from himself, loosened social bonds, and thereby contradicted morality. So far as the admission of nonkosher foods into the Christian's diet and other nonessential questions were concerned, Paul's doctrine was liberal, but otherwise his views were "dogmatic, exclusive." Paul preached that "he who is not for Christ is against him," and rejected all unbelievers, thus abolishing "the natural ties of humanity." Feuerbach argued that "Faith is essentially intolerant, [and] necessarily passes into hatred, hatred into persecution."[31] "Can I love anything higher than humanity?," Feuerbach inquired. But "Christ, as the consciousness of love, is the consciousness of species," he concluded, and he who loves man "for the sake of man" is a Christian, and indeed is "Christ himself."[32] These were ideas that Eliot welcomed.

Feuerbach's materialistic humanism was founded on a left-wing Hegelianism which held that not Hegel's Mind but Praxis—man's activities in his struggle to develop his powers and subject nature to his purposes—was the motive force of history. Feuerbachian man would exert his will to achieve improvement. When men had secured this new comprehension of the historical process, they would cease to be the puppets of historical necessity. The young Marx wrote sympathetically of the Feuerbachian version of Hegel. At the time of the appearance of Feuerbach's work, Marx even argued that a necessitarian historical materialism would in a final synthesis be negated by its dialectical opposite, leaving men no longer subject to unconscious "laws" but able to formulate their own conditions of living. Man's alienation—not from God, as the religious believed, but from man's own true self and from humanity, as both Feuerbach and Marx held—would then cease. Both these left-Hegelians urged that a knowledge of the laws of history and sociology would enable men to assist in molding a future society along lines compatible with what progress had in store for mankind. They called for a state more acceptable to a well-instructed social conscience, even as they pictured a utopia free of the compulsion of circumstances.[33]

When asked in later years to whose influence she could trace the first unsettling of her religious views, George Eliot did not refer to German philosophers: she pointed to Sir Walter Scott.[34] On another occasion she noted a novel by Bulwer-Lytton where an atheist behaved virtuously, and wrote of how, when she had read the book at age thirteen, she had been "considerably shaken" by the possibility that "religion was not a requisite to moral excellence."[35] Elsewhere, Eliot described her initial shock at the revelation by her Methodist aunt of the lack of scrupulous morality among those who otherwise had strong religious feelings; she had been startled to discover, for example, that even the most enthusiastic Methodists could lie without a qualm. She might have been reminded not only of Scott's portraits of religious hypocrisy in *Woodstock,* but also of how, in the case of Balfour of Burleigh in *Old Mortality,* a fanatical determination to impose the true faith could produce undoubted vice. On the other hand, the apparently unsaved could conduct themselves not only according to the standards of chivalric virtue (which she admired) but with a moral sensitivity.[36] Scott's creed had been one of religious tolerance. And Eliot, with sensitive sympathy, told a young friend that "the great lesson of life is tolerance," one of "live and let live."[37]

Other influences beside Scott—or Strauss or Feuerbach—were at work in bringing Eliot to this position. The historian and essayist Thomas Carlyle, whom she described as "a grand favorite of mine," had played a role. Although he was not "orthodox," she wrote of Carlyle when she was still a believer, "his soul is a shrine of the brightest and purest philanthropy, kindled by the live coal of gratitude and devotion to the Author of all things."[38] When she met Carlyle's American admirer the philosopher-poet Ralph Waldo Emerson in 1848, she pronounced him "the first *man* I have ever seen."[39] A former Unitarian with Swedenborgian leanings, Emerson, like Carlyle a mystic and a transcendentalist, was an opponent of materialism and necessitarianism.

The arguments of the philosophical necessitarians might be more scientific than those of believers in free will—just as the theological structure of Calvinist predestinarianism possessed a stronger intellectual base than that of its free-will Arminian opponent—but Eliot found necessitarianism and Calvinism deficient in terms of human sympathy. When only seventeen, and still "a strong Calvinist" (she recalled in 1859 after the publication of *Adam Bede*), she had concluded that her Methodist aunt's moral authority was to be found in "the spirit of love which clings to the bad logic of Arminianism." This was the spirit Eliot found in Feuerbach. Eliot described her aunt as "very loving—and . . . a truly religious soul, in whom the love of God and love of man were fused together." Eliot had talked a good deal with Dissenters previously, but they had all shared with her the doctrines and outlook of Calvinism; her aunt, however, was an Arminian, a believer in the efficacy of works as well as grace, and in the possibility of salvation for all. In the course of "little debates" on free will and determinism, on works and grace, not her aunt's logical deficiencies but her underlying moral "superiority came out."[40]

While George Eliot shed her Evangelicalism, she did not retreat to a version of eighteenth-century free thought, with its rejection and condemnation of the religious heritage. She disapproved of the Voltairean dismissal of religion as the dwelling place of fools and knaves, and later was critical of rationalists, like the historians H. T. Buckle and W. E. H. Lecky, whom she saw as too cavalier in their dismissal of revealed religion and its accompanying emotions. "I do not share Mr. Buckle's opinion that a Scotch minister's groans were a part of his deliberate plan for keeping the people in a state of terrified subjection," she wrote in 1865: "[T]he ministers themselves held the belief they taught, and might well groan over it." Following the arguments of conservative writers—and of her own version of the politics of inheritance—she urged a recognition of the strength of "our sentiments," religious and other, which she called "organised traditions" drawn from "the life lived . . . before we were here," and which justified so many of our actions. "A mind at all rich in sensibilities," she continued, was made uneasy by "an undistinguishing attack on the coercive influence of tradition." She urged a better regard than that which rationalists were usually willing to grant for "the mysteries of inheritance" and "the dependence of one age upon another."[41]

If she was ready to defend the religious heritage against the rationalists, she was equally prepared to attack the bigotry of some members of the clergy. In an 1855 article Eliot denounced the ugly side of Evangelicalism as it appeared in the sermons of Doctor John Cumming, one of the more popular preachers of the day. Cumming, she wrote, displayed an inability to sympathize with "the disinterested elements of human feeling," and indeed with human feelings generally. As a Feuerbachian, Eliot thought that the idea of God was "really moral" only when God was "contemplated as sympathising with the pure elements of human feeling" and as "possessing infinitely" the qualities that we think "moral in humanity." But she maintained that "Dr Cumming's God is the very opposite of all this."[42]

But even Evangelicalism, with its constraining doctrines, might have a good side. In the third of the *Scenes of Clerical Life* (1857), the novella *Janet's Repentance,* Eliot described the transforming power of religion, the superiority of feeling to ideas, in a well-presented Evangelicalism. In this story, Eliot wrote to her publisher John Blackwood in June 1857, the conflict was one between "*ir*religion and religion," between "immorality and morality," not as some might think between Anglican bigotry and Evangelicalism. Her "irony" was directed not against opinions but against human "vices and weaknesses." The benign Arminian theology of the Anglican layman Dempster was accompanied by a persecutorial spirit, while the Calvinistic, hell-fire Evangelical preacher Tryan behaved as a minister sympathetic to the emotional needs of his parishioners.[43]

Certainly, in the novella Tryan identifies Christianity with a "too narrow doctrinal system," and sees "God's work too exclusively in antagonism to the world, the flesh, and the devil." The narrator notes that his "intellectual culture was too limited" (chap. 10). But he is a sensitive human soul who rejects the calculations and "complacency of statistics" of so many in the Arminian party, however rational, and relies instead on an "emotion" that is "obstinately irrational" in "caring for individuals" (chap. 22). In the tale, Eliot credits Evangelicalism, not unlike the older Dissent, with bringing into the local society the "idea of duty," "that recognition of something to be lived for beyond the mere satisfaction of self." The Evangelicals encouraged men to acquire "a principle of subordination, of self mastery," making them "no longer a mere bundle of impressions, desires, and impulses." Eliot praised the effort of the religious to subdue "selfish desires" and to achieve a "Christ-like compassion" (chap. 10).

If in *Janet's Repentance* Eliot suggested that even a "narrow doctrinal" Evangelicalism had possibilities for good, in *Adam Bede* she celebrates the union of a relatively benign theology and the sympathetic conduct of its preachers and pastors. She delights in both the complacent Anglican latitudinarianism of Parson Irwine, a man of wide-ranging human sympathies, and the evangelical Arminianism of the Methodist lay preacher Dinah Morris. The time is 1799 and Methodists from the stony mining and manufacturing districts of the north are coming to preach in the country village of Hayslope. Dinah wishes "to bring home to the people their guilt, their wilful darkness, their state of disobedience to God," but she sees herself as primarily wishing to assure the alienated poor of the possibility of "the divine peace and love" in their own lives (chap. 2). Parson Irwine is perhaps more interested in the local hunt than in either his pastoral duties or theology. He believes "the custom of Baptism [is] more important than its doctrine." But more than compensating for what the world regarded as these pastoral or doctrinal deficiencies, Irwine is "tender to other men's failings, and unwilling to impute evil" (chap. 5). On the other hand, Irwine's Evangelical successor, Ryde, "insisted strongly on the doctrines of the Reformation, . . . visited his flock a great deal in their own homes, and was severe in rebuking the aberrations of the flesh." His parishioners, however, do not love Ryde as they had loved Irwine. For as Eliot's protagonist Adam Bede observes, "It isn't notions sets people doing the right thing—it's feelings" (chap. 17).

When Adam Bede in his youth had visited the meetings of Methodist preachers, we are told, he could always find a logical loophole in the Arminian argument. He disputed so insistently one day with a Wesleyan class leader that the Methodist charged him with intellectual vanity which the devil was using against "the simplicity o' the truth." Upon consideration, Adam came to agree that "whether folks are saved all by God's grace, or whether there goes an ounce o' their own will to 't, was no part of real religion at all" (chap. 17). "Sympathy" was "the one poor word which includes all our best insight and our best love," the narrator observes toward the end of the novel (chap. 50).

In the end, Eliot saw the necessitarian doctrines of the Calvinists as a prime target. Although sympathy had in some part redeemed Tryan's Evangelical theology in *Janet's Repentance,* she continued to denounce rigid determinism in religion as a force for evil. After hearing the evangelist Charles Haddon Spurgeon speak at the Park Square Chapel in London in November 1870, Eliot excoriated his "Grocer's-back-parlour view" of Calvinism which stressed predestination—an abject determinism, even fatalism, that Eliot felt unworthy of an enlightened humanity.[44] His was the Evangelicalism of Doctor Cumming, or of Bulstrode in *Middlemarch.*

By the last third of the century Calvinism was no longer the most influential disseminator of necessitarian opinions among educated Victorians. Science was successfully preaching this doctrine to agnostics and atheists, and liberals, particularly advanced liberals, saw science as their ally against the stultifying power of the past. Mrs. Henry Ponsonby (a granddaughter of Earl Grey, the Whig prime minister who secured the passage of the Great Reform Bill of 1832, and the wife of the private secretary to Queen Victoria) wrote George Eliot in October 1874 on the difficulty she had experienced in reconciling her scientific outlook with her "approval for moral greatness and beauty and purity in the high ideals you would set before us."[45] In her reply, Eliot observed that the "consideration of molecular physics," which seemed to justify a "hideous fatalism," had nothing to do with the human condition, and ought not to obstruct any movement to "a higher strain of duty." Only by "the modified action of the individual beings" could "the progress of the world" be advanced. Nor should her correspondent's loss of faith in immortality lower her view of the sympathy she owed her fellow creatures, each of whom had suffered because of the nature of human life.[46] The following August she wrote Mrs. Ponsonby that every new day presented an opportunity "for exerting one's will." "I shall not be satisfied with your philosophy," Eliot declared, "till you have conciliated necessitarianism—I hate the ugly word—with the practice of willing strongly, willing to will strongly, and so on."[47]

In the nineteenth century it was the conservatives and the religious who championed free will while doing battle against the scientific necessitarianism of the liberals. The chief upholders of the conservative politics of inheritance—Coleridge and his school—were believers in free will, even as their chief opponents, the Benthamites, upheld necessity. It might be argued that, in insisting on the importance of political tradition, the conservatives were employing the national inheritance as a counter to the new secular ideologies associated with a liberal determinism. But there were ambiguities to be resolved, for we shall see that these conservatives often appeared to argue that race and the national tradition constituted a prime and almost irresistible influence in determining the life of a people.

In an essay on George Eliot published after her death, John Morley, who began his career as a virtual Comtist (or at least a Comtian fellow traveler), described Eliot, whom Victorian liberals saw as one of their own, as more a conservative Coleridgian than a liberal. He explained that "the conservatism of . . . [Eliot's] artistic moral nature was shocked by the seeming peril to which priceless moral elements of human character were exposed by the energumens of progress."[48] We must see to what extent a characterization of Eliot as a Coleridgian is justified.

There was a wide recognition and understanding of the term "Coleridgian" by educated Englishmen, and we can readily recover Morley's meaning. In stressing this dichotomy between the philosopher and poet Samuel Taylor Coleridge and liberals, Morley was following the lines set down by John Stuart Mill in two well-known essays, one on the utilitarian philosopher Jeremy Bentham (1838) and another on Coleridge (1840). Mill regarded Bentham and Coleridge as the mentors of all who thought seriously concerning philosophical and political issues; they were "the two great seminal minds of England in their age," one liberal, the other conservative. Every thinking Englishman, Mill argued, was either a Benthamite or a Coleridgian.[49] Morley, a friend and admirer of Mill, thought of himself as essentially a Benthamite, as a liberal who like Mill valued both progress and order, but whose greater sympathy was for progress.

Bentham was "the great *subversive*," Mill had declared in his 1838 essay, "the great *critical* thinker of his age and country," a "negative philosopher" on the model of Voltaire and Hume who questioned all that was "false in contemporary society." But Mill believed that Bentham belonged to a group of "systematic half-thinkers," people incapable of understanding some of the most important aspects of human complexity. For the determinist Bentham, men were creatures of circumstances, guided entirely by self-interest, by a desire to seek pleasure and avoid pain. "Man is never recognised by him as a being capable of pursuing spiritual perfection as an end," Mill continued. Bentham never admitted the existence of conscience. For him such concepts as "'Principle,' 'Moral Rectitude,' 'Moral Duty,'" had little meaning. Bentham's ethical system had nothing to say concerning "regulating the nicer shades of human behaviour," of sexual or family relations, for example, "or any other social and sympathetic connexions of an intimate kind." And if Bentham's neglect of conscience, sympathy, and "the nicer shades of human behaviour" were not sufficient to disqualify him from serving as a mentor for any poet or writer of fiction, what Mill described as "his contempt for the pleasures of imagination, and for the fine arts" would have been.[50]

Bentham had even gone so far as to base his ethical system on a "felicific calculus," as he called it, a conception that George Eliot in 1857 dismissed with disdain. The utilitarian believed that quantities of pleasure and pain could be placed on a scale that took account of their intensity, duration, certainty, and so forth, and that the sums might be so precisely calculated that a legislature could mold its statutes to conform to the utilitarian criterion of securing the greatest good for the greatest number. In *Janet's Repentance,* Eliot lamented that "certain ingenious philosophers of our day" could take offense at the idea that pleasures and pains were only "slightly influenced by arithmetical considerations." When a mother "is hanging over her last dead babe," Eliot remarks, she can but find "small consolation in the fact that the tiny dimpled corpse is but one of a necessary average, and that a thousand other babes brought into the world at the same time are doing well, and are likely to live." Such a "complacency in statistics" might be "highly rational," she notes, but emotion was "obstinately irrational" in its "caring for individuals." This was "the inherent imbecility of feeling" not understood by this "great philosopher." The "man who knows sympathy" understood the "transcendent value in human pain, which refuses to be settled by equations" (chap. 22).

Both Morley and Mill saw themselves as most of all representing, as had Bentham, the thinking of the eighteenth-century liberal Enlightenment, and not, like Coleridge, the thinking of Edmund Burke and the German idealists who had turned against the Enlightenment. Yet both, particularly Mill, were also responsive to parts of the counterrevolutionary philosophy of Coleridge, with its conservative emphasis on order and on the value of the past. The "German-Coleridgian doctrine," Mill wrote, was transcendental, mystical, intuitive—in contrast to the Enlightenment's sensualism, rationalism, and determinism. Understanding how thin was the crust of civilization, Coleridgian conservatism sought to put men under a *"restraining discipline"* so as to induce them to subordinate "personal impulses and sins" to "the ends of society."[51]

Coleridge and "the philosophers of the reactionary school," Mill further observed, took the inherited past into careful account, and did not share the "disrespect in which history was held by the French *philosophes"* and by Bentham. The eighteenth-century philosophers had attempted to construct a social science—in Bentham's case a science of legislation—but had failed to do "justice to the Past," to appreciate the important role played by traditional "institutions and creeds" in individual and social life. Like Burke, and most unlike Bentham, Coleridge believed that "any doctrine" inherited from the past, no matter how apparently irrational, was "not altogether a fallacy" but must have some basis for existence, must fulfill or have fulfilled "some natural want or requirement of human nature," and therefore that such a doctrine deserved the careful examination, and indeed the respect of the living.[52]

The Coleridgian school particularly stressed the idea of nationality. It was the German romantic Herder, at the end of the eighteenth century, as we have seen, who had first written that each nationality was unique, and that each nation must be governed by laws appropriate to its own character and development. Burke argued along similar lines, as did Coleridge. In his essay on Bentham, Mill scolded the liberal philosopher for neglecting what Coleridge had insisted upon,[53] that what "alone ennobles any body of human beings to exist as a society" was a "national character" that served as "a strong and active principle of cohesion." Not, Mill added, "nationality, in the vulgar sense of the term," that is, "a senseless antipathy to foreigners" or "an indifference to the general welfare of the human race, or an unjust preference of the supposed interests of our own country." What Coleridge had in mind, in Mill's words, was "a feeling of common interest among those who live under the same government, and are contained within the same natural or historical boundaries." The people of a nation must "set a value on their connexion" and "feel that they are one people, that their lot is cast together, that evil to any of their fellow-countrymen is evil to themselves."[54] These views of Coleridge, with which Mill clearly sympathized, would become those of George Eliot.

Many liberals, like their Enlightenment predecessors, had no conception of such sentiments, and were actually cheered by their recognition that the forces of national cohesion were waning, Mill further observed.[55] They were individualists and cosmopolitans with no particular sympathy for their own country, speaking good only of humanity in general. Eliot's complaints against the liberalism of her contemporaries would be expressed in similar terms.

Coleridge's politics were deeply rooted in his conception of the inheritance from the past and in his idea of nationality. In his most systematic work on political theory, *On the Constitution of the Church and State* (1830), Coleridge saw the state as composed of interests represented by the forces of Permanence, the landed classes who preserved the nation's priceless national tradition, and the forces of Progression, the mercantile classes who favored reform. The rich merchant, when he bought land, "redeems himself by becoming the stable ring of the chain, by which the present will become connected with the past; and the test and evidence of permanency afforded." Even such remnants of feudalism as primogeniture and hereditary titles counteracted "the antagonistic and dispersive forces, which the follies, the vices, and misfortunes of individuals can scarcely fail to supply." Coleridge noted with approval, on the side of the forces of Permanence, "the proverbial obduracy of prejudices" of a peasant class that resisted even the innovations that would improve their condition.[56] (Such a view, we shall see, was shared by both Riehl and Eliot.) Coleridge insisted on the primacy of the "heritage" of the state and the church and called on the clergymen of the established church, assisted by academics, once again to take up the duties of a "national clerisy": that of preserving the national heritage and "continuing and perfecting, the necessary sources and conditions of national civilization."[57] This was Coleridge's politics of inheritance.

Two other writers defined the politics of inheritance and national tradition in England, established its metaphors, and shaped its emotional tone. The first was Coleridge's immediate intellectual predecessor, the eighteenth-century Whig Edmund Burke; the second was the nineteenth-century Tory novelist and statesman Benjamin Disraeli, who, as we shall see, may have played a significant role in Eliot's intellectual and political development. There were in addition two continental writers, both of whom had won Eliot's high praise, who wrote in similar terms and tones, and who we know to have exercised a considerable influence on her: Auguste Comte and W. H. Riehl.

Burke, the father of modern British conservativism, made the metaphor of inheritance the dominant one for his politics. Burke was horrified by the French Revolution, and by the ease with which many English radicals and Dissenters, and even some Whigs, welcomed that event. In his *Reflections on the Revolution in France* (1790), Burke denounced the destruction of historic French institutions by the revolutionaries, their insults to the monarchy, and their attacks on church property. At this early stage in the history of the revolution, when both English and French liberals still hoped for the creation of a limited monarchy on the pattern established by England's Glorious Revolution of 1688, Burke correctly predicted that this violent attack on national political traditions by fanatics intent on establishing a theoretic, doctrinaire polity would result first in terror and then in a military dictatorship.

In the *Reflections* Burke insisted on both the ordinary meaning and the metaphor of inheritance. An early section of the work dealt approvingly with England's traditional law of bequest, and suggested that by no other polity could "our liberties . . . be regularly perpetuated and preserved sacred as by *hereditary right.*" He was disturbed at "the total contempt" of radicals for "all ancient institutions" which they seemed ready to set aside for "a present sense of convenience or . . . inclination."[58] (These were the sentiments, even the phrases, of the Dodson view of inheritance in Eliot's *Mill on the Floss,* as we have seen.) In the revolution of 1688 Englishmen had wished only "to derive all we possess as *an inheritance from our forefathers,*" without "any scion alien to the nature of the original plant." England's lawyers and legislators made no claims on such "abstract principles as 'the rights of men.'" They preferred "positive, recorded, *hereditary* title" to "theoretic science." From the time of Magna Carta onward, Englishmen had asserted their "liberties as an *entailed inheritance* derived to us from our forefathers, and to be transmitted to our posterity—as an estate specially belonging to the people of this kingdom, without any reference whatever to any other more general or prior right." Thus England had "an inheritable crown, an inheritable peerage, and a House of Commons and a people inheriting privileges, franchises, and liberties from a long line of

ancestors." Thus it was that Englishmen held and transmitted their privileges and liberties just as "we enjoy and transmit our property."[59]

"In this choice of inheritance," Burke declared, England had adopted
"the image of a relation in blood," demonstrating the people's regard for
the country's laws and constitution as one with "our dearest domesticities"
and "family affections." The country gave "reverence to our civil institutions" on the same principle that we do to individuals, because of their age
and descent. If Englishmen acted with a full consciousness of their
history—"as if in the presence of canonized forefathers"—the "spirit of
freedom" would not lend itself to "misrule and excess."[60]

The following year, in 1791, Burke defended the sentiments of chival-
rous sentiment against the naked theoretic reason of fanatic systems-
makers. For him, as it would be for Eliot, feelings were more important
than thought. If men looked more deeply into events they would discover
that "our feelings contradict our theories, and when this is the case, the
feelings are true, and the theory is false."[61] When the people rose against
the government from "a sense of grievance," they would subside when that
grievance received a remedy. But if they rose because of a "theory of
government," which might become "as much a cause of fanaticism as a
dogma in religion," if they rose from "speculative grounds," from "system," their "mind will be heated as much by the sight of a scepter, a mace,
or a verge as if . . . daily bruised and wounded by those symbols of
authority."[62] Only by the "moral sentiments" of a few among them could
we "put some check on their savage theories." But could such sentiments
long survive the inculcation of a creed that wished to destroy all prejudice?
The principles of these fanatics "always go to the extreme"—"with them
there is no compromise." For Burke, compromise was at the heart of the
English political tradition.[63]

When as Tory prime minister Benjamin Disraeli accepted a peerage
from Queen Victoria in 1876, he selected the title of Beaconsfield, after the
location of Burke's estate; it was the title that Burke would have taken if
circumstances had not hindered his elevation to the House of Lords. The
Jewish-born Disraeli began his career as a radical but soon turned to the
Tories as the more congenial party. In his early novels—the political trilogy
of *Coningsby, Sybil,* and *Tancred*—Disraeli stressed the importance of the
national inheritance, and lamented that the Tory party, which ought to be
the national party, had neglected this ideal.

The principles of politics presented by the Jewish financier Sidonia in
the first and last books of the trilogy—loyalty to ancient traditions, a sense
of nationality, and a consciousness of responsibility for the condition of all
members of the community—were Disraeli's own. These were at present
the principles of the Jews, Disraeli observed, whom Sidonia in *Coningsby*
described as "essentially Tories" (bk. IV, chap. 15). Once they had constituted the political faith of all Englishmen. This had been before the mechanical spirit of Benthamism and liberalism, that of the age of utility, had
put them to flight. Sidonia stressed the importance of "the national charac-

ter," and decried the efforts of makers of utopian systems who wished to replace the organic development of the nation with abstractions. Society could not be reconstructed "on a purely rational basis," as liberals believed, on "a basis of material motives and calculations" (IV, 13).

In *Sybil,* the second novel of the trilogy, Disraeli depicted an Owenite socialist who "can spare no pang for the past." The Owenite is pleased to see ideas of family and home disappearing; for him "the domestic principle" had "fulfilled its purpose," and the "irresistible law of progress" will soon replace it by a "new Jerusalem" where men will not live as families and in their own homes but in socialistic communities (III, 10). What the British workingman wished for, on the other hand, were practical reforms; and Disraeli's spokesman in the novel hopes the socialist would "sink his high-flying philosophy and stick to old English politics" (II, 16). The Owenite is described as "a visionary, indulging in impossible dreams, and if possible, little desirable" (V, 4), and his idea of community is more like "a jail" (VI, 5).

Two continental writers, both familiar to Eliot, approached these questions in a fashion similar to that of the English adherents of the politics of inheritance. One, of course, was Auguste Comte. Comte's mentor in this matter was Joseph de Maistre, the antirevolutionary French political theorist who saw Burke as one of his predecessors. Comte saw revolutionary doctrinaires as people who were seeking the violent overthrow of the past, and believed this goal accounted for their hostility to the inheritance of property. The socialistic and communistic writers, Comte declared, had sought to re-establish in utopian and consequently disruptive and unrealizable forms the organic community that the Reformation had destroyed. Their lack of a sufficient "social instinct" resulted from their "anti-historic spirit."[64] For this reason they did not appreciate the importance of inheritance as the natural means by which one generation transmitted the fruits of its labors to the next generation. Even "the best socialists" saw only a "Present without roots in the Past," and this "would carry us headlong towards a Future, of which they have no definite conception."[65] Comte stressed the importance of the family, united through the generations by the principle of inheritance, as a transitional stage leading mankind from self-love to social love. In a Positivist society, he declared, the sense of duty would be substituted for the sense of right, as in a family, and the future society would see "the subordination of Politics to Morals."[66]

Comte had a traditional conception of the nation, of a *patrie,* even as he put forward a cosmopolitan vision of the future that the triumph of a Positivist state would make practicable. The idea and reality of a fatherland would continue to have an important place even after a Comtist victory. The *patrie* was not merely "the necessary forerunner" but was also "the permanent support of the idea of Humanity," intimately connecting man with his milieu, and serving as a way station between family and humanity. It was "the permanent seat of all those moral and intellectual impressions, by whose unbroken influence the individual destiny is moulded." Today,

Comte wrote, when the industrial society sees "classes imperfectly connected with one another"—this being "the chief problem of modern
civilisation"—"the idea and feeling of patriotism," which is "being more
and more impaired by the revolutionary tendencies of our time," is the
only force that might combine the efforts of individuals into collective
activity. The idea of fatherland, however, is "now in danger of being
swallowed up in that of Humanity." Only a Positivist society could provide
the remedy when it achieved control of "all aspirations after universal
association, which are too vague to be practicable." It is therefore necessary
that "our memories of the past, our feelings as regards the present, our
wishes for the future" should revolve about the fatherland and its needs
and aspirations. This was "a public activity capable of being carried on by
successive generations."[67] Comte's religion of humanity predicated "the
substitution of the [Positivist] Catholicism of Paris for that of Rome."
After "the revolution of the West" that would usher in the Positivist state,
Paris would become "the spiritual capital of Humanity"[68]—a testimony,
perhaps, to Comte's love of his *patrie*.

Eliot agreed with Comte regarding the importance of the nation and
national feelings, and its utility in energizing sympathy with a larger community; in this, she differed not only from those who espoused the cosmopolitan liberalism of the England of her day, but also from the even more
defiantly cosmopolitan English Positivists who, we shall see, were more
prepared to advocate class warfare than to preach national solidarity.

Other parts of Comte's doctrine, however, aroused Eliot's resistance.
A critical element of the Positivist creed—with its roots in the rationalism
and cosmopolitanism of the eighteenth century, despite Comte's stress on
the importance of the past—was the conviction that there existed an abstract, theoretical science of society, a generalized, deterministic sociology
applicable to all peoples. Positivists believed that seemingly exceptional
cases were of little significance except to obscurantists of the metaphysical
school: this metaphysical resistance to social science, Comte added, reflected religious preconceptions as well as an antagonism to the goal of
bringing humanity under the aegis of a common, Positivist morality and
polity, the next stage of mankind's progressive development. Eliot had
doubts about a social science of this kind. She was more sympathetic to
the position of the German historical school, particularly to the views of
W. H. Riehl, who ridiculed the idea of a social science. She wrote favorably
on Riehl for the *Westminster Review* in 1856, two years before any of her
fiction had appeared.

An opposition to a deterministic social science, which was her later conviction, had not always been Eliot's position, as we know, and, indeed, we
cannot entirely escape the probability that she felt drawn to two quite
contradictory points of view in the 1850s. During this period, for example,
she wrote in terms that would have won the approval, in conception if not
in details, of determinists such as Comte and Charles Bray. In a letter to

Bray in 1857, for example, Eliot criticized H. T. Buckle—whose first volume on the *History of Civilization in England* had just been published—for insisting that "there is no such thing as *race* or *hereditary transmission* of qualities!" Such "unphilosophic opinions," she wrote, were particularly surprising to her because Buckle was a determinist, and should therefore have known better.[69]

Similarly, her essay on "Woman in France: Madame de Sablé," written for the *Westminster Review* in 1854, traced the source—"the primary one, perhaps"—of the "more abundant manifestation of womanly intellect" in France to "the physiological characteristics of the Gallic race." Among this race, women had a "small brain and vivacious temperament," making it possible for the more "fragile system" of women to "sustain the superlative activity requisite for intellectual cleverness." The "larger brain and slower temperament" of English and German women made for a more "generally dreamy and passive temperament." So "the *physique* of a woman may suffice as the substratum for a superior Gallic mind, but is too thin for a superior Teutonic one." Women might absorb ideas, but they lacked the physical "energy required for spontaneous activity." These "more than unfavourable external circumstances" accounted for the failure of women to make original contributions to art, science, and philosophy. (As we shall see, Eliot's position resembled the physiological argument for female inferiority that Comte set forward in his correspondence with J. S. Mill; Mill stressed the historical and social limits under which women labored.) As secondary causes for the intellectual superiority of French women, Eliot cited social circumstances: the "laxity of opinion and practice" so far as marriage was concerned, and the "stimulating effect of the meeting of the sexes in *salons,* generally under the aegis of women." "Gallantry and intrigue" served "better to arouse the dormant faculties of woman than embroidery and domestic drudgery," she observed.[70]

There was, we see, a significant racial element in Eliot's discussion of Gallic and Teutonic peoples. What might be called a natural historical—even at times zoological—view of mankind was not uncommon at the time, and without adopting such an extreme opinion, she entered into its phrases and spirit. She and Lewes had passed three months in Weimar in 1854, and in June 1855 Eliot wrote a *Fraser's Magazine* article in which she spoke of the "usual heaviness of *Germanity,*" even whose "stare was slow, like that of herbivorous quadrupeds." Later in the piece she noted, on the evidence of a miniature of Schiller, that the author had "the fine wavy, auburn locks and the light-blue eyes, which belong to our idea of pure German race."[71]

The Jewish contribution to German music and poetry was a subject of critical controversy in Germany at the time of Eliot's visit. In a *Fraser's Magazine* article in July 1855, Eliot discussed the aesthetics of Richard Wagner's music-drama[72] without mentioning Wagner's assault on the German-Jewish Meyerbeer for exerting a pernicious influence on German music—a "Jewish" striving for vulgar, tawdry effect. (Wagner's essay appeared in 1850 and attracted considerable attention, although its author did not publicly claim it as his own until 1869.) But Eliot herself, in the intellectual mode of the time, was quite prepared to accept distinctive German and Jewish cultural characteristics as meaningful. In an article written in 1856, for instance, she praised the "German wit" of Heinrich Heine, who, though "half a Hebrew"—Eliot mistakenly described the poet as having been "happy in his mother, who was not of Hebrew, but of Teutonic blood"—had wonderfully combined "Teutonic imagination, sensibility, and humour" with French *"esprit."*[73]

We should understand these opinions, which may put off a late twentieth-century reader, in terms Eliot would set down in a *Pall Mall Gazette* article in 1865. In this piece, she wrote of distinctive national views of things, and like the future Mordecai of *Daniel Deronda* expressed pleasure that "the human race has not been educated on a plan of uniformity." It was the "partition of mankind into races and nations, resulting in various national points of view or varieties of national genius, which has been the means of enriching and rendering more and more complete man's knowledge of the inner and outer world." "It would have been a dreary issue for mankind," she concluded, "if the division into nations" had culminated in "an identity of mental products."[74] Eliot's 1856 article on Riehl had anticipated such opinions. In this review, Eliot accepted Riehl's dismissal of the possibility of a deterministic social science, and yet made room for the quasi-deterministic passing on of a distinctive national and racial character.

Riehl's reputation has undergone a considerable change in the last century. In an essay on Eliot, an admiring Lord Acton described Riehl—a Rhinelander and a once-celebrated professor, writer, and lecturer on the history of civilization—as "an author worthy of such a commentator."[75] A generation later G. P. Gooch's authoritative study of nineteenth-century historiography described him as the great pioneer of German *Kulturgeschichte.*[76] After the Second World War, however, this favorable view gave way to a more critical perception of Riehl as a racist whose writings served as an inspiration for the Blut und Boden populism that became one of the sources of German national socialism.[77]

In her review of Riehl's "natural history" of Germany, Eliot argued that social questions did not properly belong to "the sphere of science"—a position that the Brays and Hennells (no less than Comte) would have seen as heretical, and one, we recall, she felt compelled to disclaim in a letter to Bray the following year. She agreed with Riehl that "the most complete equipment of theory" was inadequate to the statesman or reformer, for "a wise social policy must be based not simply on abstract social science" but on a "Natural History of social bodies," a subject that dealt with the "innumerable special phenomena," with "the peculiar characteristics of the nation, the province, the class."[78]

Eliot dismissed what she ironically termed "the splendid conquests of modern generalisation" which caused men "to believe that all social questions are merged in economical science" and that social relations might be based on rational, mathematical calculation, as the liberal (and later Marxist) adherents of a science of political economy believed. She hit also at the "aristocratic dilettantism" of romantics (like Disraeli and his Young England party, although she did not name them) who believed they could "grow feudal fidelity and veneration . . . by an artificial system of culture." Neither the political economists nor the advocates of the "good old times" had based their views on "a real knowledge of the People."[79]

Reliance on abstract theory concerning social classes had resulted in harmful distortions, she continued. Those who created such "images" as "'the masses,' 'the proletariat,' 'the peasantry,'" and who theorized and legislated for such social bodies without possessing much "concrete knowledge" of them, were deliberately blinding themselves to reality.[80] Eliot noted French radical theorists and writers of the 1840s—citing the novelist Eugène Sue as an example—whose "idealised proletaires" misrepresented social groups in the supposed interest of "a moral end." How much better than such utopian thinkers was Sir Walter Scott, when he "takes us into Luckie Mucklebait's cottage, or tells the story of 'The Two Drovers,'" giving readers a realistic picture of the lower classes in all their "coarse apathy" and "suspicious selfishness," and succeeding better in "linking the higher classes with the lower." (One should note that in "The Two Drovers" Scott displayed what he saw as the sharply different national characters of Scotland and England.) It was a "miserable fallacy that high morality and refined sentiment can grow out of harsh social relations, ignorance, and want; or that the working classes are in a condition to enter at once into a millennial state of *altruism*, wherein every one is caring for everyone else, and no one for himself." Eliot was striking a blow not only against the French romantic revolutionaries but also against the Comtists who believed that the proletariat would serve as the moral conscience of the future Positivist stage of society; her use of the word "altruism," which Comte had coined, made her target specific.[81]

Eliot clearly agreed with Riehl that the peasant was a special bulwark of conservatism, guided as he was by inherited custom which "with him holds the place of sentiment, of theory, and in many cases of affection."[82] The peasant rejected the rational, "bureaucratic plan," the "patent machinery of State-appointed functionaries, and off-hand regulations" favored by "modern enlightenment." His views were practical, not inspired by "the spirit of modern revolution" or "the abstract theorising of the educated townsmen," but by a "narrow and personal impulse, towards reaction." Indeed, the outlook of the peasantry was "highly irrational and repugnant to modern liberalism."[83] But neither Riehl nor Eliot regarded these conditions as grounds for complaint. For Riehl, and, as certain of her later writings would confirm, for Eliot too, these were admirable sentiments.

While granting that the peoples of the Continent felt the "vital connection with the past . . . more vividly" than Englishmen for whom "Protestantism and commerce" had to a greater extent modernized society, Eliot believed that English life was also "in its core intensely traditional." In

politics too, she stressed, as Burke and Coleridge had, the necessarily binding character of a historical national inheritance. There was an "analogous
relation" between the moral tendencies of man and the "social conditions
they have inherited," she observed. Man's nature had "its roots intertwined
with the past, and could only be developed by allowing those roots to
remain undisturbed while the process of development is going on."[84] Eliot
agreed with Riehl that only "purely rational men, free from the sweet and
bitter prejudices of hereditary affection and antipathy" could form "a
purely rational society." But to find such men was "as easy as to get
running streams without springs, or the leafy shade of the forest without
the secular growth of trunk and branch."[85]

Riehl, believing all this, and consequently in Eliot's eyes neither "the
doctrinaire [n]or the dreamer," had described his views as "social-political-
conservatism."[86] Riehl had noted the failure of the German revolutionary
movements of 1848 "conducted from the point of view of abstract democratic and socialistic theories," with the *parti pris* of such theories in favor of
"a bureaucratic system which governs by an undiscriminating, dead mech-
anism." A successful social policy, on the contrary, Eliot observed, again
agreeing with Riehl, had to be based on the actual state of the people. The
French socialists had at least studied the life of the factory operatives—but
they had then gone on to make this "single fragment" of "Parisian proletaires or English factory workers" the basis of a theory describing all society. This was inherently foolish. For Riehl, Eliot noted, "*a universal social
policy has no validity except on paper,* and can never be carried into successful
practice." The same social theory could not apply to the different national
societies of Europe, and even less to the more varied societies of the world
as a whole. For German, French, English, and Italian society were "altogether different" from each other.[87] Riehl's position, as described approvingly by Eliot, was the position of Coleridge and Burke, not that of liberals, utilitarians, socialists, or Comtists.

In concluding her essay, Eliot praised Riehl's "admirable volumes" and
pronounced his conservatism free of "the partisanship of a class," of "a
poetic fascination for the past," and of "the prejudice of a mind incapable
of discerning the grander evolution of things." Riehl's was the conservatism of "a clear-eyed, practical, but withal large-minded man," writing in
opposition to "democratic doctrinaires who have their nostrums for all
political and social diseases." These doctrinaires were an "intellectual proletariat," a well-educated class for whom there was no employment and who
consequently constituted "the most dangerous seeds of disease." The
"communistic theories" of this class, Eliot noted, quoting Riehl directly,
represented "the despair of the individual in his own manhood, reduced to
a system."[88] In this last, we may see an allusion to the determinism underlying so many of the schemes of the radical systems-makers; such a determinism was in contradistinction to the call of the German philosophers
(and of Coleridge and Carlyle) for an assertion of individual will which
might overcome what seemed necessity.

Perhaps as noteworthy as Eliot's praise of Riehl's argument is the incompleteness of her discussion of his book. In what seems a remarkable lapse, Eliot failed to mention in an otherwise reliable account of Riehl's views the German writer's deep prejudices. These were hardly surprising; indeed, they were shared by almost all of the German *völkisch* writers who proclaimed the virtues of their own nation and national character by making unpleasant comparisons with other nationalities—particularly with such pariah groups as Jews and Gypsies.

Riehl had written at some length about Jews, employing traditional stereotypes that would receive even wider currency in the following century. Unmentioned by Eliot was Riehl's contention that Jews—whether as intellectuals or businessmen—had no place in the life of the German nation. Riehl took special note of Jewish journalists and intellectuals, describing them as rootless revolutionaries who had turned the press against established society because of what Nietzsche later called *ressentiment*. Jewish journalists thirsted for revenge against the state and the police, forces that hounded their very existence, moving them to a fierce hatred of society. But, Riehl continued, it had been the original group of the Jewish intellectual proletariat ("jüdischen Geistesproletariats") of the 1840s, most of them journalists (Karl Marx among them, though Riehl did not specifically mention him), whose all-encompassing hatred against society and the state had shaped the feelings of the press as a whole. These Jewish litterateurs had been in the forefront of the revolutionary activity. Riehl portrayed them as adrift: having abandoned Judaism without embracing Christianity, they saw no source of authority either in the German state or the Hebrew theocracy.[89] These journalists were "the Cossacks of modern civilization."[90] Riehl thought no better of the "wandering, haggling Jews" of the "commercial proletariat," who shared their social position and its opprobrium with the wandering Gypsies; these Jews peddled baubles to the peasants, and though performing no legitimate economic role often ended up as uncaring capitalists, whose selfishness invited retribution. They were embedded in their benighted past and sought no place in the modern state. On the other hand, the Jewish intellectual, having broken with his former *Volkstum,* did seek such a role. But lacking a genuine social position—not possessing either a peasant or a proletarian consciousness—these uprooted cosmopolitans could only look to a future revolution.[91]

Why had Eliot not discussed these issues in her admiring essay on Riehl? Was anti-Semitism seen as so inescapable among classes of continental—particularly German—writers that one could omit such details almost as one might omit lapses of style? There may have been a similar forgetfulness in her discussion of Wagner. But forgetfulness on this question is not a satisfying answer when dealing with the future author of *Daniel Deronda*. Eliot may have known that if these opinions were included in her summary of Riehl's work, her support of Riehl's position on the national character would find far less favor from many British liberals and Positivists, who constituted her principal audience. And it was they whom she primarily wished to convert to the politics of inheritance and nationality, for Tories were on the whole already inclined to such a position. Certainly, it was sufficiently daring to stress the importance of national character in cosmopolitan liberal circles without unnecessarily attracting the charge (for Eliot, a false one) of an anti-Semitic tribalism—not necessarily because Jews were much loved, but because the public expression of such sentiments was seen as vulgar and continental.

Rather than regarding Eliot as a Victorian liberal, and as has been the convention, a liberal whose views were somewhat qualified by a Comtian positivism, one can gain a better understanding of her politics, and of her writings, if we see her as a conservative, enlarged and modified by a heterodox positivism. Not that Eliot did not share many of the interests of Victorian liberals and Positivists. But these interests did not constitute the principal thrust of her outlook. One may better comprehend her position if we take into account her deep sense of dependence on the past,[92] her commitment to the English political tradition, and her vision of the English nationality—and even her sympathy with what Coleridge had described as "the proverbial obduracy of prejudices" of the peasant class. Closely related to such a social and political posture, as we have seen, was her stress upon free will in place of a deterministic social science. Such convictions were hardly the hallmarks of either liberalism, or of the Comtian positivism often regarded in Victorian times as a radical wing of liberalism. All this may have been what Morley had in mind when he called her a Coleridgian.

But Eliot was sufficiently liberal to appreciate liberty, not only that of conscience in the manner of the German idealists but also what has been called the "negative" liberty from interference by the state. While prepared to accept certain of the communitarian values of a Comtist society, she was not willing to acquiesce in the quasi-totalitarian polity that Comte had envisioned. Such an ambivalence helped to create the uncertainties felt by many Comtists reading her novels concerning the extent to which she was truly sympathetic to their doctrine.

3

The Positivist Novel

In the early 1820s the financial speculator and social theorist Henri de Saint-Simon attracted a group of talented young followers, among them Auguste Comte, by virtue of his personality and his doctrines. In his final years Saint-Simon preached a "nouveau Christianisme," a religion with a stern morality but no deity. After his death in 1825, his successors, presided over by a *Père Suprême*, governed the disciples, proclaiming a vaguely socialistic ethic that aimed at raising the condition of the proletariat, and, preaching free love, at liberating women from marital servitude. By the time the French government brought their leaders to trial in the early 1830s, for attacks on the family and property, many writers and intellectuals in Europe had come to sympathize with parts of Saint-Simon's doctrine: among these writers were George Sand, Heinrich Heine, J. S. Mill, and Thomas Carlyle.[1] In the 1840s both Mill and G. H. Lewes became admirers of Saint-Simon's former secretary Auguste Comte, who claimed authorship of the more "scientific" aspects of Saint-Simonian belief. (When Saint-Simon had turned to the construction of a new religion, Comte left him in disgust.) Mill was particularly impressed by Comte's view of historical development and his mastery of the logic of the sciences.[2]

In 1842 Comte completed a six-volume work of philosophy that portrayed the history of thought in terms of three progressive stages. The first, the theological stage—when all events, natural and social, were attributed to supernatural causes—had reached its apogee in medieval Europe when the Catholic church had been supreme; in this stage, according to Comte, there had been an organic society, in which all men agreed on the fundamentals of religion, society, and politics. The Protestant Reformation initiated the second stage, characterized by uncertainty and strife. Now men could no longer accept purely theological explanations of natural phenomena. This was an age of transition, a metaphysical stage, in which what had previously appeared certain was hurled into a perpetual flux. Since intellectual and moral certitude had vanished, men invoked liberty of conscience and popular sovereignty as political principles: previously unquestioned assumptions became subjects of debate. By the end of the eighteenth century the development of the principal sciences (mathematics, astronomy, physics, chemistry, and biology) had moved beyond the stages of theological and metaphysical explanation to a new scientific stage. The specialists in each of these fields were now in essential agreement. Only social questions remained embedded in controversy. Comte claimed that he had at last made the study of society a proper social science, eliminating the need for further debate and making it possible for a new, organic society to emerge. In the future Comtian society a united and self-confident public opinion could be relied upon to suppress error just as medieval public opinion had extirpated heresy.

Comte detailed an elaborate liturgy and rituals for a religion of humanity, which would be the established faith of the future Positivist state. If revealed religion in the form of Catholicism had marked the theological stage, and first Protestantism and then Deism characterized the metaphysical stage, the final Positivist era would be one in which humanity— Comte's philosophizing of Christianity, akin to the efforts of Strauss and Feuerbach—would become the object of worship. The days of the new Positivist calendar would celebrate the great writers, thinkers, and scientists of the past: Shakespeare, Racine, Descartes, and Newton would be the saints of the new era. While women would not formally hold either spiritual or temporal office, they would represent the feelings of love and sympathy that characterized the Positivist faith, and undertake to represent its altruistic ethic in the home and in the community.

Comte even constructed a set of Positivist sacraments clearly modeled upon those of Catholicism. Though Comte himself had parted with Saint-Simon because the latter had taken what he regarded as a retrogressive step to create a new religion, he was attempting the same thing. The biologist T. H. Huxley, indeed, would later describe Comtian positivism as Catholicism without Christianity. The somewhat bizarre character of the liturgies of the religion of humanity recalled Robespierre's efforts during the French Revolution to construct a religion of reason.

In the early 1840s Mill and Comte carried on an extensive correspondence. What began for Mill as an acceptance of Comte as a philosophical colleague—even a mentor—ended in disillusion. The principal subject of contention was the so-called woman question. For Comte, women in the future organic, Positivist society would occupy a position much the same as the one they had occupied under the earlier organic society of medieval Catholicism: they would be symbols and sources of love and compassion, and objects of adoration, as Mary had been in the Middle Ages. Comte idealized the society of medieval Catholicism. He even denounced the Protestant remedy of divorce, a device he regarded as characteristic of the uncertainties and conflicts of the metaphysical stage. Sometimes Comte made his rules even more stringent than those drawn by the Catholic church: the Positivist society would not only forbid divorce but also deny remarriage for those whose spouses had died.

A determinist, Comte believed that character was permanently fixed by the facts of individual physiology. For Comte, virtually all women and members of the working class were bound by their physiological constitutions to an inferiority in intellect, character, and physical strength— whereas for Mill individuals could rise by their own efforts above repressive limitations. The issue was one of a deterministic belief in the shaping power of heredity versus a conviction that the individual will could play an essential role in shaping one's destiny. For Mill, society, not biology, had placed women and laborers in subordinate positions: he held that through self-development these disadvantaged groups could improve their circumstances.[3]

Mill had still other grounds for displeasure when he examined Comte's political opinions. The illiberal sides of Comte's doctrine—not only his views on the permanent inferiority of women and the working classes, but his antipathy to free speech, freedom of conscience, and democratic government—had been present in his earlier exposition of Positivist philosophy. However, the full dimensions of the authoritarian regime Comte envisioned emerged with startling clarity only in the four volumes of the *Politique positive*, published in the early 1850s. Here, clearly, despite all Comte had previously urged concerning the importance of links with the historical past, he prescribed a utopian state, *de novo*, one antagonistic to liberty and to the politics of inheritance.

Comte's future Positivist state was to be divided into three classes: there would be a patriciate of financiers and capitalists presiding benevolently and protectively over a vast industrial proletariat; at the apex of the pyramid, above the patriciate, Comte placed a "priesthood" of scientists and intellectuals headed by a high priest of humanity. This intellectual elite would constitute the spiritual power. The proletarians, in alliance with the women, would join the high priest and his priestly associates in maintaining a spiritual watch over the behavior of the patriciate, the possessor of the temporal power, both political and economic. The Positivist ethic to be enforced by the spiritual power was *altruism*, a word Comte coined by latinizing the French *autrui*, meaning "others." The enemy was the self-seeking egoism of the metaphysical stage. The high priest of humanity would employ the pressure of public opinion to govern a Comtian republic of virtue.[4]

Both Mill and Lewes parted company with the French Positivist on these issues. In 1865, eight years after Comte's death in 1857, Mill wrote two lengthy articles on Comte's ideas. While still expressing admiration for his views on philosophy and history,[5] the author of *On Liberty* now denounced Comte's political vision as a nightmare for all who valued freedom and individuality—the fruits of England's national political inheritance. Mill could not accept a society where no opinion contrary to that of the ruling class would be permitted, and where the pursuit of individual happiness in any form would be needlessly discouraged, indeed, exorcised, by a system of ethics that saw the asceticism of a besieged camp as the only legitimate morality. (On a number of these issues, Mill's longtime philosophical antagonist Thomas Carlyle held opinions much like those of Comte.) Mill acknowledged that Comte had ably defended the spiritual and moral advantages of medieval society against the thoughtless denigration of the Middle Ages offered by the writers of the liberal Enlightenment. But while Mill approved of this rendering of historical justice to the organic society of Europe's past, he could only shudder at Comte's effort to revive what he viewed as the repressive medieval spirit of conformity.[6] Lewes, we shall see, would agree with this indictment.

The Positivists were interested in allying themselves with writers whose works would bring the Comtian message to the reading public. In general, Comte was hostile to the idea of literary men exercising any political influence, for fear that this would result in anarchy. "In the normal state of human nature," he cautioned, "Imagination is subordinate to Reason as Reason is to Feeling."[7] Yet Comte saw an appropriate territory for a Positivist writer: the writing of historical novels. Scott and the Italian Manzoni had blazed a path, and Positivists (who possessed an understanding of history) could do splendidly by following their example.[8]

Comte was also prepared to offer advice to poets. With the coming of a Positivist society, Comte wrote, poetry could assume its "true social function," which was "idealizing Humanity" and expressing "the gratitude we owe to her, both publicly and as individuals." Comte called for a future Italian poet to contribute an epic that would preside over "the close of the Western Revolution" just as Dante's epic had presided over its beginning. That poem, which he suggested should be entitled "Humanity," would depict "in succession all the phases of the preparatory life of the race, up to the advance of the final state." And Comte proceeded to describe each of the thirteen cantos of the epic—"thirteen, a trebly prime number" was "the proper number of cantos for any systematic epic."[9]

There was good precedent, then, for the English Comtist Frederic Harrison to urge George Eliot to produce a Positivist novel and even to prescribe its structure. But even before she was encouraged to do so, Eliot had written what many readers regard as her only political novel. That work, *Felix Holt, the Radical,* published in 1866, has been described as a novel "saturated with Comtism" by a noted historian of ideas.[10] But Harrison had had his doubts.

Eliot had presented a copy of *Felix Holt* to Harrison to thank the barrister for his assistance in clarifying legal questions associated with the inheritance tangle of her story. Harrison hastened to acknowledge the gift. He expressed admiration for the work, which he saw as "a romance constructed in the artistic spirit and aim of a poem." Harrison observed that he wished to regard *Felix Holt* as a Positivist work, and he believed that "the right people have I think read it in the right way so far as they could." But there was a difficulty: for "each party and school are determined to see their own side in it," he wrote to Eliot—"the religious people, the non-religious people, the various sections of religious people, the educated, the simple, the radicals, the Tories, the socialists, the intellectual reformers, the domestic circle, the critics, the metaphysicians, the artists, the Positivists, the squires, are all quite convinced that it has been conceived from their own point of view."[11] Harrison's complaint, it would appear, was that Eliot had written too well developed a novel, instead of a work more clearly propagating Positivist doctrine.

Harrison hoped to persuade Eliot—whom he regarded as sympathetic—to write a work that would be less ambiguous, and would more fully embody the Comtian view. He did not ask that Eliot "directly" expound Comte, or that she present a portrait of a society that "should have subjectively and objectively realized in its completeness a Positive system of life." He sensibly took it for granted that "no true art is directly didactic or dogmatic." What he wished was "that the grand features of Comte's world might be sketched in fiction in their normal relations though under the forms of our familiar life." A future Positivist society would make use of the ordinary social institutions and roles that represented the functions of "the temporal and the spiritual power": "the home, the school, the temple, the workroom, the teacher, the ruler, the capitalist, the labourer, the wife, the mother, the child." There was "no human passion which it supposed absent or which it will not set itself to govern." Harrison wanted Eliot to depict a society in which these could all develop naturally and normally— one "where the moral and practical forces are sufficiently elevated to control without arousing too strong resistance, and where the good forces are sufficiently strong to show their value by practical results."[12]

Harrison even offered Eliot a setting, a group of stock characters, and the outline of a plot for such a work. He suggested setting her story in "a corner remote from disturbance," far from the centers of the modern commercial society. Normandy might do or Quebec, where "something of the social tone of Catholicism lingers." Such a social tone was "indispensable" for a discussion of Positivist relations. Yet Harrison postulated that "Revolution and Progress" must have sufficiently "penetrated" the locale so as to have destroyed "all strictly dogmatic religion." Perhaps "a secluded manufacturing village" near Rouen might be a possibility, where Catholic and feudal "doctrines and rights" had passed away but the *"social* spirit of both remained: the positive fruits of science and industry" would be present but without "the negative solvent";[13] this negative solvent was not specifically described by Harrison, but Comte had depicted liberal ideas and class conflict in this fashion.

In such a society, all classes would be present. One might expect to find what Harrison called "the normal capitalist," the Comtian ideal of the benevolent possessor of the temporal power, as well as the quite different "actual capitalist." One would also find "a rural capitalist," perhaps, in Harrison's words, "a transformed French noble with the best sentiments of feudalism surviving and none of its vices." Harrison envisioned Eliot portraying the priestly power of the traditional society yielding to the local physician, who would represent science and the spiritual power of the Positivist world. The physician "should gradually acquire a free spontaneous and entirely moral ascendancy over both capitalist and labourer." He would found schools to introduce science and progress without "coming into conflict" with the church. Armed by "the conscience" of the capitalist and "the confidence" of the people whom "he taught and healed," the physician could "exercise moral control of the best kind."[14]

Harrison understood that the modern society of industrial England might not retain much of the paternalistic social tone of an idealized feudalism or Catholicism. But he suggested that "it would not be impossible" to find these elements in France. It was important that the modern elements in Eliot's novel not be sufficiently strong "to shake the controlling forces to pieces." The "humanising powers" of a "vigorous and disciplined" order in the hands of "a scientific leader" could keep passions and evils under control. For example, he suggested that Eliot might depict an industrial strike that would awaken "the darker passions" of class conflict, a conflict that would then yield to common moral principles and "the active intervention of a trusted teacher." Domestic tragedies could be "curbed" by "more systematic intervention" of the women of the community, who Comte had suggested would supplement the spiritual power of the Positivist priesthood. Such a novel, Harrison concluded, would show the possibility of "healthy moral control over societies"; it would portray "the infinite scope and power of wealth used morally," and would "easily illustrate the superiority of the new to the old life."[15]

George Eliot replied with pleasure to Harrison's praise of *Felix Holt,* but noted the "tremendously difficult problem" of accomplishing the work he had outlined. She had conceived her task as a writer to be that of making "certain ideas thoroughly incarnate" as if these had been discovered "in the flesh" of living beings and not as intellectual abstractions. Art had to deal with life "in its highest complexity," and thus it was "the highest of all teaching." If writing moved from "the picture" of these complexities to "the diagram" of a utopia, "it ceases to be purely aesthetic" and "becomes the most offensive of all teaching." It would not necessarily be offensive to set forth "avowed Utopias," but such a book would be scientific, not aesthetic, in character. It could not "work on the emotions," or "'flash' conviction" by "aroused sympathy."[16]

What Frederic Harrison did not appear to have noticed was that George Eliot had already written a work that resembled his outline, though it parted from his design in significant respects. This was her first novel, *Adam Bede* (published in 1859, seven years earlier), Eliot's portrait of an organic, paternalistic community beginning to feel the effects of modern ways. The novel had no man of science as a protagonist, as there would be in *Middlemarch,* but it did have an entrepreneurial builder, armed with the bourgeois faith that God helps those who help themselves. It is he who acquires the "free spontaneous and entirely moral ascendancy" with which Harrison endowed the physician in his model Positivist novel. A latitudinarian Anglican clergyman supports the builder, though as the purveyor of a commonsensical sympathy rather than a medieval ethic. Factories exist at some distance from the setting of the story, but Eliot's tale includes two rural capitalists, an "actual" landlord, rapacious and self-seeking, belonging to an older generation, and his grandson and heir, the "normal capitalist" incorporating the benevolent traits of the Positivist ideal. Domestic tragedies are curbed by a spirit of compassion and community, as in Harrison's outline, as are small evidences of class conflict, though of a nonindustrial type. And Eliot's scene was an English Midlands village at the end of the preceding century, not the Normandy of the 1860s.

In the village of Hayslope in 1798, Arthur, the grandson and heir of old Squire Donnithorne, seduces Hetty Sorrel, the niece of a tenant farmer. Young Donnithorne, though infatuated with the beautiful Hetty, knows he cannot marry her. Adam Bede, a young builder, respected by the local farmers and his fellow villagers but idolized by Arthur, loves Hetty, despite her frivolous character, and wishes to marry her. When Bede discovers that the young squire has improperly aroused Hetty's affections, though he is as yet unaware of her seduction, he strikes Arthur down. Adam fears that having been encouraged to love Arthur, Hetty will no longer be content to marry at her own social level. Nonetheless, when Donnithorne leaves for the army, Hetty agrees to marry Adam. A few months later, now expecting Donnithorne's child, she flees the village in search of her lover. Not finding him, she is first tempted to commit suicide, but after giving birth she instead strangles her child. Tried for murder, she is found guilty. At the last minute, her sentence of hanging is commuted to transportation after a plea by a penitent Donnithorne. Adam Bede, loving Hetty despite all, has been crushed by these events.

Here is the old regime in all its wicked dimensions. Yet Eliot did not come to curse; indeed she almost blesses this world. Adam Bede is no village Danton waiting to smash the quasi-feudal social system in order to usher in the new society of liberty, equality, and fraternity. Instead, he is a respecter of customary authority. We may see the novel as an almost idyllic portrayal of traditional society just at the moment it is turning modern, and as more redolent of a conservative regard for the past than of Harrison's Positivist formula.

Eliot drew none of her characters as social or political stereotypes. She deliberately refrained from viewing her characters "from a lofty historical level"; she did not think of them "as an embodied system or opinion" (chap. 5), but as individuals. Arthur Donnithorne is a weak man who permits his infatuation to overcome his scruples. What he wishes above all else is to live respected and loved by his tenantry. When Arthur inherits the estate, the tenants are convinced, there would be "a millennial abundance of new gates, allowances of lime, and returns of ten per cent" (chap. 7). Arthur's vision of the future is similar: a well-meaning, good-natured man, even a man of conscience, he sees the estate as "made up of a prosperous, contented tenantry, adoring their landlord, who would be the model of an English gentleman" (chap. 12). When he becomes aware of the great injury he has done Hetty, he exiles himself to the army. When his grandfather dies, Arthur leaves control of the estate to the latitudinarian clergyman Irwine, a good and gentle man much loved by his congregation and the tenantry. Donnithorne, moreover, entrusts certain of his interests to Adam Bede, who forgives the new squire once he sees his genuine repentance. And with the assistance of Irwine and Adam, Arthur's hopes for the estate seem about to be realized.

Hayslope's society is a hierarchical one. How can Arthur fail to overwhelm Hetty, "a simple farmer's girl, to whom a gentleman with a white hand was dazzling as an Olympian god" (chap. 4). This, as Adam understands, places a special responsibility on the young squire's shoulders. When Captain Donnithorne and the clergyman Irwine come to visit the farm of the tenant Poyser, even the irreverent and sharp-tongued Mrs. Poyser is anxious "to conduct herself with perfect propriety." The narrator notes, "For in those days the keenest of bucolic minds felt a whispering awe at the sight of the gentry, such as old men felt when they stood on tiptoe to watch the gods passing by in tall human shape" (chap. 6). Yet Mrs. Poyser was no friend of abject deference when injury was intended. "I know there's them as is born t'own the land, and them as is born to sweat on't," Mrs. Poyser declares, "and I know it's christened folk's duty to submit to their betters," but only "as fur as flesh and blood 'ull bear it." She will not "make a martyr" of herself "for no landlord in England, not if he was King George himself" (chap. 32). (Eliot tried to reproduce the actual tone and accents of provincial speech and the speech of an uneducated peasantry much as Scott had done, and she had praised Scott for his skill in doing so in her article on Riehl; other English writers were to follow her example, notably Mark Rutherford, her admirer and disciple, and of course Thomas Hardy.)

In *Adam Bede* Eliot constructed a pastoral of a self-regulating, organic English society of the old regime. Not mere law but mutual sympathy governed Eliot's traditional community. In her view, the defects of the system could be counteracted by remedies within the system itself. Adam himself, like Mrs. Poyser, is a man of the transition, sufficiently a peasant to feel deference to his superiors, yet ready to speak out against not merely wrongdoing but wrong management. Unlike Eliot's other artisan hero, Felix Holt, who lived a third of a century later, he is not "a philosopher, or a proletaire with democratic ideas, but simply a stout-limbed, clever carpenter with a large fund of reverence in his nature, which inclined him to admit all established claims unless he saw very clear grounds for questioning them." "He had no theories about setting the world to rights"; the "word 'gentleman' had a spell for Adam" (chap. 16).

The new industrialism of the mills and the mines, however, Eliot noted, was accompanied by an age of doctrines: Reformation theology reappeared in the established church as Evangelicalism, and there was a spate of both revolutionary and reactionary social and political creeds. The new age would be one of tormented soul searching and social conflict, an age "made squeamish by doubts and qualms and lofty aspirations." Traditional society "never went to Exeter Hall, or heard a popular preacher, or read 'Tracts for the Times' or 'Sartor Resartus,'" the narrator notes (chap. 52). For Eliot, the older society had been a happier one, for the modern age was too much concerned with ideas and not enough with feelings.

The Comtists complained of the age of seemingly endless doctrinal controversies that had followed the destruction of the happy unity of the medieval, organic society; superficially, this appeared to be Eliot's opinion as well. But the Positivists saw science and the religion of humanity as the fountainheads of a new sense of organic community and unanimity of belief, and preached the future rule of a spiritual priesthood of scientists and intellectuals—and this was hardly Eliot's position in *Adam Bede*. In contrasting the old society with the new, she was more the traditional conservative, the oldfashioned Tory, than the Positivist. She seemed to prefer the older society, "happy" in its inability to know the causes of things, preferring "the things themselves," to the new society "prone to excursion trains, art museums, periodical literature," and even "to scientific theorising, and cursory peeps through microscopes" (chap. 52). Riehl, not Comte, was her mentor in such matters—not the *völkisch* Riehl, but a Riehl suitably tailored for English consumption. *Adam Bede* was molded so as to fit better into the British politics of inheritance and tradition than into a Positivist formula. This was also true of *Felix Holt*.

In *Felix Holt* Harrison might also readily have discovered elements of the Comtian outlook. Like Felix, the Positivists saw the proletariat as a special target for their mission. The workers were the dangerous class. Alienated by the decline of traditional communitarianism, they posed a crude and barbarous threat to an orderly industrial society. The leaders of the proletariat frequently spoke the language of class warfare and incited the workingmen to violent revolution. Revolution, Comte had warned, would prove catastrophic to the hope of improvement; this hope was dependent on the moral regeneration of the proletariat, a necessary prelude to that class becoming a support, along with women, of the spiritual power in a Comtian society.

Felix Holt's mission was not to awaken the working classes to their grievances, but to give them a sense of self-respect and to mend their bad habits. "I want to be a demagogue of a new sort," Holt tells Esther Lyon, one "who will tell the people they are blind and foolish, and neither flatter them nor fatten on them." Felix has no desire to rise above his class. Like Comte, whose view of society included a relatively fixed order, he delights in workers as workers. They were a class "in which a man may be better trained to all the best functions of his nature than if he belonged to the grimacing set who have visiting-cards" (chap. 27). Like Comte himself, Holt seeks first of all the proletarian's moral improvement.

When *Felix Holt* appeared in 1866, a sometimes violent campaign to extend the suffrage was in progress, and radical Liberals like John Bright and Comte's English followers, Frederic Harrison among them, were campaigning in Parliament and in the streets to secure votes for workingmen. In this effort, these London-based Positivists were moving in a direction different from Comte, who had not only disapproved of universal suffrage but who dreaded any stirring up of the working classes as an incitement to dangerous revolution. The English Positivists during the late 1860s and 1870s, as we shall see in the next chapter, were to a remarkable degree under the influence of the class-warfare doctrines of many socialists in clear deviation from orthodox Comtian doctrine. Harrison and other British Positivists—their French counterparts by and large retained Comte's perspective—at this time preferred to ignore Felix's warning, very much in the spirit of Comte himself, that while the working-class "Caliban is Caliban, though you multiply him by a million he'll worship every Trinculo that carries a bottle" (chap. 27).

Felix's view, of course, was not too different from that of many Whigs and Tories who opposed the idea of extending the suffrage. Felix wished to give the worker a share in life, but not the "power to do mischief—to undo what has been done with great expense and labour, to waste and destroy, to be cruel to the weak, to lie and quarrel, and to talk poisonous nonsense." This was the "power that the ignorant number have," an "ignorant power" that came in the end to "wicked power." This was to see the working classes realistically, as Eliot had observed in her Riehl article, not romantically, as she complained that Eugène Sue and George Sand had done. The power to do good must come not from mere engines like parliaments, from mere voting, or from secret ballots, Felix added, but from "human nature,—out of men's passions, feelings, desires." The power that worked political engines for good or for bad was "public opinion," he added, "the ruling belief in society about what is right and what is wrong, what is honourable and what is shameful" (chap. 30). All this was the soul of Comtian doctrine.

Why, then, was Harrison not content with the service Eliot had rendered to the Positivist cause in *Felix Holt*? Since Harrison and other leaders of British Comtism had moved considerably to the left of Comte's political agenda, Harrison could only complain that there was nothing in the novel with which a Tory or a Whig might not agree. George Eliot's friend and publisher, the Tory John Blackwood, confirmed this judgment. After hearing Disraeli's speech to the workingmen on the use of their vote in late

1867, he asked Eliot to write an article on the subject. "It strikes me," he wrote her, "that you could do a first rate address to the Working Men on their new responsibilities." Blackwood even suggested that this address "might be signed Felix Holt."[17] Eliot happily complied.

The spirit of "Address to Working Men, by Felix Holt" was certainly that of the novel proper, but Eliot elaborated the arguments more pointedly. The politics of inheritance, of tradition and nationality, implicit in the novel, were explicitly presented in their most conservative form. The "Address," first published in *Blackwood's Magazine* in early 1868, could only have made an increasingly revolutionary Harrison more unhappy.

Holt began by refusing to compliment workingmen as a class. This had become the habit of radical politicians and the English Positivists. There was no reason to believe, Holt continued, that "a Sheffield grinder is a better man than any one of the firm he works for,"[18] a clear reference to a contemporary case involving two Sheffield grinders hired by their union secretary, Broadhead, to murder a recalcitrant employer. (We shall see that a number of English Positivists would publicly sympathize with Broadhead.) Insofar as life was characterized by ignorance and vice, all classes bore a share of the blame, Felix continued. There was a "law by which human lives are linked together," a "fine widespread network of society" binding not merely all the living as if in one body, but even different generations. "A society, a nation" was "held together" by mutual dependence and a sense of "common interest." To be sound, the members of such a society must think of "the general good as well as their own," must think first not of "Class Interest" but the interest of all in the nation.[19]

Eliot, speaking through Holt, did not deny the reality of class interests. In an "old society," like England's, "there are old institutions," and "among them the various distinctions and inherited advantages of classes" which "have shaped themselves along with all the wonderful slow-growing system of things made up of our laws, our commerce, and our stores of all sorts, whether in material objects . . . or in knowledge." However, to attempt a sudden overthrow of the class system without having a better alternative would be "fool's work." What was necessary, Holt urged, was to turn "Class Interests into Class Functions or duties," to persuade each class "to perform its particular work under the strong pressure of responsibility to the nation at large." (This had been a leading theme of Coleridge, Carlyle, and of Disraeli's Young England party of the 1840s.) All classes must put "knowledge in the place of ignorance, and fellow-feeling in the place of selfishness."[20]

It was important to preserve public order, Holt declared, and this would always be in danger when great changes were taking place. He spoke as a workingman radical, not an upper-class radical with "a title or a French cook." Workingmen had to resist the blandishments of "dishonest men who professed to be on the people's side." There was "a set of Roughs," "the hideous margin of society," and good and wise men must recognize that "the fundamental duty" of government was to maintain order and "enforce obedience" to the laws. The preservation of order was not, as many appeared to think, merely in the interest of the selfish aristocratic or middle classes. It was in the common interest to restrain "the savage beast in the breasts of our generation," and to avoid a repression that would "sweep us down in the ignoble martyrdom of fools."[21]

Holt reminded the workingmen of the benefits they received from "what I may call the common estate of society." This was "wealth of a more delicate kind," which they might "more unconsciously bring into danger, doing harm and not knowing that we do it." This was the "treasure of knowledge, science, poetry, refinement of thought, feeling, and manners, great memories, and the interpretation of great records, which is carried on from the minds of one generation to the minds of another." The "security" of this national inheritance required the maintenance of public order, and a "certain patience" with the ways of accumulating wealth in which workingmen were "more likely to discern the evil than the good of." Workingmen must not be too impatient with inherited inequities lest by an overly rapid effort to eliminate them they should only bring about "the too absolute predominance" of the worst class of men and "debase the life of the nation."[22]

Workingmen must recognize "the supreme unalterable nature" of many things in life (of "selfishness, stupidity, sloth") if they are to succeed in their efforts at gradual improvement, Eliot's spokesman Holt continued. It was "bigoted" and "narrow" and "unprofitable" to blame whole classes for evils that "patience must bear." It was only wise to take into account "the selfishness and weaknesses of human nature." A mere change in political institutions would not destroy ignorance and vice; only a sense of parental duty and responsibility would do this. He urged the workers to educate their children, a duty in which too many of them had been deficient; good leaders must set workers against "wickedness in low places" as well as in high. In this way, by recognizing the necessity for communal feeling and cooperation in time of peace as in time of war, Englishmen could shape "the rules of fellowship" to the concept of a "common good."[23]

Holt entreated workingmen not to "injure your inheritance and the inheritance of your children," as they would by a precipitate stoppage of the sources of "leisure and ease." To do this would be as "short-sighted" as France and Spain had been when "in jealousy and wrath, not altogether unprovoked," they banished "races and classes that held the traditions of handicraft and agriculture." (This reference not only to the Huguenots but to the Jews and Moors of late fifteenth-century Spain may have been prompted by Eliot's involvement at this time in the writing of *The Spanish Gypsy*.) The better "endowed classes, in their inheritance from the past"— "this treasure which is held in the minds of men"—"hold the precious material without which no worthy, noble future can be moulded." Privilege, even though often "abused," had value to society as "the nurse of excellence." This was a part of "the great law of inheritance" to which "we have to submit ourselves."[24]

Here too there seemed little, except in emphasis, to which orthodox Comtists might take exception, though, as noted earlier, many English Comtists were on their way to taking a more extreme position. Their having joined advanced liberals in mounting grand demonstrations of workingmen to compel Parliament to extend the suffrage helped to spur Matthew Arnold, like Eliot fearful of mob violence, to denounce the followers of system-makers like Comte. In a *Cornhill Magazine* article in July 1867 Arnold attacked Frederic Harrison by name, noting his hostility to high culture, and explaining it by stressing Harrison's awareness that culture was "the eternal opponent of the two things which are the signal marks of Jacobinism—its fierceness and its addiction to an abstract system."[25] This was not an entirely fair estimate of Harrison's *public* position at this time, though in three to four years time it would come closer to being so. Eliot certainly did not neglect the second term of Comte's motto of devotion to "Progress and Order." And she defended the nation's cultural inheritance—which she defined in a letter to Harrison as "the highest mental result of past and present influences"—against both proletarian fierceness and systems overly flattering to the workingmen, even as she had in her 1856 essay on Riehl.[26]

But if it was still possible for Harrison to see Eliot as a quasi-Comtist or a Positivist sympathizer after reading *Felix Holt,* it was an act of self-delusion for him to have thought of her in such terms after publication of her 1865 poem "A Minor Prophet," which offered a distilled version of the message of her novel *Romola,* published two years earlier. Of course, Harrison may not have read the poem, or, if he had, may not have fully comprehended its relevance, since it was directed against utopias, and since Comte's followers did not see their future Positivist society as a utopia—though Eliot did. It is more difficult to understand Harrison's failure to see *Romola* (which he did read) for what it was: an *anti*-Positivist novel, describing the transformation of a one-time sympathizer into a clear opponent.

In her poem "A Minor Prophet" Eliot depicted an enthusiast "whose ancestors in Cromwell's day believed / The Second Advent certain in five years" but who was now persuaded that the adoption of a vegetarian diet would bring about a state of perfect harmony. Such doctrinaires

> Somewhat too wearisomely on the joys did insist
> Of their Millennium, when coats and hats
> Would all be of one pattern, books and songs
> All fit for Sundays, and the casual talk
> As good as sermons preached extempore."

Eliot herself could not share such crotchets and hopes:

>   . . . Bitterly
> I feel that every change upon this earth
> Is bought with sacrifice. My yearnings fail
> To reach that high apocalyptic mount

> Which shows in bird's eye view a perfect world,
> Or enter warmly into other joys
> Than those of faulty, struggling human kindness
>   . . . I cleave
> To nature's blunders, evanescent types
> Which sages banish from Utopia.

Eliot, ever conscious of human limitations, was prepared to respect the good intentions and to some degree share the hopes of enthusiasts, but she was wary of the results of their efforts. She feared that in their insistence on exalting virtue and eliminating vice, the utopians would suppress liberty, individuality, and personal happiness.

This had been the theme of her novel *Romola,* concerning the religious reformer Savonarola's late-fifteenth-century republic of virtue. It had also been the subject of Sir Walter Scott's *Woodstock,* a novel about Cromwell's Commonwealth published in 1826, of Edward Bulwer-Lytton's *Rienzi,* which appeared in 1836, and of G. H. Lewes's 1849 biography of Robespierre. It is probable that both Scott and Bulwer-Lytton had had Robespierre's republic—in particular its fanaticism and accompanying terror—in mind when writing their novels, and Lewes was no doubt also affected by the sharp hostility to Robespierre found in Thomas Carlyle's 1837 history, *The French Revolution.*

In two of his novels Scott had described efforts to establish republics of virtue and the ideological rigidity and heartless persecutorial fanaticism that followed. In *Old Mortality* he presented the Covenanter fanaticism of Balfour of Burleigh, and in *Woodstock* he portrayed the fanatical Cromwellite Bletson, an intellectual and rationalist, a Harringtonian democrat, as well as a secret atheist who hopes to use the revolution to advance his views. While Puritan enthusiasts hope for a millennial rule of saints, Bletson seeks "a reign of philosophers." Scott dismissed Bletson's "theoretical politics." His vision of "a pure democratical republic" could not work in so large a country as Britain, Scott observed, where wealth was unequally distributed and the great majority of the population was not fit for citizenship. But Scott noted with sorrow that even though events had long ago proved the impracticality of Bletson's principles, "the miscarriage of his experiment no more converts the political speculator, than the explosion of a retort undeceives an alchemist" (bk. I, chap. 11).

The writer and Liberal politician Edward Bulwer-Lytton modeled his historical novels on those of Scott, whose views on the dangers of republics of virtue he shared. In the early fourteenth century Cola di Rienzi had attempted (like the later Jacobins of the French Revolution) to restore the ancient virtues and glories of the Roman Republic by establishing himself as tribune of a revived Rome. Bulwer-Lytton's Rienzi is a fanatic and a mystic, not "a mere demagogue" but someone who has "brooded over the past" and is dominated by "one master passion," in his case, a regeneration of the Romans and the establishment of a *buono stato,* a commonwealth in which the "lawful heritage" of liberty and equal justice the ancient Romans had enjoyed will be restored to their descendants (IV, 1). At first Rienzi is successful, but the realities of power and his fanaticism soon undermine his popularity, and his cruel and tyrannical behavior alienates a people not prepared for liberty (II, 4). A mob sets fire to his residence, seizes him when he attempts to flee in disguise, and murders him—a fate not unlike Tito's in *Romola*.

Religion was the binding element of the polities established by Rienzi and Cromwell, as it was of Savonarola's Florence. Bulwer-Lytton portrayed Rienzi as having joined "strong religious feeling" to "political enthusiasm"—"the religious feeling of a premature and crude reformation." (I, 6n). Inspired by "the daring but wild doctrines" of Arnold of Brescia two centuries earlier, Rienzi's "faith bore a strong resemblance to the intense fanaticism of our own Puritans of the Civil War" (IV, 3), wrote Bulwer-Lytton, who invoked Cromwell as a later specimen of Rienzi three times in the course of the novel (IV, 3; V, 5; IX, 4). Like the Cromwell of Scott's *Woodstock* (and Tito in *Romola*), Rienzi wears a "secret corselet" of mail to protect himself against assassins (V, 1).[27]

In his biography of Robespierre (written before he had met Eliot), Lewes sought to counter the benign image of Robespierre as the "sea-green incorruptible," glorified in France during the 1848 Revolution by the socialist historian Louis Blanc and the poet Lamartine, and in England by the Irish Chartist Bronterre O'Brien. O'Brien had portrayed Robespierre as "one of the greatest of Men and most enlightened of Reformers that ever existed in the World."[28] But Lewes, in contrast, argued that Robespierre was "a fanatic who would sacrifice everything to the triumph of an idea," his conception of a republic of virtue. Robespierre shared with certain contemporary philanthropists, Lewes noted, that union of a "perfect heartlessness towards every individual with a sentimental sensibility towards the mass."[29] Robespierre was neither "a great [n]or good man": he was "a political Fanatic" who cared nothing about "the agony of a few thousands, compared with the triumph of an opinion."[30] He was a "theorist," who saw men as "simple units in a calculation," not as "complex beings, having many wants, many passions, and much foolishness." Men do not and "will not act as you tell them," and "your Republic which went so smoothly upon paper cannot live a day."[31] The Terror was his instrument, and by its means, Lewes concluded, he became "the worst of dictators—a religious dictator."[32] Lewes may have had in mind Robespierre's attempt to install the worship of the Goddess Reason, whose fête Lewes described at some length in his biography.

Lewes urged the subject of Savonarola on Eliot when the two were traveling in Italy in 1860. By that time, Lewes had already been repelled by Comte's politics and by the rituals associated with Comte's religion of humanity. I will argue that Eliot perceived the essential core of the Positivist utopia—in which the social interest would far outweigh, indeed overwhelm, that of any individual—in Savonarola's state, and that she viewed

Savonarola as the Robespierre (and the Comte) of the theological era even as Comte saw himself as the high priest of a modern, scientific version of a medieval organic society.[33] So many of the friends of Eliot and Lewes were Comtists that some disguise of her intentions seemed necessary to avoid offending those who had treated them with kindness when social barriers had been erected against them because of their unconventional relationship.

Nineteenth-century liberals had a generally favorable view of Savonarola. In John Stuart Mill's *On Liberty,* for example, Savonarola appears as a forerunner of the Reformation, and along with the Lollards, the Waldensians, and the Hussites, as "instances of truth put down by persecution."[34] In Savonarola's denunciation of the corrupt Renaissance papacy and in his puritanical insistence on simplicity in dress and ornamentation, one might easily see a harbinger of Luther and Calvin, and the reformers' wish to turn their backs on the greedy commercial society of quattrocento Italy and return to a virtuous primitive Christianity. Moreover, like the Old Testament prophets he regularly invoked, Savonarola had urged his followers, the Piagnoni, to do works of charity and provide justice to the poor. His plan of government revived the liberties of Florence so long suppressed by decades of Medici rule, and he gave his city a regime modeled on the free and representative institutions of Venice, though more democratic and without the doge.

It is not surprising that Eliot's initial portrait of Savonarola as a proto-Protestant should have been a generally favorable one, though her depiction of his state's later stages replayed the critiques of the governments of Rienzi, Cromwell, and Robespierre made by Bulwer-Lytton, Scott, and Lewes. All three writers had described regimes characterized by a mystical fanaticism, religious as well as political, that sought a return from a profligate and disorderly present to a virtuous past. Both Rienzi's and Savonarola's republics, moreover, were experiments in the puritanism that Cromwell's Protectorate established. Rienzi's Rome, Cromwell's England, and Robespierre's France—all failed utopias—were prepared to follow the paths of virtue marked out by the imagined models of either ancient Rome or a primitive Christianity. Eliot saw this as the reason for Savonarola's failure as well. The vanity, self-interest, and self-absorption of the populace contributed to the fall of these republics of virtue, as did the pride and fanaticism of their leaders. And Eliot believed that they deserved to fail because their utopian designs ran contrary to what she believed to be mankind's deepest needs and aspirations.

Eliot's *Romola* was a genuinely learned work, and Eliot took greater pains to ensure the historical accuracy of its perhaps too overflowing detail than her mentor Scott had probably shouldered in any of his novels. In the early days of the enterprise, Lewes described Eliot's deep "personal sympathies with the old reforming priest," who in the final decade of the fifteenth century had attempted to rid Florence of its corruption and transform it into a virtuous state.[35] The work proved a more difficult one to write than any of her previous books, and she struggled through every part of it. She suffered periods of despondency and depression, though Lewes reported in August 1861 that the novel was "slowly crystallizing into what will be a magnificent programme."[36] She began it, she later wrote, as a young woman and completed it as an old one. In 1877 George Eliot would reread *Romola* for the first time in ten years. There was "no book of mine about which I more thoroughly feel that I could swear by every sentence as having been written with my best blood, such as it is, and with the most ardent care for veracity of which my nature is capable." The tale had often made her "sob with a sort of painful joy" as she reread certain passages.[37]

In introducing *Romola,* Eliot set the theme: a Stoic virtue, embodied in Savonarola and also in Romola, in opposition to an Epicurean levity. The man of virtue was "a man of public spirit," of "care for a common good," a man who believed "*that* life to be highest which is a conscious voluntary sacrifice" ("Proem"). The heroine, Romola, comes from an old Florentine family and has been raised by her scholar father in the "lofty spirit" and "grand severity of the stoical philosophy." Yet, even so, her main motive has not been the inflexible rule of this philosophy but love, "the law of her affections" (chap. 36). She has loved her father and loves her husband, Tito, who has escaped from the pirates who captured both him and his foster father. Tito's classical learning has won the approval of Romola's father and established a place for him in Renaissance Florence. Yet Tito has grave moral defects, notably ambition, lust, and greed. His defects lead him to deceive a pretty peasant girl, Tessa, into a mock marriage and to refuse any recognition of his foster father, Baldassare, when the old man is led prisoner into the city.

A French army has invaded Florence and has ended the tyrannical Medici rule, and a new republican government has been established under the influence of the prior of the Dominican monastery, Savonarola. Savonarola's message to the bustling commercial city, whose citizens have long devoted themselves to selfish sensual and material interests, is that of a Christian (and Stoical) virtue. Florentines "must postpone their private passions and interests to the public good," he proclaims. He urges the adoption of a popular rather than an aristocratic form of government; in this way the "public will" might "counteract the vitiating influence of party interests." Savonarola himself is a man with "no private malice," seeking "no petty gratification." By transforming Florence into "a pure community," he wishes to make it "worthy to lead the way in the renovation of the church and the world" (chap. 35).

Knowing herself deceived by Tito, Romola disguises herself as a nun and leaves Florence. Once she has made her escape from the city, she experiences a "sense of freedom and solitude." But she is met along the way by Savonarola, who declares that God has commanded him to stop her flight "from the lot God has laid upon you." The monk denies Romola's right to choose for herself, and to "have no rule but your own will."

Romola's "mind rose in stronger rebellion," and she refuses to acknowledge any "right of priests and monks to interfere with my actions." However, Savonarola's glance conveys to Romola an "interest in her and care for her," and in his gaze "simple human fellowship expressed itself as a strongly felt bond." To replace freedom, Savonarola offers duty and "the bond of a higher love." Romola, he declares, is "blindly seeking the good of a freedom which is lawlessness," for she wishes to follow her "own will" rather than "the law you are bound to obey." To desert Tito is to violate her marital vows, and even a base, pagan "duty of integrity," not to mention holy matrimony, should be enough to keep her in her place. (Savonarola is depicted, like Comte, as opposed both to divorce and the remarriage of widows and widowers.) She must feel "the glow of a common life," and see "the history of the world as the history of a great redemption" in which she, like Savonarola, is "a fellow-worker." Savonarola enjoins Romola to help in the "great work" of purification that will make Florence "the guide of the nations." Romola must crucify her "selfish will," and accept a higher love (chap. 40).

Romola comes to understand that just as Tito committed a great crime by denying his father, she herself would have sinned by deserting Tito. But she will later feel "the demands of inner moral facts." The "stifling predominance" over her of a husband she despises has made the continuation of her marriage "simply a degrading servitude." "I too am a human being," she will tell Tito; "I have a soul of my own that abhors your actions" (chap. 58). That "the law was sacred," Romola well understood; but she also states, "Yes, but rebellion might be sacred too" (chap. 56).

Nonetheless, Romola makes her choice of personal and civic virtue in preference to unfocused freedom and alienating solitude. She returns to the city and to Tito, and joins the Piagnoni (the young men and women dedicated to the crucified Christ and to the new regime of virtue) in their efforts to purify Florence. No longer does she suffer the "frequent loneliness" of her home, for now on every street she is greeted "with looks of appeal or of friendliness" (chap. 43). She takes upon herself a life of philanthropy, of concern for the poor, and all her former "tenderness" toward her dead father and Tito has "transformed itself into an enthusiasm of sympathy with the general life." The goal of life seems no longer to be her personal happiness, but "the diminishing of sorrow." She shares Savonarola's concern for "liberty and purity of government in Florence" and for "a universal regeneration." She now finds in communion with the church the "satisfaction for moral needs" that her past life had "left hungering." By her altruism, she is able to transform her sadness into "a life of active love" (chap. 44).

The life of Florence as a whole has been transformed by Savonarola and the Piagnoni. Companies of Discipline composed of the leading citizens of the city march in their separate units in shrouds of distinctive colors, with a slit open for their eyes: "They had dropped their personality, and walked as symbols of a common vow" (chap. 43). Although some citizens inevitably resent those who wished "to lay on them a strict yoke of virtue" (chap. 45), the force of public opinion, the chief instrument of Savonarola's as of Comte's utopia, has brought the citizenry to accept the new moral regime. On the last day of Carnival the Piagnoni organize a ceremony, the "Burning of the Vanities." Objects of art or books thought to be immoral, playing cards and gaming boards, musical instruments, rouge pots and wigs are all placed in a great bonfire as trumpets sound. Bands of "young-inquisitors" go from house to house demanding that citizens contribute their jewels so as to relieve the distress of the poor. The method employed—"to coerce people by shame, or other spiritual pelting"—is successful, and citizens feel obliged to conform (chap. 49).

Certain citizens, however, are beginning to have doubts. The narrator grants that in many ways the circumstances in Florence have improved, for "there is no kind of conscious obedience that is not an advance on lawlessness." Yet Romola, at first reluctantly, becomes concerned when the painter Piero di Cosimo warns her that "your Piagnoni will make *l'inferno* a pleasant prospect to us, if they are to carry things their own way on earth." Would her classicist father have approved of the burning of the books of Ovid or Boccaccio or Petrarch?, she asks herself. Yet how can Romola not think well of a religious enthusiasm that makes for a greater "sympathy with pain, indignation against wrong, and the subjugation of sensual desire" (chap. 49)? On all matters, moreover, it has become her habit "to reject her impulsive choice, and to obey passively the guidance of outward claims" (chap. 51).

Just as Robespierre would argue that the intervention of foreign enemies of the revolution, assisted by royalist sympathizers at home, made necessary the Reign of Terror, so the regime of the Piagnoni is transformed by the growing hostility of the papacy and the French king. At the beginning the voice of "peace, charity, and oblivion of political differences" has prevailed, but the Piagnoni now begin to seek out enemies of their regime, and they find one in Romola's godfather, Bernardo del Nero (chap. 52). Del Nero not only believes a less democratic government would prove more effective, but also retains a nostalgic regard for the banished Medici. Romola's "affection and respect" for del Nero makes her resist "the division of men into sheep and goats by the easy mark of some political or religious symbol." Feelings are more important than ideas; ideas must be "taken in a solvent of feeling." She rejects "the denunciatory exclusiveness" of Savonarola because she now sees "the complexities in human things." For a considerable period Savonarola's "grand view of human duties" has persuaded Romola to accept the narrowness of much of his doctrine. But now the "practical effect" of this narrowness comes into conflict with a strong force within her. She begins to acknowledge to herself that the regime of the Piagnoni was "a fanaticism from which she was shrinking with newly startled repulsion" (chap. 55).

Eliot ably charts the difficulties experienced by a member of a political or religious sect in freeing herself from its trammels. Savonarola had "opened to her [Romola] the new life of duty" and inspired her to fight "for principle against profligacy." After Savonarola's excommunication by the pope for the heresy of wishing "to make the Christian life a reality," Romola, despite her growing doubts, is more especially determined not to desert him. In Savonarola's excommunication she sees the "hostile vice" of the Borgia pope, "lustful, greedy, lying, and murderous," in battle against Savonarola's "public virtue and spiritual purity" (chap. 55).

The cry is raised that "the Republic was in danger"—the same cry as that which guided the Terror of 1794—and that leniency would encourage the enemies of the state. Del Nero and four of his friends are arrested and sentenced to be executed. There is some hesitancy about burning men of illustrious families, and the justices await some signal from Savonarola. Romola hopes that Savonarola will be merciful, despite Tito's opinion that the Dominican has "got into the practice of preaching that form of human sacrifice called killing tyrants and wicked malcontents" (chap. 58). Still, Romola determines to seek out Savonarola in the hope of securing clemency for her godfather. He assures her that in this case to grant mercy would be "treason against the common good." New circumstances call for severity (chap. 59).

Romola engages Savonarola in a dialogue concerning the individual conscience and the ends of power. Following Antigone, Romola announces that this was "a moment when the soul must have no guide but the voice within it." The "power-loving" Dominican, "accustomed to seek great ends that cast a reflected grandeur on the means by which they are sought," resents her words. Yet he is caught between his own "never-silent hunger after purity and simplicity" and the "tangle of egoistic demands, false ideas, and difficult outward circumstances" originating in the necessities of power. He tells Romola that the lives of the five count for little compared to "the cause of freedom, which is the cause of God's Kingdom upon earth." Del Nero may have "certain human virtues," but he is an enemy of the cause. Savonarola's appeal might well have prevailed with Romola in the past, but her love for her godfather now makes her bitter. Does Savonarola know "so well what will further the coming of God's Kingdom" that he dares to take a life "despite the plea of mercy,—of justice,—of faithfulness to your own teaching?" Romola reminds the Dominican that his enemies accused him of seeing only what would "strengthen your own party." "The cause of my party *is* the cause of God's Kingdom," Savonarola replies. "God's Kingdom is something wider," she declares, "else, let me stand outside of it with the beings that I love" (chap. 59). Del Nero is executed.

Romola has lost "her trust" in Savonarola. She now sees the "inconsistent details" of his doctrines and believes he wishes only to extend his power in Florence. While she looks at "individual suffering" with "the eyes of personal tenderness," he sees them with those of "theoretic conviction." His identification of his cause with that of God she now sees as egoism. Yet is not such an identification consistent with "all energetic belief"? And is

Romola now permitting "tender fellow-feeling for the nearest" to undermine "the larger aims without which life cannot rise into religion" (chap. 61)?

Disillusioned with Savonarola, Romola flees Florence a second time and unsuccessfully attempts suicide. After this failure, she reviews the situation and again sees her great obligation to Savonarola for having "waked a new life in her" (chap. 69). His errors and lies were "entwined with noble purposes and sincere beliefs" in which "self-justifying expediency" was interwoven with "the tissue of a great work" (chap. 64). While he undoubtedly "sought his own glory," Romola is now convinced that he is working "for the very highest end,—the moral welfare of men—not by vague exhortations, but by striving to turn beliefs into energies that would work in all the details of life" (chap. 71).

If this is a valedictory eulogy for Savonarola, and for the role he played in Romola's life, it is also one for Comte and for the influence the French Positivist had on Eliot. Yet both men were the prisoners of an abstract philosophy they wished to impose on an understandably reluctant humanity. They were utopians and fanatics. In Eliot's novel Machiavelli cynically observes that since Savonarola's "universal renovation" did not prove possible merely by securing "a free and pure government" and "making all Florentines love each other," then "it must be done by cutting off every head that happens to be obstinately in the way" (chap. 60). This had been Robespierre's way, and Cromwell's, and Rienzi's, and might become Comte's as well. Mill and Lewes believed Comte and his followers were so much dedicated to the sacrifice of the individual to the general good as to be inveterate enemies of liberty and individuality. This was Eliot's view of Savonarola. Despite her attraction to the virtuous order of an organic community, Eliot's strong concern for liberty and individuality—and for a society based on orderly development, not revolutionary, utopian abstraction—enveloped her in what may have at times seemed an irreconcilable conflict.

It was to counter the doctrines of self-styled "reformers" such as Comte, whose ideas he believed to be "really liberticide," that led Mill to write *On Liberty* in 1859.[38] In his essay on *Utilitarianism* three years later Mill condemned Comte's narrow view of happiness as self-sacrificing altruism. While Mill enjoined a virtue that sought the common good, he rejected Comte's insistence that all desire for personal happiness must be set aside as antisocial.[39] It was in what Comtists might call the metaphysical spirit that Mill (and Romola, and Eliot) recoiled at the course taken by Savonarola, just as Lewes had condemned the course followed by Robespierre.

In a study of Eliot published some fifteen years after her death, Frederic Harrison, while praising her earlier works, found *Romola* "too elaborate, too intricate, too erudite." Many later critics have reacted similarly. "In my opinion," Harrison continued, "it marks the decline of her genius"; "I cannot count any of the later books as equal to the earlier books." He concluded that Eliot's effort in *Romola* "to frame in a complex background of historical erudition an ethical program of even greater complexity and subtlety . . . was a task that might have tried even greater powers than hers—a task in which Goethe and Scott may have succeeded, but which Goethe and Scott were too truly the born artists to attempt."[40]

Was Harrison as a literary critic unhappy with Eliot's artistic performance, or was he as a Comtist displeased with what Lewes had called her "magnificent programme"? Harrison may not have consciously perceived *Romola* to be intentionally anti-Positivist; he may rather have thought that what seemed to be its anti-Comtian implications were a consequence of the writer's secret doubts and inadequate literary powers. Certainly *Romola* did not keep Harrison—three years after that book's publication—from asking Eliot to write a Positivist novel.

One might note, finally, that Eliot had already addressed the central theme of *Romola* seven years earlier, in an 1856 discussion of Sophocles' *Antigone*. She had, moreover, here anticipated the way in which she would treat the subject, for her interpretation of the relationship between Antigone and Creon foreshadowed her treatment of that between Romola and Savonarola. Sophocles' tragedy, she wrote, had portrayed "the conflict" between custom, tradition, and personal feeling, on the one hand, and "obedience to the State" on the other. Readers will recall that Creon, the king of Thebes, forbade a proper burial to his enemy, Polyneices, the brother of Antigone, without which Polyneices could not enjoy the peace of the world below. Antigone begged Creon to permit her to bury her brother, despite his being an enemy of the state. In Eliot's words, "Here lies the dramatic collision: the impulse of sisterly piety which allies itself with reverence for the Gods, clashes with the duties of citizenship." Both "principles . . . at war with each other" were valid, Eliot noted. Creon insisted—as would Savonarola when Romola begged for the life of her godfather, accused of treason—"on the duty of making all personal affection subordinate to the well-being of the State." Creon believed it necessary "to the welfare of the State that he should be obeyed as legitimate ruler, and becomes exasperated by the calm defiance of Antigone."[41]

Eliot set down as "superficial" any interpretation that depicted Creon as "a hypocritical tyrant" and Antigone as "a blameless victim." Both Creon and Antigone saw themselves as contesting for the right principle, though each was conscious of the strength of the contending one. At bottom, Eliot noted, in Sophocles' drama the struggle was "between elemental tendencies and established laws" which sought to bring "the outer life of man . . . gradually and painfully . . . into harmony with his inward needs." "Reformers, martyrs, revolutionists, are never fighting against evil only; they are also placing themselves in opposition to a good—to a valid principle which cannot be infringed without harm." When you "preach against false doctrines, you disturb feeble minds and send them adrift on a sea of doubt," she observed, perhaps remembering her doctrinaire freethinking days; when you "cultivate a new region of the earth," then "you exterminate a race of men."[42]

For Eliot, in *Romola,* both the Florentine Antigone and the Renaissance Creon were contending for valid principles—as were both she herself, with her concern for the individual and his or her happiness, and Comte, with his larger interest in the welfare of society and the state as a whole. "Wherever the strength of a man's intellect, or moral sense, or affection brings him into opposition with the rules which society has sanctioned, *there* is renewed the conflict between Antigone and Creon." In her Florentine novel Eliot inclined her argument in Romola's favor, but not unreservedly so. For, as she had observed in her 1856 essay, "[S]uch a man [as the woman Antigone] must not only dare to be right, he must also dare to be wrong—to shake faith, to wound friendship, perhaps, to hem in his own powers." "Like Antigone," she continued, "he may fall victim to the struggle." But he can no more be thought "a blameless martyr" than "society . . . can be branded as a hypocritical tyrant."[43]

Eliot, I wish to suggest, drew from *Antigone* what was, as she wrote in her final paragraph, the "best moral" to which Sophocles' Chorus had pointed: "[T]hat our protest for the right should be seasoned with moderation and reverence, and that lofty words . . . are not becoming to mortals."[44] This moderation would become the tone of her treatment of many political questions, and would lead to understandable confusions concerning her message. In *Romola* Eliot leaned to the individual against the despotism of the state: in *The Spanish Gypsy* and *Daniel Deronda,* as we will see, her heroine, in the first book, would yield her personal happiness to the larger demands of her people, and in the second her hero would find individual fulfillment and happiness by accepting the transcending national mission set before him. Eliot may have intended a distinction between the state, on the one hand, and the nation (that is, the people, the society, the nationality) on the other—between the state and what one may term the implicit populism of the politics of national inheritance.

In *Middlemarch* Eliot would defend a central element of Britain's politics of inheritance. For her, as for other perceptive liberals and conservatives, the national political tradition called for a compromise of interests, an ideal that Eliot had already discussed in Felix Holt's "Address." Positivists rejected the pursuit of such an ideal as a cowardly timidity that prevented England from emerging from the doldrums of the metaphysical stage.

4

Positivism and the Politics of Compromise in *Middlemarch*

George Eliot's *Middlemarch*, which was published in 1872, is not generally regarded as a political novel, as is *Felix Holt*, nor was it designed to be one, but its politics are clear—sometimes explicitly so, sometimes immediately below the surface of the narrative. In *Middlemarch* Eliot promotes the politics of compromise, the traditional politics of the nation (the politics, in the Hegelian phrase, of the English *Volksgeist*), which form an essential part of Eliot's politics of inheritance. In this work, as we shall see, Eliot also added to the shades of meaning in her philosophy of inheritance.

The chief intellectual opponents of the politics of compromise in the England of the 1860s and 1870s included John Morley, a Comtian sympathizer though not a doctrinaire Positivist, as well as the more orthodox followers of Auguste Comte (Richard Congreve, Frederic Harrison, E. S. Beesly, and their friends), who established themselves in London as the spokesmen of the Positivist sect. Among the leading defenders of compromise was Eliot's friend and mentor, Herbert Spencer, who formulated a philosophy of positivism even as he denied any Comtian influence upon his thinking, and, indeed, criticized essential parts of the Comtian Positivist ideology.

We must try to distinguish between those who accepted the general outlook of positivism—a scientific and philosophical position that decried the mysticism, religiosity, and intuitionism of the past—and those who embraced the Comtian Positivist program. Writers like Spencer and Mill in England and Taine in France thought of themselves as exponents of a philosophical positivism, though they owed no particular allegiance to the sociology and politics of Comte. True Comtists accepted virtually all their master's opinions, including even the liturgy and rituals of the religion of humanity. Neither of these camps can be rigidly defined, and we can no more avoid confusions in labeling them than did their own contemporaries.

At this time, as we shall see, English Comtian Positivists assumed a more radical position than had their master Comte, for they put aside Comte's cautions concerning the need to preserve order in favor of a doctrine that called for revolutionary class war. In attempting to locate Eliot in the context of contemporary political and social thought, I must give special attention to the way the English Comtists were reshaping Positivist politics during the period in which Eliot was writing *Middlemarch*.

The Franco-Prussian War in 1870 and the 1871 Commune—the proletarian government set up in Paris after France's defeat—created divisions between the orthodox London Positivists and mere sympathizers like Lewes, Mill, and Morley. The London Positivists favored British military intervention in favor of France and cheered the Commune. The sympathizers, however, believed France had properly paid the price for Napoleon III's arrogance, and were put off by the communism and proletarian rule of the Commune. Frederic Harrison chided Morley, in a January 1871 letter, because he had been persuaded to follow Mill's postulate of moderation: "Mill teaches you all to chop logic in politics," he wrote Morley, "but you ought to feel with a mysterious force of nature."[1]

Morley replied by accusing Harrison of having deviated from Comte's doctrine. He noted that Harrison had set politics as "one of the hysterical arts," rather than as "the Master-Science of Society" that Comte had envisioned.[2] The Positivists, Morley wrote in a subsequent letter in April, were followers of "an absolute method," and impaired by "the vices of French political thinking."[3] While acknowledging his own intellectual debts to Comte, Morley denied he was a Comtist.[4] Earlier he had dismissed the London society by concluding, "There is not a Positivist among you. There are only two in England—Mill and George Eliot."[5] (Morley probably intended to assign these two to the category of a more tenable non-Comtian positivism, though he might also have been referring to the growing radicalism of the London Positivists, at variance with the outlook of Comte himself.)

There was clearly a discrepancy between Eliot's public position as, at the very least, a Comtian sympathizer and the substantially non-Comtian, and even anti-Comtian, thrust of her writings. In order to partially account for such ambiguities, it is important to examine her friendships with Herbert Spencer and the Richard Congreves.

Maria Congreve was the friend Eliot most valued after she and Lewes decided to live together, and Maria's husband, Richard, was one of the leaders of British Comtism. Eliot had first encountered Mrs. Congreve as the daughter of the physician who had treated her father during his last illness. Eliot met Maria Congreve again when Eliot and Lewes set up their rather unconventional household. The Congreves welcomed the Leweses into their circle, virtually all of whom were Comtists, at a time when many of Eliot's previous friends treated her as a social pariah. Eliot's affection for Mrs. Congreve was great; their correspondence gives abundant evidence of her love and of her determination to keep their friendship flowering.

Comtism was an especially sensitive issue for the Leweses. Once a complete believer, Lewes remained an admirer of the Comtian philosophy. In 1866 he publicly dissented from Comte's "scheme of sacerdotal despotism," and proclaimed himself "a reverent heretic."[6] The reverence made it possible for Lewes to keep his antipathy for Comte's politics from interfering with his respect for Comte's philosophy. Eliot too gave evidence of this reverence. In a letter to Maria Congreve written in early 1867, Eliot described herself and Lewes, at Biarritz, as both reading the *Système* after breakfast, he one volume, she another, "interrupting each other continually with questions and remarks." This morning occupation kept her in a "state of enthusiasm through the day—a moral glow." "My gratitude increases continually for the illumination Comte has contributed to my life," she declared.[7] The terms in which Eliot's "gratitude" were expressed very likely warmed the letter's recipient, as they were probably meant to do.

Herbert Spencer, on the other hand, had always been a skeptic, and with the passage of time he became increasingly hostile to Comtian doctrine. Spencer became a leading critic of Comte's philosophy and view of the state, and, as we shall see, an advocate of the traditional British politics of compromise, the politics that Comtists blamed for the failure of Britain to progress to a more scientific, Positivist society. George Eliot had loved and even proposed marriage to Spencer before she accepted Lewes as her husband, and Spencer continued to be important to her, and she to him.[8] It would be surprising if a certain jealousy—on the part of both Lewes and Spencer—did not affect the relationship of the three. The Leweses' friendship with Spencer was nearly severed in 1864 after Lewes accused Spencer of being unwilling to acknowledge an important intellectual debt to Comte. After a long correspondence the breach was healed.[9] From that time onward, Spencer later wrote, Comtism became "a tacitly tabooed topic between the Leweses and myself—the only topic on which we differed, and which we refrained from discussing."[10]

Eliot was determined not to revert to her earlier sectarianism, and she now had more intimate reasons than ever to avoid an obviously polemical position. The shedding of her Evangelical opinions had "left her mind in an attitude of antagonism which lasted for some years," Herbert Spencer wrote of her in his *Autobiography,* but "her natural feeling was a longing to agree as far as possible."[11] She had for some time been prepared to subordinate herself to a husband: while in Geneva in 1849 she wrote to the Brays about her forthcoming return to England, "the land of duty and affection," and confessed that the "only ardent hope I have for my future life is to have given to me some woman's duty, some possibility of devoting myself where I may see a daily result of pure calm blessedness in the life of another."[12] She needed to maintain her close friendship with Spencer. If both her union with Lewes and her friendships with Spencer and Mrs. Congreve were to prosper, she might well have felt the need to tread lightly on the question of Comtian doctrine.

Lewes had made both his critique of and his intellectual debt to Comtian positivism a matter of public notice. In 1852, before the beginning of his relationship with Eliot, Lewes had published a series of articles on Comte's philosophy, and the following year he revised and enlarged them for his volume *Comte's Philosophy of the Sciences*. The work, published before the appearance of Comte's more clearly authoritarian *Politique positive*, expressed the devotion of a full believer, independent enough to express certain small doubts, but nonetheless convinced that Comte was "the greatest thinker of modern times."[13] Comte was "a philosophic socialist," Lewes further observed, who founded his views on "actualities," and hence he had vindicated private property, leaving to others "the pleasant fields of Utopia."[14] Yet he also noted that Comte believed that "communism is the *goal* towards which society tends," though it was not "a path by which the goal may be reached."[15]

In late 1864 a number of advanced liberals with Comtian leanings determined to found a journal to represent "progressive" opinion. They chose Lewes to serve as editor of the new *Fortnightly Review*. Lewes intended the *Fortnightly Review* to promote the politics of moral regeneration, not the politics of revolution; he would preach the politics of *Felix Holt*, we might say, which Eliot was writing at this time. In January 1865, in a letter to a Comtian sympathizer, Lewes declared that the journal's public would not "tolerate a negative or aggressive spirit in reference to the fundamental principles of Government and Religion." He added that though "we have no ism, Theological or Political to advocate," the journal's "motto, Progress and Order must inspire us."[16] This, of course, was the motto of Comte and his followers.

In January 1866 Lewes wrote an article on Comte for the *Fortnightly Review* that expressed decidedly more reservations than had appeared in his 1852 essays; by this time the *Politique positive* had appeared, and Lewes had been persuaded by Eliot, with whom he had now lived for a decade, that Comte's predicted Positivist society was indeed a utopian dream. As "a reverent heretic," he wrote, he now distinguished between the author of the *Philosophie positive,* whom he admired, and the author of the *Politique positive,* where "the philosopher" had become a high priest. Altering his earlier view, he could no longer regard the politics and religion of the Comtists as a scientific forecast but only as "a magnificent utopia and a prophetic vision of what the Religion of the future may become."[17] He had changed his earlier opinion, he noted, when he learned "from the remark of one very dear to me"—clearly George Eliot, though she was not named—"to regard it [Comte's society] as an utopia," offering "hypotheses rather than doctrines, suggestions for future inquirers rather than dogmas for adepts,—hypotheses carrying more or less of truth, and serviceable as a provisional mode of colligating facts, to be confirmed or contradicted by experience."[18]

As Comte grew older, Lewes continued, he had become more and more convinced of "an apostolic mission," and metamorphosed into an "imperious pontiff," which Lewes characterized as an "unfortunate fatality which seems attached to deep convictions in certain powerful and arrogant natures."[19] Comte had imitated "the intellectual despotism" belonging to "all priesthoods."[20] When Comte had adhered to the objective method Lewes had followed him "as a disciple," but when Comte became an autocrat, "arbitrarily arranging individual and social life according to his subjective conceptions" and creating a "scheme of sacerdotal despotism," Lewes became "a spectator" and even "an antagonist."[21] Lewes's position was essentially the same as the one Eliot had offered three years earlier in *Romola*.

In October 1866 Lewes wrote another *Fortnightly Review* essay, this time on "Comte and Mill," in which he again attempted to distinguish what was properly science in Comte's work from what was mere doctrine. Comtian "doctrine," in the views of its adherents, had been "systematically established," and the followers of Comte's (as of any) ideological system felt secure against any attack by outsiders.[22] Lewis argued that Comte had sacrificed science to achieve "unity" and a "desire for synthesis," and as his "pontifical pretensions grew" his "impatience to construct a system" led him into basic errors.[23] Comte was convinced he had "seized the truth—so is every theorizer," Lewes observed. His disciples accepted this truth because it cohered to the system, and, Lewes concluded, "I do not imagine that my objections will shake their confidence."[24]

Many liberal Englishmen of advanced views—the *Fortnightly Review*'s public—were attracted to the Comtian outlook. What drew them was its presentation of itself as a "scientific" faith. Comte had provided a critique of revealed religion, seen as the great obstacle to progress, as well as a scientific view of history that made the past more comprehensible and predicted a happy future for society. Moreover, he had constructed a polity designed to replace the theological and feudal one, with its monarchy and a nobility of birth that belonged to Europe's past; such a political system would transcend England's metaphysical halfway house of feudal forms, liberal shibboleths, and creaky parliamentarianism, with which advanced liberals might easily find fault. Rule by a spiritual priesthood of intellectuals and professional men (and a temporal patriciate of financiers and capitalists) would triumph over a long-worn-out metaphysical religion and a quasi-feudal polity. Thus, Comtian political doctrine opposed itself at virtually every point to England's traditional politics of inheritance.

The soon-to-be victorious middle classes were those strata of society to which advanced liberals generally belonged. These liberals saw the coming of an elite paternalism as the only way to avoid revolutionary violence, as the means to secure not only progress but order. One might say that the quasi-Comtism of many Victorian liberals resembled the quasi-Marxism of certain of their twentieth-century descendants. In the 1930s and afterward one might frequently encounter the view that a Communist was merely a liberal prepared to follow his convictions to their inevitable conclusion, a conclusion justified by the "scientific" character of Marx's (as earlier of Comte's) view of history and society.

Positivists such as J. H. Bridges, Frederic Harrison, and the Congreves publicly identified themselves with the radical wing of British Liberalism. Though the antiliberal, antidemocratic Comte intended to do away with such relics of the metaphysical era as freedom of speech and freedom of conscience in his Positivist polity, the English Comtists supported free speech so that they could preach their cause. They joined advanced liberals in demanding the disestablishment of the Church of England, and with similar motives called for a public, secular system of education in opposition to the existing one largely in the hands of the Anglican church. Also like these liberals, they were antiaristocratic, devoted to humanitarian causes, and, as members of an international church, both cosmopolitan and staunchly anti-imperialistic. These views led the governing classes to regard them, one contemporary has told us, as "un-English." The respectable classes were shocked that men of good family who had been trained at the universities—the chief Comtian leaders were products of Wadham College, Oxford—should express sympathy with Irish Fenian terrorists, and even with those trade unionists who adopted violent methods. Although in theory the English Positivists favored Comte's benevolent despotism, in practice they advocated workingman suffrage in the 1860s as an immediate measure to counteract socially irresponsible aristocratic governments.[25]

The leading British Comtists, however, were far removed in temperament and ultimate program from even the more advanced liberals, who were, after all, defenders of liberty. Justin McCarthy, a sophisticated observer, described the Comtian Positivists as believers in "a sort of celestial despotism," which would provide homes and jobs, and all else for the people, while still, though in some unspecified way, protecting their liberty. McCarthy saw them as detesting any form of voluntarism in favor of state direction of every aspect of society.[26]

Not even McCarthy, however, was fully aware of how far most English Comtian leaders were at this time from being liberal defenders of moderation, liberty, individualism, laissez-faire, and parliamentary government. Usually somewhat surreptitiously, and then for a brief period more openly—though the full dimensions of their position were not fully grasped by contemporaries—they appear to have turned their backs entirely on order, for Comte the essential complement to progress. Although they ostensibly continued to be defenders of stability and private property, in time they became so enraged at the shortsightedness of the bourgeoisie that they advocated proletarian violence and even revolution.

When the Congress of the Socialist International met at Geneva in 1866, the *Fortnightly Review* published an article by Lewes. Although a moderate who opposed class warfare, Lewes expressed the sympathy of advanced liberals for the International and welcomed the founding of that revolutionary organization as the coming of age of the working classes. He compared the Geneva session to the 1789 meeting of the Estates General.[27] During the time of the Commune of 1871, a number of the leading Positivists extolled the dictatorship of the proletariat established by the workingmen of Paris against the capitalists, even as did Karl Marx and other spokesmen for the Socialist International.

Edward Spencer Beesly, professor of history at University College, London, was the Positivist most closely associated with the International; he had, in fact, presided over the meeting in September 1864 that created that organization. Through his activities in the International he became a friend of Karl Marx. Marx had a low opinion of the Positivists, but he believed Beesly—despite the latter's Comtian defense of private property—to be an exception. Beesly was in turn one of Marx's most fervent English admirers. In September 1870 he attributed much of the success of the International "to Dr. Karl Marx," whose knowledge of European history and the "industrial movement" was "without a rival."[28]

In 1865 and 1866 Beesly wrote articles for the *Fortnightly Review* on the two revolutionaries who had conspired against the Roman Republic during Cicero's consulship and after. In 1865 Beesly defended Catiline (long regarded as a villain by the educated classes, who absorbed that view in studying the orations of his antagonist Cicero) as a progressive who had fought a reactionary party "whose interests were bound up with order." In Rome, as in contemporary England, Beesly wrote, while there was "no love lost between the business men and the [aristocratic] governing class," there was "a tacit understanding" between them "to divide the spoil." While Catiline was the leader of the party of "the masses," Cicero had been the bought tool of "the reactionary party." Beesly had contempt for Cicero as a mere man of letters, "a coward and a babbler," out of his depth in the role of first magistrate of "a military commonwealth." Catiline, on the other hand, was a good deal better: he was "the man of action, who would rather see a thing done than hear it talked about," and who possessed "an intellect of the practical sort, quick, decisive, intuitive." Beesly noted that the "practical statesman" Louis Napoleon (whom Comtists admired as the last representative of the great French Revolution) had seen Catiline's virtues more clearly than the literary men who preferred Cicero.[29] In a subsequent essay, in 1866, Beesly portrayed Cicero's enemy Clodius as the champion of the "masses of men" who had "a claim to justice no less well-founded than individuals," and whose enemies were "the high-born, the wealthy, the educated." Beesly's great hero was a noble and wise proletariat.[30]

There existed then, as now, a modish middle-class sympathy for revolution, provided that revolution was sufficiently removed in time and place. Lewes thought Beesly's articles on Catiline "first-rate."[31] Even Anthony Trollope, not often identified with revolutionary opinions, found them (in a letter to Lewes) "admirable"—though he qualified his praise by adding that he preferred Cicero's form of patriotism to that of the conspirator. If Beesly had been "more historic and less enthusiastic," Trollope observed, Beesly would have noted Cicero's personal freedom from corruption, which entitled him "to deal heavily with a demagogue." Nonetheless, Trollope concluded by describing himself as "so given to rebellion in politics that I am delighted to see and hear any Catiline defended, and any Cicero attacked."[32]

Even before Beesly became involved in the activities of the Socialist International, the English Positivists had begun to think of trade unionism and the proletariat as sacred causes. In supporting a building strike in 1859, for example, Congreve had defended unions as a necessary form of "self-defence" for the working classes against the power of concentrated capital and the exploitation of labor by an unfair division of profits. As an orthodox Comtist, of course, Congreve insisted that his posture was "pacific to the exclusion of violent methods."[33]

While the country's leading trade unions rejected violence, some smaller trade clubs in the Midlands, particularly in Sheffield, did not hesitate to use terror, and even murder, to gain their ends. The various grinders' unions in Sheffield became especially notorious for their custom of "rattening," the seizure of the tools of workingmen who refused to join, or were in arrears to a trade club. If depriving the artisan of his tools proved an insufficient remedy, the Sheffield unions would toss gunpowder into his grinding wheel or down his chimney. Serious injuries inevitably resulted. There had been intermittent outbreaks of such activity in the 1840s and in 1861, and the terror was renewed and increased in 1865 and 1866. What aroused the most public notice were the confessions to murder, in June 1867, of members of the various grinders' unions. William Broadhead, the secretary of the Saw Grinders Union, gained special attention because he hired two union members who murdered, in a particularly gruesome manner, a Sheffield employer believed to be hiring too many young apprentices. There was an outcry on the part of the press that something be done to stamp out such activity.

Here was a test for the Positivists concerning the seriousness of their commitment to order. Professor Beesly, the first to respond, defended Broadhead against unfair treatment by the press, and in somewhat combative terms. At a meeting at Exeter Hall called in July 1867 by the London trade unions to condemn what became known as the "Sheffield outrages," Beesly, to the satisfaction of many in his workingman audience, did not adopt the apologetic tone of the preceding speakers. "Murder was a great crime," he declared, but men like Governor Eyre (who had brutally suppressed a Jamaican rebellion in 1865 in which many blacks had been killed) were praised for having "committed his crimes in the interests of employers, as Broadhead committed his in the interest of the workmen of

Sheffield." The audience cheered.[34] Beesly's activities in the Socialist International, as well as his earlier defenses of Catiline and Clodius made his position unsurprising to the public, and the greater part of the press attacked him in severe terms.

But Positivists and advanced liberal papers (like the *Daily News*) rushed to Beesly's defense. A week after Beesly's Exeter Hall speech, Richard Congreve, in a pamphlet condemning Broadhead's crimes and "all recourse to violence," nonetheless applauded Beesly's motives in defending the union movement. Congreve envisioned a "contest between labor and capital," which he foresaw as "long and bitter," and offered his sympathy to "the proletariate" in its struggle with "the territorial and moneyed aristocracy."[35] In July 1867 someone (Eliot believed it was Beesly himself) sent the Leweses a copy of Congreve's pamphlet on the Broadhead case and Beesly's defense of the union leader. Eliot read the pamphlet aloud to Lewes, and she reported to Mrs. Congreve that "we both felt a cordial satisfaction in it."[36] It is difficult to determine how great a role Eliot's friendship for Maria Congreve played in her expression of this sentiment. But Eliot's sympathy for Beesly did not extend to the secretary of the Saw Grinders; in Felix Holt's "Address" to the workingmen, as was noted earlier, there was a specific reference to the saw grinders' violence, and not a friendly one. Indeed, it may well be the case that the "Address" was written in response to the "Sheffield outrages." After publication of the "Address," the *Daily News* was highly critical of Eliot's tract.[37]

The Positivists had been turning to labor, and to the trade unions as the chief weapon of working-class activity, because they saw workingmen as the coming political power. In 1868 Frederic Harrison delivered a lecture on the political function of the working classes in which he not only defended the proletariat as an oppressed class, but also attacked Britain's liberal system of government. Both positions were, of course, in line with the orthodox Comtian outlook, but appeals to revolution were hardly what Comte had prescribed. The parliamentary system, "an enfeebling system of detail and compromise," must be brought to an end, Harrison declared.[38] The rich and the poor could not compete at elections on equal terms. The working class—"the Revolutionary element" in English politics—understood this truth and was determined to "purge the Constitution of the country from the deep-seated disorder of 'Parliamentarianism.'"[39] What would replace this "creation of old class law"? Harrison argued that government should be placed in the hands of an able elite. With such an elite in power, Harrison advised, the working classes need not fear "over-legislation" (a term coined by the laissez-faire Spencer). Harrison urged, rather, that "for real and efficient control" the working classes must "look to the State."[40]

Marx had spoken harshly to Beesly about the main body of Positivists, and Beesly had defended his Comtian associates. The chief point Marx and the Comtists held in common, he wrote Marx in June 1871, was "our indignation against the individualist theories of the propertied classes and their anti-social conduct." "We both believe," Beesly continued, "that the working class suffer terrible wrongs at the hands of the middle class, and that the social question is more important than the political." Though they might differ on whether private property was to be abolished, Marx and the English Positivists shared a "common foe." When Marx insisted that in these matters Beesly was different from other Positivists, Beesly cited Frederic Harrison as being in entire agreement with himself, "though in writing he is inclined to be too diplomatic, in my opinion, and to spare the susceptibilities of the middle class."[41]

Certainly, Harrison's opinions, and his language in a private letter he wrote in support of the Commune to John Morley in March 1871, seem indistinguishable from those of Marx at his most doctrinaire, and most colorful. The French professional and commercial classes were "mere adventurers" ready "to use any weapon, especially lying, fraud, legal and parliamentary chicanery" to maintain the status quo, Harrison began, adding that "society as it is now constituted is not worth keeping together." So much for Comte's order. What was modern society, Harrison asked, but "the right to grind out of the workman, his wife and child the uttermost farthing; to leave him naked, half-starved, ignorant, filthy." "No death or torment" was "worse than they deserve . . . *ces bougres du bourgeois.*" Harrison denied the legitimacy of parliaments and voting: "The lying sham called universal suffrage" was "one of the tricks of the *bougres.*" Let the best men govern, he observed, proclaiming—again more in the spirit of Marx than of Comte—that the two million workingmen of Paris were the best men. The bourgeoisie called itself a majority because they had "hocussed a lot of peasants." But "majority or not we won't have them," Harrison fumed; "legitimate government be damned." "In an epoch of revolutions every government is but the issue of a fresh *coup d'état*"; "but election or not," he concluded, "I deny that suffrage is the source of right altogether"—"I fall back on force."[42]

In May and August 1871 Harrison published two articles in the *Fortnightly Review* in support of the Commune: his arguments resembled Marx's treatment of the subject in *The Civil War in France,* read to the International in May 1871. While as a Comtist he found the communism of the leaders of the Paris workingmen "incompatible with human nature," Harrison nonetheless saw the Paris revolution as "the greatest of all class struggles" and "a regeneration of our social life."[43] In more orthodox Comtian fashion, he repudiated "the dogma of universal suffrage," and condemned government by suffrage as "the election of the superior by the inferior" and thus as "inherently vicious." He praised the Commune's dismissal of a representative assembly, in favor of a "simple executive council" organized for action, not mere talk, as a display of "the political sagacity of the working class."[44] The "struggle of the workman against the capitalist" was the beginning of "a new social order," he declared. Harrison insisted that the people of Paris were not really communists. They merely shared "the faith that capital and its holders must adapt themselves to

nobler uses, or they had better cease to exist," and, again reverting to
Comtian phrases, he called for "a true education, a new morality, and an
organised religion of social duty."[45]

In a second article Harrison defended the Communards against
grossly exaggerated charges of inhumanity, incendiarism, and vandalism.
Why had there been no outcry about the undoubted massacres perpetrated
by "the party of Order" when it tried to repress the Commune?[46] The
success of the Commune, he argued, would put an end to wars and "Imperial Chauvinism,"[47] and would establish an industrial system in which "the
principal, in some cases the whole, results of common labour" did not
become the "special perquisites of capital." The Commune stood for the
"ideal . . . of government by and for the working classes"—he did not
use the phrase "dictatorship of the proletariat"—and for a state in which
selfishness and competition were not regarded as "the whole duty of
man."[48] Another prominent Positivist, J. H. Bridges, also defended the
Commune, but in less vigorous terms than those employed by Beesly and
Harrison.[49]

In the early 1870s, as we have seen, the leading English Positivists—
particularly Beesly and Harrison, though Congreve clearly agreed on many
issues—both privately and publicly, put forward a social and political program that resembled that of the Marxists of the Socialist International, one
very different from what Eliot, and Britain's leading political theorists,
believed to be England's traditional, historical course: its politics of national inheritance and, most notably, its politics of compromise.

The politics of Eliot's *Middlemarch* must be seen against the background of
English liberal and Positivist thinking in the 1860s and 1870s. The novel
merits special attention if we are to grasp Eliot's view of the English
parliamentary system about which the London Positivists (and certain
advanced liberals) were so critical. An essential part of the parliamentary
regime, as it traditionally operated in England, was the compromise of
contending interests; Burke, Coleridge, and Mill, as well as Eliot's friend
Herbert Spencer, praised the uses of compromise. The Comtian sympathizer John Morley, on the other hand, joined the leading Positivists in
denouncing compromise as an obstacle to genuine progress. Herbert
Spencer's and John Morley's works on the subject appeared after the 1872
publication of *Middlemarch*—Spencer's in 1873, and Morley's in 1874—so
they could not have directly influenced Eliot. But the major points of
contention had been well represented in the earlier Positivist rejection
of the spirit of Britain's parliamentary tradition, as well as in the writings of
generations of theorists who supported this tradition. We may assume that
Eliot was familiar with the arguments on both sides of the question. Both
Spencer and Morley presented their opinions in a systematic fashion, making clear the stakes in the controversy as they would have appeared to Eliot.
Spencer's views on compromise were cast in a way that makes them easily
recognizable as supporting the politics of national inheritance.

The "policy of compromise," Spencer declared in his *Study of Sociology* (1873), was one "especially" characteristic of England, and one "essential" to a society undergoing "the transitions caused by continued growth and development." Spencer understood that contemporary society had inherited from the past many "illogicalities and imbecilities," "ideas and institutions proper to a past social state," but "incongruous" in the new. Yet such a "perpetual compromise" was "indispensable" to the "normal development" of society. Spencer insisted that any state of transition had to be a "compromise between the requirements of past and future, fulfilling in an imperfect way the requirements of the present." He observed that the failure to recognize both the value of past institutions and the inevitability of compromise to healthy political development characterized "too much the reformers, political, religious, and social, of our own time," even as it had "those of past times."[50]

In a Burkean or Coleridgian mode, and much in the spirit of Mill's essays on Coleridge and Bentham, Spencer observed that men who were "eager to rectify wrongs and expel errors" were possessed by so great "a consciousness of the evils caused by old forms and old ideas" as to make impossible any awareness of "the benefits these old forms and old ideas" provided. An unfortunate "one-sidedness" impelled both those who rashly attacked inherited institutions and those who with "an unreasoning bigotry" defended them. In England, he wrote, there was a great need for "both-sidedness." In the spirit of Eliot's essay on Riehl, written nearly two decades earlier, Spencer cautioned that the radical reformers not only presented an exaggerated picture of prevailing "injustices, and abuses" but gave the impression that the governing classes were entirely responsible for injustice and that the lower classes were "blameless." These radicals appeared to argue that were the "selfishness of the governing class forcibly extirpated," all would be well. However, selfishness was not peculiar to those in power but was to be found in all strata of society, since it was rooted in human nature. Unfortunately, Spencer concluded, "the destructive tendency" of the radical reformers was balanced by "but little constructive tendency," and they had too little understanding that "along with forms which are bad," there was "a large amount of substance which is good."[51]

In his writings, of course, Comte had also denounced the destructive tendencies of revolutionary reformers unable to value the virtues of past ideas and institutions. Though Comte's English admirers sometimes repeated such cautions as a matter of form, we have seen that they often accompanied such disclaimers with a denunciation of bourgeois society's abuses for which they blamed both the aristocrats and the capitalists, while eulogizing a sinless proletariat. Moreover, we have noted that left-Positivists like Beesly and Harrison depicted the parliamentary system as so irredeemably corrupt that revolution seemed the only remedy.

John Morley, Lewes's successor as editor of the *Fortnightly Review,* agreed with Harrison, Congreve, and Beesly on the perils of a policy erected upon the enervating spirit of compromise. Morley published his essay *On Compromise* in 1874. (Viscount Samuel, one of the prominent Liberal party leaders of the early twentieth century, later testified that *On Compromise* constituted, along with Mill's *On Liberty,* the greatest influence on him when he was at Oxford in the 1890s.[52]) In this tract, Morley was prepared to meet the needs for rousing talk and radical social analysis that enabled middle-class advanced liberals, feeling somewhat guilty about contemporary social arrangements, to adopt a pose of intellectual and moral superiority without provoking violence.

Morley prided himself on possessing "both-sidedness"—Morley's intellectual hero Mill (following Goethe) had called it "many-sidedness"—a position foreign to many of the readers of the *Fortnightly Review.* In his *Recollections* Morley recalled an essay he had written on the emigré opponent of the French Revolution Joseph de Maistre, whom some called a French Burke. Morley's appreciation of that "powerful genius" of "reactionary principles" had given "something of a shock to what I may call the regulation free-thinkers of the *Fortnightly Review,*" he later noted, adding that "I was privately refreshed by George Eliot's remark to a friend, that it showed a quite unexpected improvement in my *Wesen,* or mental disposition."[53] Eliot may have been too polite to have observed to this friend that Comte had also praised de Maistre; this though Morley had even quoted Comte's remark that "De Maistre has for me the peculiar property of helping me to estimate the philosophic capacity of people, by the repute in which they hold him."[54] The *Fortnightly Review's* editor was hardly likely to fail a test of both-sidedness to which he possessed Comte's key.

Morley's *On Compromise,* on the other hand, proceeded decidedly in a more one-sided *Fortnightly Review* manner. Quoting Burke's statement that "all government, indeed every human benefit and enjoyment, every prudent act, is founded on compromise," Morley insisted that these "words of wisdom and truth" were more suitable for the French than for the British, who he thought altogether too ready to accept compromise. In more moderate fashion than the Positivists, Morley made room for some kinds of compromise. For Morley, a sensible compromise did not mean "the undisputed triumph of one set of principles" (as of religion in England) or "the mutilation of both sets of principles" to produce "a *tertium quid*" involving "the disadvantages of each, without securing the advantages of either."[55] On this last, Morley had especially in mind the Liberal enactment of the Education Act of 1870, an act that extended the role of the established church in the teaching of the young, and which in Morley's view had set back indefinitely the possibility of achieving a secular system of education. Nonbelievers were seriously delaying progress by making concessions to prevailing public opinion, merely in order to gain the votes of a new working-class electorate, still under the influence of an obscurantist religion.[56] To follow "the political spirit" of compromise was not merely dishonest and hypocritical, but was positively harmful to all social values, Morley added.[57]

In addressing himself to the rejection of what he saw as spurious compromises, Morley was anxious to avoid the label of fanatic or sectarian.[58] He knew the low esteem in which "abstract theory and general reasoning" or the "spirit of political generalisation" had had in England since the French revolution of 1848. And he noted Mill's approval of "the English feeling for compromise."[59] Still he believed, as did sectarians like the Positivists, that compromises were positively harmful, morally and socially, and urged radicals to refrain from making them in the future.[60]

For Comte, the history of France constituted the ideal type of historical development, while the history of England was decidedly eccentric. France was the pioneer, the cutting edge of European social and political movements. In 1789, France's decision to overthrow the ancien régime and to engage in the politics of liberty, equality, and fraternity had opened the revolutionary path for other European societies. But England was trapped in the cul-de-sac of the "metaphysical stage" of politics, what Harrison and Morley called "the system of compromise," a stage that the continental countries had escaped as they moved directly from the theological polity to the positive polity. For the Comtists, England's parliamentary machinery was an antiquated relic of earlier centuries, designed to maintain the rule of the traditional governing classes. Such a view underlay the adulation the English Positivists felt for the Commune, as it did the support many English advanced liberals had long bestowed on French revolutionary movements.

George Eliot, despite her sympathy with democratic movements and her close relationship with the world of liberal intellectuals, resisted such opinions. Her restrained reaction to the French revolution of 1848, which occurred when she was twenty-nine, is revealing. She approved the French dismissal of Louis Philippe, but dreaded an English sequel to the Paris revolt. While at this time somewhat prepared to indulge in the idealization of the French working classes, as painted by Eugène Sue and George Sand, seven years later, in her essay on Riehl, she expressed doubts as to the accuracy of their portrayals. She feared that the English working classes contained "so much larger a proportion of selfish radicalism and unsatisfied, brute sensuality (in the agricultural and mining districts especially) than of perception or desire of justice, that a revolutionary movement would be simply destructive—not constructive." She expressed this same position in *Felix Holt*. Not the least important part of Eliot's outlook was her acceptance of Britain's parliamentary system, recalcitrantly "metaphysical" to Comtists. Eliot believed that France might be well served by revolution but insisted that the British constitution could only accommodate "the slow progress of *political* reform"—it was "all we are fit for at present." Genuine social reform was undoubtedly on the way, "but we English are slow crawlers," she declared.[61]

All Eliot's novels give some evidence of political purpose. In *Adam Bede,* we see the simple politics of a traditional, patriarchal society. *Felix Holt* called for a cleansing of the parliamentary politics of England's old

regime by means of a moral regeneration of all classes. In *Romola* Savonarola's utopian, proto-Comtian state challenged the selfish and atomis-
tic Florence of the Medicis, and Eliot depicted the defects of Savonarola's
system in its suppression of freedom and individual happiness. And in
Middlemarch, I shall suggest, Eliot embraced, although somewhat hesi-
tantly, the meliorism of nineteenth-century Britain's parliamentary state,
and with it a po'ity devoted to liberty and to compromise, the bugaboo of
the Comtists. She accepted Britain's "metaphysical" regime, again revealing her preference for Mill's and Spencer's moderate positions—and for
the traditional politics of inheritance of Burke and the conservatives—over
Comte's utopian plan.

   In *Middlemarch,* set two years before the passage of the Reform Bill of
1832, which considerably extended the suffrage, Eliot contrasted three
political models. Sir James Chettam, the best of landlords, embodies the
patriarchal ideal of traditional society. The second model, that of the Victorian polity—the parliamentary contention of class interests, and of compromises and piecemeal reform—has Will Ladislaw for its spokesman. The
third is represented by the proto-Comtist and scientific model upheld by
Tertius Lydgate. Two of Dorothea Brooke's suitors, Sir James Chettam
and Will Ladislaw, represent, respectively, the paternal and the liberal
modes; the Saint-Simonian Tertius Lydgate, who in an earlier version of
the plot, it has been suggested, Eliot may have intended for a more active
role as a suitor, represents a third (Tertius?), utopian mode. It is Ladislaw
who eventually triumphs, along with his politics of compromise.[62]

   In introducing *Middlemarch,* Eliot's narrator presents the sixteenth-
century Spanish Saint Theresa walking "hand-in-hand with her still smiling
brother to go and seek martyrdom in the country of the Moors." Theresa,
we are told, was fortunate in the clarity of her mission, and found her
"epos" in returning the Carmelite Order to its earlier rigor, and in establishing a new ascetic order of *Descalzos,* or Barefoot Ones, who wore
sandals of rope, slept on straw mats, ate no meat, and lived on the charity of
the faithful. "Later-born Theresas," like *Middlemarch*'s heroine Dorothea
Brooke, the narrator declares, "were helped by no coherent social faith and
order which could perform the function of knowledge for the ardently
willing soul" ("Prelude").[63]

   Like Romola and Saint Theresa, Dorothea wishes to improve and to
purify the world, and she persuades her wealthy neighbor Sir James Chettam, who hopes to marry her, to better the condition of his tenants. In the
paternalistic fashion of the traditional society of *Adam Bede,* Dorothea
wishes to make the cottages of the poor "fit for human beings from whom
we expect duties and affections" (chap. 3). Dorothea also convinces Chettam to adopt new techniques to "raise the productivity" of his land, noting
that "it is not a sin to make yourself poor in performing experiments for the
good of all," to which her guardian, Mr. Brooke, responds that "young
ladies can't understand political economy" (chap. 2).

Dorothea eventually marries Edward Casaubon, a pompous, blood-less, middle-aged clergyman-scholar, because she idealizes him as an intellectual who will introduce her to the Stoic and Alexandrian philosophers whose ethical ideal, the elevation of the common good over petty, personal interest, resembles her own. She seeks "a binding theory" to bring "her own life and doctrine" into connection with this intellectual heritage (chap. 10). Casaubon's scholarship, however, proves to be narrow, futile, and incommunicable, and Dorothea's marriage to him rapidly degenerates. Dorothea even regrets the relative well-being of Casaubon's rural parish, for she would have preferred a parish with "a larger share of the world's misery, so that she might have had more active duties in it" (chap. 9).

After Dorothea marries Casaubon, Chettam turns for comfort to her younger sister Celia, whom he marries. Despite his disappointed love, Sir James continues his work of improvement, still with Dorothea's assistance. His is the voice of the traditional, paternalist order. "I do think one is bound to do the best for one's land and tenants, especially in these hard times," he declares (chap. 38). Dorothea's guardian, Brooke, serves as a middle-class foil for Chettam. A Whig landowner of good family and a follower of the self-interest doctrines of the political economists, he neglects his duties as a landlord. Brooke favors suffrage reform (which Tories like Chettam oppose), and calls himself a philanthropist, yet he permits the housing of his tenants to decay even while he exacts maximum rents.

The ethic of a commercial society is breaking down traditional values. When Brooke decides to stand for Parliament, the local Tory organ remarks on the contradiction between his reforming pretensions and his conduct as a landlord. His experiences on the hustings reveal to him how unpopular he has become. ("Brooke doesn't mean badly by his tenants or anyone else," Chettam charitably observes, "but he has got that way of paring and clipping at expenses." "I do wish people would behave like gentlemen," Chettam declares, "feeling," the narrator notes, that "this was a simple and comprehensive programme for social well-being" [chap. 38].) No less important in terms of marking the decline of the traditional, hierarchical structure is Brooke's solicitation of the votes of local farmers and tradesmen whom he invites to dinner at his home. The very existence of rich farmers who own the acres they themselves cultivate (and are therefore, as the vicar's wife unhappily comments, "monsters—farmers without landlords—one cannot tell how to class them" [chap. 34]) reveals the period's social changes. Before the agitation for reform had "done its notable part in developing the political consciousness," the narrator tells us, there had been "a clearer distinction of ranks and a dimmer distinction of parties." Since the agitation, however, there has been a "general laxity" about social forms that came from the habit of people like Brooke "talking too much in the form of ideas"—rather than yielding, as Chettam did, to social feeling (chap. 10).

Tertius Lydgate, the representative of (a pre-Comtian) Saint-Simonianism, may be regarded as the partial realization of the character called for by Frederic Harrison, a decade earlier, in his outline of a Positivist novel. Related to the family of a Northumberland baronet, Lydgate has determined on a career as surgeon and general practitioner, which he hopes will provide the means for carrying on his prime purpose, medical research. Middlemarch doctors, he understands, do not possess "a scientific culture" as do doctors in France (chap. 13): they persist in what Comte described as the metaphysical stage of biological thinking, and still live in "the heroic times of copious bleeding and blistering." Seen by some as "a sort of philanthropist" (chap. 10), Lydgate had considered "joining the Saint-Simonians" when he was a medical student in Paris. "Though he did not agree with all their doctrines," he had hoped to aid their effort "to advance the social millennium." Lydgate's "nature" demands "the most direct alliance between intellectual conquest and the social good" (chap. 15).

In the 1830s the Saint-Simonians had made themselves somewhat ludicrous in the eyes of their contemporaries by their efforts to dignify prostitutes as the most oppressed of women and the conscience of the race. We are told in *Middlemarch* that when he was a Saint-Simonian sympathizer in Paris, Lydgate had fallen in love with a Provençal actress, a profession regarded as little better than that of a prostitute, who he later discovers has murdered her husband. Lydgate determines that "henceforth he would take a strictly scientific view of woman" (chap. 15), but he is taken in hand by Rosamond Vincy, the narcissistic and beautiful blonde daughter of a local manufacturer. She charms Lydgate, whom she sees as a gentleman, despite his impecunious condition; she makes him put aside his desire to pursue a scientific career, a path he might follow only if unfettered by marriage.

Casaubon's poor cousin Will Ladislaw counterposes an artist's and a liberal's philosophy of individual happiness to Lydgate's utopianism, as well as to Dorothea's ethos of Stoic duty. He tells Dorothea that she has "some false belief in the virtues of misery" and wishes "to make [her] life a martyrdom." "The best piety is to enjoy—when you can," he declares, cautioning Dorothea against "the fanaticism of sympathy" (chap. 22). But while favoring happiness over a martyr's sense of duty, Ladislaw is no irresponsible pleasure seeker. He rejects the advances of Rosamond Lydgate, after she becomes bored with her husband; and he leaves Middlemarch after Casaubon's death when he learns that because of the clergyman's jealousy, Casaubon's will enjoins that Dorothea is to be disinherited if she marries Ladislaw. Ladislaw is unwilling to compromise Dorothea, whom he loves, even though her income apart from Casaubon's legacy would easily support a marriage. He intends to follow the path of "self-culture" (as charted by the contemporary German idealist philosophers, and later by Mill in his *On Liberty*), while sympathizing in politics "with liberty and progress in general" (chap. 46).

Ladislaw is a liberal intellectual, not a radical, but a defender of the parliamentary politics of compromise. Having achieved some success as Brooke's election agent, and as the editor of a liberal paper in Middlemarch, he sees the emerging, more-democratic society as one in which his political and journalistic talents might prosper. He is a moderate—not the sort of journalist of whom Riehl had complained. Ladislaw's politics differ sharply from those of Lydgate. Lydgate was "sarcastic on the super-stitious faith of the people in the efficacy of 'the bill'" (chap. 46), that is, the Reform Bill of 1832. He can only sneer at the way liberals like Ladislaw encourage "the superstitious exaggeration of hopes" about any particular measure "as if it were a universal cure," and what he sees as Ladislaw's belief that "society can be cured by a political hocus-pocus." Only by the advance of science in all spheres, most particularly by the scientific study of society, by a moral regeneration of that society, particularly of its leaders, can a genuine progress be achieved—for that would be a progress accom-panied by order. Lydgate is impatient of halfway measures and compro-mise. On the other hand, Ladislaw seeks gradual, piecemeal reform on all fronts and thinks it foolish to "wait for wisdom and conscience in public agents." Only if all classes, not merely the landowners, are represented in Parliament can a rough political justice be achieved. "The only conscience we can trust to is the massive sense of wrong in a class," he proclaims, "and the best wisdom that will work is the wisdom of balancing claims" (chap. 46). Ladislaw is the expositor of England's politics of parliaments and compromise—and thus of Eliot's politics of national inheritance.

Dorothea faces a moral and political choice, and she rejects Lydgate's doctrinaire views. Although she admires the young doctor, she chooses to follow, no doubt for personal as well as political reasons, the conservative-liberal Ladislaw. Yet Lydgate is not a fanatic: "In warming himself at French social theories he had brought away no smell of scorching"; he held no "extreme opinions" and was at bottom a part of the "established order," espousing no really radical views about "anything but medical reform and the prosecution of discovery." Lydgate "would have liked no barefooted doctrines," the narrator suggests, no doubt with Saint Theresa's Descalzos in mind, "being particular about his boots" (chap. 36). He is less a true Positivist than a fellow traveler of the movement.

Similarly, in embodying the quest for individual happiness and self-culture, Lydgate's opponent Ladislaw is no extremist. Neither anarchist nor libertine, Ladislaw seeks, insofar as possible, to join pleasure and vir-tue; improvement will come out of the maelstrom of parliamentary poli-tics, the balancing of claims. Will and Dorothea eventually marry. Ladislaw, we are told, will become "an ardent public man" and reformer, and will be honorably elected to Parliament by a constituency that has paid his expenses, avoiding one impediment of the old system ("Finale"). (John Stuart Mill had insisted on such an arrangement when he contested the election for the borough of Westminster in 1865.) Ladislaw is a bourgeois Felix Holt, and like the heroine of that novel, his bride willingly gives up an inheritance to join him in his mission.

A number of minor characters display varieties of corrupt forms of political virtues. The underside of Comte's benevolent banker-led patriciate is suggested by the Evangelical banker Bulstrode. Comtism might be viewed as a secular Evangelicalism, extolling duty, opposing individual enjoyment, and believing in the subordination of the individual to a puritanical public opinion. Like Savonarola in his worst moments, the pious Bulstrode wishes "to gain as much power as possible" so that he might use it "for the glory of God," and he seeks to impose an ascetic life on others by denouncing the very "few amusements which survived in the provinces" (chap. 16). Brooke is well-meaning, but he has been corrupted by the philosophy of a commercial society, and must be cozened into fulfilling his duties by the pressure of opinion and his own political ambitions. Through the character of Fred Vincy, who fantasizes about inheriting land and becoming a gentleman-farmer, and thereafter devoting himself to drinking, hunting, and gambling, Eliot portrays the underside of the paternalistic image.

The nineteenth century had the hard-working entrepreneur as its ideal, and the woman Fred Vincy loves, Mary Garth, chastises Vincy as "contemptible" for his dreams of inheritance and his narrow view of duty. "When others are working and striving, and there are so many things to be done," she asks, "how can you bear to be fit for nothing in the world that is useful?" (chap. 25). Mary's father, Caleb, is a Middlemarch Adam Bede, a builder, a valuer, and an agent who is concerned not so much with money but with active enterprise, a life of "sublime labour" (chap. 24). The modern concern for enterprise is at the opposite pole from the earlier society's absorption with inheritance, a subject that Eliot pursues further in her novel.

In *Middlemarch* Dorothea Brooke offers a philosophy of inheritance not unlike that of the Dodsons, with strong undertones of Eppie and Esther Lyon, but with certain surprising variations. Eliot probably startled her liberal readers when she has the narrator note that, after initial misgivings, Dorothea has come to accept the rightfulness of feudal primogeniture and entail. As a child, we are told, after a troublesome probing, Dorothea was persuaded of "the historical, political reasons why eldest sons had superior rights, and why land should be entailed." (Burke, the reader may recall, had defended such a position.) In feudal times inheritance was not conceived as "a question of liking," the narrator observes, but as one of "responsibility." Mere "liking" belonged to the looser ways of a commercial society, concerned with the interests of the moment; responsibility connected people with their predecessors by blood or law and ensured the orderly progress of society. Here, *in nuce,* were the foundations of the politics of inheritance.

"All the energy" of Dorothea's "nature went on the side of responsibility," we are told. By "responsibility" Dorothea meant "the fulfilment of claims founded on our own deeds, such as marriage and parentage" (chap. 37). As presented in earlier novels—and in Eliot's view of the relationship between God and the Jews—Eliot's heroine saw the overriding duty of parents to endow, though as in the case of Eppie in *Silas Marner* or Esther Lyon in *Felix Holt,* the legatee might for moral reasons relinquish her claim. But an heir deprived of his or her right, Dorothea believed, even after the lapse of some generations, continued to possess a moral claim.

A key element in the background of *Middlemarch*'s plot is the disinheritance of Will Ladislaw, a disinheritance in which bigotry and fraud triumphed over responsibility. Ladislaw's paternal grandmother, we are informed, was disinherited after her marriage to an impecunious Polish musician, a circumstance that proved advantageous to her sister, Casaubon's grandmother, and ultimately to Casaubon himself. "What a wrong, to cut off the girl from the family protection and inheritance only because she had chosen a man who was poor," Dorothea declares. Casaubon's sense of moral obligation leads him to pay for Will Ladislaw's education. In this Dorothea believes him to be acting properly, to have "shown a sense of justice in family matters," for she sees her husband as owing "a debt to the Ladislaws—that he had to pay back what the Ladislaws had been wronged of" (chap. 37). She feels so strongly on this score, indeed, that she wishes Casaubon to alter his will to right this wrong. Casaubon himself, hostile to Will Ladislaw and suspicious of Dorothea's interest in him, is unwilling to make such a change.

A second disinheritance lies hidden in Ladislaw's past. Will's mother, Sarah Dunkirk, was the daughter of Calvinistic dissenting parents; her father was a pawnbroker, as well as a fence for stolen goods. When Sarah discovered her father's illegal activities, we are told, she ran off in moral horror. Dunkirk soon brought into his business an able young member of his sect, Bulstrode, who persuaded himself that he could employ his new affluence to serve as God's instrument. After Dunkirk's death, Bulstrode married the widow, and frustrated her attempts to locate her daughter Sarah: thus Bulstrode became Mrs. Dunkirk's sole heir.

Will Ladislaw is given an opportunity to rectify the injury done him, but rejects it with contempt, thereby disinheriting himself, as Eppie and Esther had in Eliot's earlier novels. A threat of blackmail impels the conscience-stricken banker to offer Ladislaw an income of £500 a year as "atonement to you" as one who has "suffered a loss through me." But Ladislaw is contemptuous of Bulstrode and the offer, and refuses to benefit from the crimes of his maternal grandfather. He speaks of wishing "no stain on my birth or connections," for "my unblemished honour is important to me" (chap. 61). But word of Ladislaw's origins and Bulstrode's chicanery gets out, much to Will's unhappiness.

Though Eliot does not explicitly set this down—and, indeed, scholars have argued the question—it may not so much be the "ill-gotten" gain that causes Ladislaw's revulsion but an anxiety to avoid the inference that his mother was Jewish.[64] To be a pawnbroker and a fence at this time was almost certainly to be thought Jewish, though, of course, there were pawnbroking fences who were not. "So our mercurial Ladislaw has a queer genealogy," the clergyman Farebrother notes: "A high-spirited young lady and a musical Polish patriot made a likely enough stock for him to spring from, but I should never have suspected a grafting of the Jew pawn-broker." A local Tory, dismayed by Ladislaw's opinions, is not surprised to find he has "any cursed blood, Jew, Corsican, or Gypsy" (chap. 71). As the news of Will's birth spreads, there are references to "young Ladislaw the grandson of a thieving Jew pawnbroker" (chap. 77). A local notable is shocked that the "frightful mixture" of Will's blood includes "an old clo——"; it is not necessary for her to complete the phrase—"old clothes-man" (chap. 84). There was, of course, certainly enough for Ladislaw to object to in his mother's family without speculating on a possible Jewish origin, but, given Eliot's concern for Jewish issues, the question cannot be neglected. "It ought to lie with a man's self that he is a gentleman," he tells Bulstrode (chap. 61). Ladislaw, of course, loves Dorothea, and wonders how this news will affect her. He has no cause for concern. "I did not believe that you would let any circumstances of my birth create a prejudice in you against me," he later tells her, "though it was sure to do so in others" (chap. 83).

It does not occur to Dorothea that Will is wrong to reject Bulstrode's offer. While legators or their agents must behave responsibly, legatees have the right to make moral choices. But was Will wrong to reject his inheri-tance in order to avoid the imputation of not merely a criminal but also a Jewish background, if we assume this to have been the case, just so that he might maintain his position as an English gentleman? We shall see that this is a proposition that Eliot attempted to answer, from another point of view, earlier in her dramatic epic *The Spanish Gypsy* and later in her *Daniel Deronda*.

Eliot may well have taken as her model for Ladislaw the young Dis-raeli, in his early radical days. Local Tories see Will as "crack-brained," as they once did Disraeli; and like Disraeli, Will's "praeternatural quickness and glibness" when speaking from a platform were resented as casting "reflections on solid Englishmen generally." What with curls round Will's head, and Will's long, radical speeches, both features of the young Disraeli, Middlemarchers, noting Will's Polish name, could only be suspicious of his "dangerously mixed blood and general laxity." Ladislaw is a foretaste of the nineteenth-century Bohemian, and Lydgate speaks of him as "a sort of gypsy; rather enjoying the sense of belonging to no class" (chap. 46), thus reiterating the suspicions aroused by Disraeli at the beginning of his politi-cal career when his radical views, unusual origins, well-tended curls, and dandyish ways excited scorn. In his later career, of course, Disraeli, like Will, would behave more respectably. Disraeli, we know, became an articu-late spokesman for the politics of inheritance, and, we shall see, probably an important (if unacknowledged) influence on Eliot.

In none of the works preceding *Middlemarch*, except perhaps *The Mill on the Floss*, were Eliot's debts to Scott—who like herself charted the transi-

tion from traditional to commercial society—more generously acknowledged. Lydgate, we are told, once knew Scott's poems by heart (chap. 27);
Mr. Brooke is a loyal reader (chap. 39); the auctioneer Borthrop Trumbull
has bought a copy of *Ivanhoe* (chap. 32); Mary Garth is Scott's particular
admirer; and Mary's brother Jim reads aloud from "that beloved writer."
Scott, finally, is described by the narrator as having "made a chief part in
the happiness of many young lives" (chap. 57).

Eliot presents the coming of a commercial society to Middlemarch on
several levels. No longer do "squires and baronets, and even lords" live
separated from their fellows on overlooking hills; they descend from the
heights to participate in civic life. "Fastidious gentlemen" like Mr. Brooke
even "stood for boroughs." There was a more visible class mobility as
"some slipped a little downward, some got higher footing." "As the old
stocking gave way to the savings bank," even "people denied aspirates
gained wealth" (chap. 11). The railway is making its way to Middlemarch,
and entrepreneurs like Garth must persuade the more traditional workingmen that improvement may prove an advantage and not merely a threat to
the sense of community they prize.

Eliot no more viewed traditional society as perfect than had Scott. The
agents of the time were not all like Mr. Garth, men of "high moral character"; she observed ironically that such a standard of virtue, uniformly
maintained by men of business, must date from a period "long posterior to
the first Reform Bill" (chap. 35). Eliot saw profound differences between
the Middlemarch of 1830 and the town of an earlier period. For one thing,
the possibilities of an individual doing good, as they had existed for Romola and for Saint Theresa, had become much more narrowly prescribed.
The reader will recall that "later-born Theresas," as the novel's "Prelude"
notes, "were helped by no coherent social faith and order which could
perform the function of knowledge for the ardently willing soul." Eliot
rejected a Comtian positivism that might have played such a role in her
life, as did Dorothea in choosing Ladislaw and his views over those of
Lydgate. The nineteenth-century politics of compromise did not fire enthusiasm.

Nor did political economy, the premier science of commercial society,
which now stood between Dorothea and her philanthropy. Annoyed at
"being twitted with her ignorance" of the subject, "that never-explained
science which was thrust as an extinguisher over all her lights," she studies
it with care (chap. 2). She wishes to "get light as to the best way of
spending money so as not to injure one's neighbours, or—what comes to
the same thing—so as to do them the most good." But the baleful conclusion of economic science is that the less one interferes in the "natural laws"
of the marketplace the better (chap. 83). Dorothea, like George Eliot, is a
girl "brought up in English and Swiss Puritanism"; a moralist above all,
"she yearned towards the perfect Right, that it might make a throne within
her, and rule her errant will" (chap. 80). The laissez-faire doctrines of
commercial society are hard for her to accept, for Dorothea has the voca-

tion of Saint Theresa in an age in which such a calling could not be
sustained.

Eliot had read Mill's work on political economy, with its praise of the
free market—the standard text of the period; Spencer's political economy
bore an even more decidedly laissez-faire character. Like Dorothea Brooke,
Eliot moved away from the paternalism of her early years to a more
Spencerian position. When in 1874 she read Mrs. Nassau Senior's report
on girls' pauper schools, Eliot wrote the author to express agreement with
her attack on the poor laws, in opposition to the English Comtists who
advocated a strong central state as the dispenser of benevolences. The poor
law system as a whole was "an evil to be got rid of as soon as possible rather
than developed," Eliot declared. Mrs. Senior's description of the typical
pauper girl as "stubborn, apathetic, capable of violence," and devoid of
human passion, particularly discomforted Eliot. Could such a creature
prove a useful "mother or sister of the race"? The way of treating paupers
was "a huge system of vitiation" in which "communistic" principle replaced "provision through individual, personal responsibility and activity."
It was "an unhappy heritage" that must not be passed down to future
generations.[65]

In *Middlemarch,* as in *Romola,* Eliot, like Scott before her, struck at
sectarianism and utopianism. Sectarians fail to resolve the issue between
means and ends in a morally acceptable way, she suggested, and they
invariably elevate their doctrine to the point where it overwhelms any
sympathy for their fellows. These were Bulstrode's great sins as they had
been Savonarola's. Bulstrode had chosen to participate in "trades where
the power of the prince of the world showed its most active devices," and
this because he had convinced himself that even the profits of diabolic
enterprise "became sanctified" by their "right application . . . in the
hands of God's servant." This "implicit reasoning" characterized not only
Evangelical belief but the views of all who used "wide phrases for narrow
motives" (chap. 61). It was the quintessential error of the ideologue. Eliot
preferred the politics of inheritance, the politics of Ladislaw—and of
Spencer.

After Lewes's death in 1878 and Eliot's marriage two years later to John
Cross (whose family had long been sympathetic to the Comtists), the
Crosses read aloud to each other Bridges's translation of Comte's *Discours
préliminaire* as well as Spencer's *Study of Sociology* and *Data of Ethics.* Eliot
had worried as to whether her Positivist friends, Mrs. Congreve particularly, might be disturbed by her rejection of a Comtian perpetual widow-
hood.[66] Harrison was pleased about the marriage, or so he wrote Cross at
this time; the Comtian prohibition of a second marriage, he observed,
rested on "a whole system of truly religious ideas" that could hardly
be imposed on persons "who stand entirely aloof from our ways and
our thoughts."[67] (In later years, however, he would describe himself as
"deeply offended" by Eliot's decision to marry Cross.[68]) Mrs. Congreve, in

friendship, was ready to accept this change in Eliot's life.[69] Loyalty bred loyalty.

One of the loyalties that Eliot took special care to display to Mrs. Congreve, and to the Positivist fellow-traveler John Cross, was one to Comte's philosophy. "I do not think I ever heard her speak of any writer with a more grateful sense of obligation for enlightenment," Cross wrote of Eliot's regard for Comte, but he added that she rejected many of his teachings, and had only a "limited adherence to the Positivist Church."[70] She saw no existing religion or political system as "final," Cross further observed, and looked to "the gradual development of the affections and sympathetic emotions" rather than to any set of laws for future improvement. Political parties run by "ignorant amateurs" and representative government controlled by numerical majorities did not appeal to her as "the last word of political wisdom," but the Positivist scheme was no more attractive. She believed that the English system, with all its faults, would have greater advantages, he added. "Neither optimist nor pessimist," she saw herself as a "meliorist," a believer in the "gradual improvement of the mass"—the politics of "detail and compromise" that Harrison had excoriated. A search for the better, with each person finding "the better part of happiness in helping another," was Eliot's prescription for society. She had no faith in a utopian "best."[71]

Cross reported that Eliot enjoyed having the works of Shakespeare, Milton, Scott, Comte, and Herbert Spencer read aloud to her.[72] In her final month of life, Eliot wrote Sara Hennell that she wished that Hennell were not "so repelled" by Spencer's writing style, since "he has so much teaching that the world needs."[73] At the time of Eliot's death, Spencer wrote to an American friend that when he had seen her on the day she became ill, she was "veering a good deal away from Comte." Though hardly a deathbed conversion of the usual order, Eliot apparently spoke of the "fundamental divergence" between Comte's view of society and Spencer's, and said that she preferred Spencer's. "She had been re-reading, with Mr. Cross," two of Spencer's works, "the *Data of Ethics* and the *Study of Sociology* (the last, indeed, for the third time), and was in general sympathy with their views," Spencer reported. He speculated that had she lived to complete the novel that she had already begun, this "influence might have been made more manifest."[74] The intimations of such a position—the veering away from Comte and the turning to Spencer—were already present in her previous writings. *Middlemarch,* as we have seen, made the turn to Spencer and his variant of the politics of the English national tradition and inheritance even more clear.

There is "no general doctrine," the narrator of *Middlemarch* concludes, that is "not capable of eating out our morality if unchecked by the deep-seated habit of direct fellow-feeling with individual fellow men" (chap. 61). Middlemarch's latitudinarian clergyman Farebrother, in a somewhat similar vein, describes the Evangelical "system . . . [as] a sort of worldly-spiritual cliqueism"; its adherents "look on the rest of mankind as a doomed carcass which is to nourish them to heaven" (chap. 17). But the novel's narrator finds the same faults in liberals and Arminians who "believe in the future perfection of our race"; in millenarians who see "the nearest date fixed for the end of the world"; and, finally, in those (like the Comtian adherents of the religion of humanity) who "have a passionate belief in the solidarity of mankind" (chap. 61).

In place of ideology—whether Evangelical, liberal, or Positivist—Eliot turned to the politics of inheritance, which she believed to be a natural growth of a nation's traditions, history, and character. She saw the spirit of compromise, as it operated in parliamentary politics, as an essential and healthy element of England's political inheritance. Compromise had produced improvement and stability. Utopian plans to abandon the nation's historic institutions in favor of a doctrinaire blueprint seemed foolish to Eliot, and, when accompanied by an unrealistically flattering opinion of the proletariat and a call for class war, highly dangerous. *Middlemarch,* we have seen, although not written primarily as a political novel, reflects on many of these questions, and put itself in the camp not of Positivist ideologues (or even of advanced liberals like Morley) but of the adherents of the national politics of compromise.

Eliot's serious doubts concerning liberal cosmopolitanism—what she described as "a passionate belief in the solidarity of mankind"—were another aspect of the politics of inheritance that distinguished her views from those of Victorian liberalism and positivism. In her epic drama *The Spanish Gypsy,* published in 1868, four years before *Middlemarch,* and in her last novel, *Daniel Deronda,* which appeared in 1876, four years after her best-known novel, Eliot wrote in terms that Comtists like Frederic Harrison believed dangerously subversive of a faith in mankind's solidarity. In these works the liberal freedom of heirs to reject an inheritance, which we have observed in her earlier novels—while still technically present—is seen as a failure to assume a duty. Indeed, the racial nature of the heirs and the character of the inheritance appear to offer them no real choice but acceptance of a national heritage even as they might attempt to transform it. The politics of national inheritance have virtually become not merely a useful and desirable course, but a morally compulsory one.

5

The Disinherited Races

In *Middlemarch* Eliot depicted the sixteenth-century Spanish Saint Theresa going to her martyrdom at the hands of the Moors with a heart "already beating to the national idea" ("Prelude"). For Eliot, as for many of the European writers of the nineteenth century, the national idea possessed a new significance. In Germany, Herder had written extensively on its importance in the lives of the people, and Hegel had described the national spirit, the *Volksgeist*, as the guiding motif of historical development. Hegel had even argued that individuals wishing to realize themselves fully must identify with the national idea and work out its implications in the shaping of their own lives. In England not only social conservatives like Coleridge but "many-sided" liberals like Mill had stressed the critical role of the national tradition and heritage. In the 1840s, as we shall see, Disraeli wrote of these matters in terms that originally repelled Eliot, though later she embraced many of his ideas. We know that the German writer Riehl addressed these questions in the 1850s in terms that gained Eliot's sympathy and contributed to the shaping of her politics of national inheritance.

In the nineteenth century nationalism seemed to be the most vital motive in European life. Groups previously content to be obedient subjects of continental Europe's dynastic monarchies, and willing to accede to the dynasty's state language and uphold its culture in order to participate in political and intellectual life, began to insist on their separate identities and dialects and thereby laid the groundwork for establishing their own distinctive national literatures and cultures; folktales and folk music were recovered by means of the previously neglected study of peasant lore.

Nationalist rumblings were already being heard during the continental revolutions of 1830 and 1848, and by the middle decades of the century perceptive writers were pronouncing the inevitable replacement of dynastic by national states. The Italian Giuseppi Mazzini was the oracle of the nationalism that attracted continental liberals, and he became the spiritual guide of the Risorgimento that unified his long-divided country. Germany's unification, achieved by a Bismarckian policy of "blood and iron," was prepared for by a long line of nationalist writers, which included the philosophers Fichte and Schleiermacher, who had aroused the nation against Napoleon at the beginning of the century, and the national economist Friedrich List and *völkisch* writer W. H. Riehl in the middle decades of the century.

A self-assured nineteenth-century Britain, with its economic and naval preponderance, saw itself as the center of a global free-trade economy based upon an international division of labor: a wide-ranging cosmopolitanism appeared to be the natural posture for such a country. Although, as we have seen, conservative writers and politicians from Burke onward had warned against the neglect of the national idea and the national tradition, especially on the part of cosmopolitan liberals who appeared dangerously ignorant of this heritage, Britain's position in the world made such a message appear not only bigoted but reactionary. Adherents of advanced groups on the left, among them the Positivists, found little place for what they regarded as outmoded national differences. The Positivist vision of the future assumed a malleability, an almost mechanical uniformity, of the people of the most advanced nations of western Europe—for Comte, the place where a future Positivist federation would be formed. This federation was seen by the Comtists as the first great step toward establishing the unity and solidarity of humanity.

There were two pan-European nationalities, the Gypsies and the Jews, who seemed to be excluded from the prevailing ambition to achieve national self-determination. Both were pariah groups, assumed to be antisocial, and often accused of being enemies of mankind. Throughout their histories in Europe they had been wanderers. Their host nations periodically forced them to leave countries they had assumed to be their homelands. Most Jews believed they were joined to their fellow Jews by religion, not nationality. A return to Jerusalem was at this time a messianic hope or a consoling metaphor, not a program of action. And Gypsies, it was generally understood, did not even possess the Jewish consolation of a brilliant past: they lived only in a present in which, their enemies charged, they cheated and stole, and in which, consequently, they were feared and reviled. The extraordinary situation of Jews and Gypsies in a Europe in which inhabitants thought increasingly in terms of "nationalities" (some already living in states and virtually all with an expectation of acquiring them) would continue to pose a European "problem," one to which nazism, in the 1930s and 1940s, offered a "permanent solution."

George Eliot proposed a very different solution, one that she believed would transform both groups into "normal" peoples, that is, into separate nationalities with states of their own, and therefore free to cultivate their own national heritages and traditions. Riehl had referred to the Jews (and to the Gypsies) as "the other," an internal, rootless adversary against whom the host nation could hone its own sense of a superior identity. Eliot, on the other hand, particularly in her later years, pictured Jews and Gypsies as "another," different undoubtedly, but capable of discovering, defining, and pursuing their own national cultures and destinies. That they would do so was for Eliot the best possible path of self-liberation, one that would enable them to overcome centuries of national disinheritance.

Frederic Harrison had urged Eliot to write not only a Positivist novel but also a Positivist verse drama. Eliot confessed that before writing *Felix Holt* she had written four acts of such a work, but then had set them aside because the ideas its characters represented overwhelmed their reality as possible living beings. But she had now returned to the play, she wrote Harrison in 1866, and she confessed, "I find it impossible to abandon it: the conceptions move me deeply. . . . There is not a thought or a symbol that I do not long to use."[1] This drama would become *The Spanish Gypsy,* and within this work the themes of inheritance and disinheritance as she had previously treated them underwent a remarkable transformation.

Eliot did not initially suggest that the ideas of her drama were Positivist, but she willingly accepted Richard Congreve's description of the play, after the work's publication in 1868, as a "mass of Positivism." When she wrote her friend Mrs. Congreve about the success of the work and the need for a third printing, she playfully observed that she was not passing on the gratifying news of the drama's popularity because she was "an egotistical author." "The news concerns the doctrine, not the writer," she declared.[2]

But Frederic Harrison, unlike the Congreves, recognized (with some confusion and irritation) that *The Spanish Gypsy,* despite its central Positivist theme of subordinating the individual to the community, contained implications repulsive to the English Comtists. Why was Eliot prepared to agree that the epic was a Positivist work? Of course, this question is part of the larger problem of Eliot's association with Comtism, and her friendships within Comtist circles. She accepted those parts of Comte's doctrine that were more or less congruent with the politics of national inheritance, but she developed her own position in a way much more congenial to these politics than to Positivist doctrine.

Sir Walter Scott, not surprisingly, had anticipated Eliot's sympathetic treatment of the Gypsy. In *Guy Mannering* Scott produced a story in which Gypsies abet the kidnapping of a child, leading to his disinheritance—thereby creating a conventional romantic tale. (In Eliot's inversion of this plot in her epic drama, a Gypsy child becomes the disinherited victim of Christian kidnappers.) In Scott's novel an ineffectual and apparently good-natured Scottish laird becomes a justice of the peace. As a result of his new sense of responsibility, he is transformed into an overscrupulous and some-times merciless uprooter of all the disorderly elements long tolerated by the traditional society, including Gypsies. In revenge, Meg Merrilies, "a kind o' queen among the gipsies"—perhaps a precursor of Maggie Tulliver in *The Mill on the Floss* when she runs off to join the Gypsies?—becomes an accomplice to the kidnapping of the laird's five-year-old son. The lad is raised in Holland by strangers and is kept from his rightful inheritance, until restored by the repentant and good-hearted Meg. But Eliot's Gypsies, we will see, are a very different lot from Scott's.

Eliot's biographer Gordon Haight has hinted that Bulwer-Lytton's *Leila,* written in 1837, was a possible model for Eliot's poetic drama.[3] There are certainly resemblances, though Bulwer-Lytton's novel centered on Jews. *Leila* was set in and about the Moorish city of Granada in 1491 and 1492, roughly the time of the action of *The Spanish Gypsy*. Boabdil, the king of Granada, has fallen into the hands of a reputed sorcerer, Alama-men, who like the astrologer of Eliot's drama is a Jew, though a concealed one. Alamamen is a man of science and reason; not given to what he sees as the superstitions of his fellow Jews, his strong commitment to his people is one based on common race and nation, not on religion. What Alamamen hopes for, and is at first promised by the Christian monarch Ferdinand of Aragon, are "rights and immunities" that Jews have not heretofore enjoyed in Europe. Because of this deprivation, the narrator tells us, the noble ambition of the Jewish race has been turned into vice; the "loathsome leprosy of avarice" has turned Jews into "huckstering bargainer[s]," into "usurers and slaves." Alamamen is convinced that once restored to their full rights, the Jews will become more virtuous.

Bulwer-Lytton's plot is standard romance, with a heavy debt to Scott's *Ivanhoe*. Alamamen has a beautiful daughter, Leila, whom he keeps in a guarded villa, but Muza, the champion of the Moslem cause, has discov-ered the girl and has fallen in love with her. She returns his love. She knows her father would prefer her dead rather than married to a Moor or Chris-tian, for, as in the stereotypical portrait of the Jew, Alamamen is a bigoted enemy to all non-Jews. His "dark misanthropy" has turned him to "treach-ery and fraud" (bk. I, chap. 5). After a series of misadventures, Leila falls into the hands of the Christians, and is taken into the protection of a noble family (III, 2). But she does not display fierce loyalty to her national inheritance, in the manner of Scott's Rebecca of York, and converts to Christianity (V, 3). Alamamen, by now revealed as a Jew, faces the Inquisi-tion presided over by Torquemada (in a scene that resembles Rebecca's trial by the Templars in *Ivanhoe*). The Jew invokes the liberal argument that a man might be "a judge of the deeds of men, but not of their opinions" (II, 7). (However, Bulwer-Lytton does not portray his Jewish characters as liberals, and seems to have viewed Alamamen as deserving of his sufferings for having himself sown the seed of religious bigotry.) Leila, now a Christian, and hopeful that her conversion might prove "in part atonement of the crime of her stubborn race," goes to a nunnery to prepare to become a nun herself. Alamamen, having escaped from Torquemada, tries to persuade Leila to leave "these hated lands" and return to their homeland in the East (IV, 4). Don Juan, the royal heir (playing the part of Boisguillebert in *Ivanhoe*), offers Leila his love and protection, but not marriage. But Leila is steadfast in her intentions. Alamamen, "the revengeful fanatic," goes to the nunnery to kill "the meek convert" for her perfidy (IV, 3). But the arrival of Muza, to whom Leila has remained devoted, prevents her murder.

It is not difficult to see Bulwer-Lytton's plot as a variation of that of *Ivanhoe,* with Christians and Moors taking the place of Norman and Saxons, though without a precise correspondence of qualities, and with the Jews in much the same position of pariah. Bulwer-Lytton has Alamamen see a return to the Palestinian homeland as the sole refuge of the Jews against persecution, as well as offering them the possibility of a moral transformation. This would certainly be, with respect to Gypsies rather than Jews, the theme not only of Eliot's epic poem, and, with Jews more specifically, also that of *Daniel Deronda,* in which we will see another variation of the Ivanhoe plot.

Victor Hugo called *Ivanhoe* "le véritable épopée de notre âge" (the genuine epic of our time),[4] and in 1820 outlined its essential features. "A half-civilized people finds itself transported, as a result of its conquests, in the midst of a yet more barbarous nation," Hugo explained, before time has brought about an equilibrium between them. The "two nations" are separated not only by their unequal civilizations, but by "the shame of defeat and national pride" on the part of the more savage, conquered nation, and by the "pride and insolence" of the conquerors. "In the midst of the two peoples stirred by mutual hatred, we find a third race," the Jews, "the object of their common contempt."[5] This theme and its variations formed the basis for a number of major novels produced by nineteenth-century writers.

Eliot referred to *Ivanhoe* in terms similar to those Hugo had used in her 1856 review of the American writer Harriet Beecher Stowe's second novel, *Dred*. Eliot observed that this novel, like Stowe's previous work, *Uncle Tom's Cabin,* had "that *conflict of races*" which Augustin Thierry, the French historian of the Norman Conquest, had in 1825 "pointed out as the great source of romantic interest—witness 'Ivanhoe.'" Stowe's novels, Eliot continued, like Scott's, depicted "a people to whom what we may call Hebraic Christianity is still a reality." Eliot suggested that Stowe's black characters had been painted in too glowing colors, losing thereby "the most terribly tragic element in the relation of the two races—the Nemesis lurking in the vices of the oppressed."[6] (One should note that for Stowe redemption for blacks could come about only through their return to Africa, just as Bulwer-Lytton saw a return to Palestine as essential to the complete rehabilitation of the Jews.)

Eliot wrote her epic drama about Gypsies, not Jews. Yet her interest in Jews was keen, and she was already on friendly terms with Emanuel

Deutsch, a Jewish scholar who taught her the Hebrew language. Perhaps Gypsies were simply more romantic and constituted a more popular subject for nineteenth-century Europeans than did Jews; the Gypsy element in Bizet's *Carmen* probably helped it to become the most popular opera of its time, and perhaps of ours as well. The Bohemian exoticism of the Gypsies and their freedom from the restraints of middle-class Victorianism made them appealing fantasy figures in a way that Jews, whose lives were severely restricted by the complex rules of their faith, could never be. Such a freedom from restraints might be a mark against Gypsies for a puritanical Eliot; certainly, as Maggie in *The Mill on the Floss* understood, Gypsies stood badly in need of redemption. If one thinks in terms of the myth of the disinherited one, Gypsies fit the bill rather well. Still, we shall see, there is an undercurrent in Eliot's verse drama that makes it seem that she also had Jews on her mind.

In her notes on *The Spanish Gypsy* Eliot observed that its theme had suggested itself to her when viewing a Titian *Annunciation*: a maiden about to marry is told she has been "chosen to fulfill a great destiny," chosen not arbitrarily, but because of a "hereditary claim on her." Eliot found this theme "grander than that of Iphigenia," and noted that it had never been previously used. The Gypsy maiden must renounce her marriage because of the "opposition of race." Eliot remarked, "I saw it might be taken as a symbol of the part which is played in the general human lot by hereditary conditions in the largest sense, and of the fact that what we call duty is entirely made up of such conditions; for even in cases of just antagonism to the narrow view of hereditary claims, the whole background of the particular struggle is made up of our inherited nature." Here was a conflict between deliberate choice and "ruthless destiny"—between whim or caprice and hereditary duty.[7]

   The Spanish Gypsy focuses on a beautiful young woman disinherited of her share in the fate of "a disinherited race." The setting is Spain during the reign of Ferdinand and Isabel, at the end of the fifteenth century. Fedalma, a Gypsy princess kidnapped by the Spaniards at the age of three and raised as a Catholic, is now eighteen. An adoring Silva, the duke of Bedmar, who leads the Spaniards in their frontier wars with the Moors, prepares to marry Fedalma despite the objections of his uncle, Isidor. This uncle, a Dominican prior and an inquisitor, regards Fedalma as a pagan, and feels that a marriage to her would defile his nephew. The Dominican plans to have Fedalma tried for heresy by the Inquisition. Silva, however, is determined to marry her.

   Ignorant of her Gypsy birth, Fedalma encounters Zarca, a Gypsy prisoner and a chief of his people, and instantly recognizes a bond with him. Zarca reveals himself to be her father, and reminds his daughter that her first loyalty should be to her blood. Zarca persuades Fedalma to renounce Silva, whom she loves, and to join Zarca in his escape. Thus nature overpowers nurture. Zarca wishes his daughter to assist him in his plan to save his people from Christian persecution, and to redeem them from their life of wandering and thievery. He plans to establish a Gypsy homeland in Africa, where he will be king. She joins him in this enterprise.

Even before she learns she is a Gypsy, Fedalma has felt stifled in the palace: she has had a "longing to be free" (Warwickshire edition, 18: 92). One day, in passing through the streets of the city, she is aroused by music in the public square. She takes up a tambourine and dances before the assembled crowd. "I did not mean to dance," she later explains to a scandalized Silva, "it happened so" (77). "Sometimes a torrent rushing through my soul escapes in wild strange wishes" (92), she explains, adding, "Perhaps I lived before in some strange world where first my soul was shaped" (96). The Gypsy inheritance is Fedalma's despite "her Spanish nurture," as Zarca will explain. She cannot "unmake" herself (132) to become a Spanish duchess. She cannot

> adopt a soul without its thoughts,
> Or grasp a life apart from flesh and blood.
>
> (133)

Fedalma acknowledges that

> in my blood
> There streams the sense unspeakable of kind,
> As leopard feels at ease with leopard.
>
> (129)

Zarca and his daughter speak the same language of blood as the inquisitor.

Silva is inconsolable when he learns of Fedalma's departure. More a Victorian liberal, or a Comtist, than a fifteenth-century Spanish grandee, Silva protests "the roaring bigotry of the herd" that the inquisitor represents. He also denounces the views on race of a Jewish friend, the scholar, Sephardo:

> To talk of birth as of inherited rage
> Deep-down, volcanic, fatal, bursting forth
> From under hard-taught reason? Wondrous friend!
> My uncle Isidor's echo, mocking me.
>
> (167)

When he had approached Sephardo for advice, he had "come for other doctrine than the Prior's" (167).

Silva follows Fedalma to the Gypsy encampment, which lies in Moorish territory, for Zarca has allied the Gypsies with the Mohammedans. Silva has come to Zarca to ask his permission "to wed his daughter as her nurture bids" (237), but Zarca interposes a sword between the two, "a sword that was baptised in Christian blood" (236). Zarca will not give his daughter to a Christian; he cannot allow Fedalma

> To be a wife amongst an alien race
> To whom her tribe owes curses.
>
> (238)

To this objection, Silva responds, again in the manner of a nineteenth-century liberal, that

> such blind hate
> Is fit for beasts of prey, but not for men. . . .
> And for the wrongs inflicted on your tribe
> By Spanish edicts or the cruelty
> Of Spanish vassals, am I criminal?
> Love comes to cancel all ancestral hate,
> Subdues all heritage, proves that in mankind
> Union is deeper than division.
>
> (238)

But then Fedalma herself rejects Silva's offer, saying

> No! I will bear
> The heavy trust of my inheritance.
> See, t'was my people's life that throbbed in me:
> An unknown need stirred darkly in my soul,
> And made me restless even in my bliss. . . .
> I must go with my people.
>
> (244)

Silva cannot part with her, and he determines to become a Gypsy for Fedalma's sake:

> I will elect my deed, and be the liege
> Not of my birth, but of that good alone
> I have discerned and chosen.
>
> (248)

Zarca doubts the possibility of such a decision:

> Our poor faith
> Allows not rightful choice, save of the right
> Our birth has made for us.
>
> (248)

To Fedalma's delight, however, Zarca reluctantly agrees to the marriage if Silva will become a Gypsy; still, Fedalma has lingering doubts, telling Silva that

> The bonds Fedalma may not break for you,
> I cannot joy that you should break for her.
>
> (251)

Zarca's Gypsies capture Silva's city of Bedmar, and, as the Gypsy leader has known from the beginning, the consequences of battle arouse Silva's repressed loyalties to his own kind. Zarca understands that this revelation will be painful to his daughter, who herself has been

> Bred by false nurture in an alien home—
> As if a lion in fangless infancy
> Learned love of creatures that with fatal growth
> It scents as natural prey.
>
> (269)

When Silva sees the slain bodies of his former comrades, and the desecration of Bedmar's cathedral, he regrets his violation of the oaths he made as a Christian knight. Blood proves so decisive that he stabs Zarca, mortally wounding him. With his dying words Zarca reminds Fedalma of their mission to establish a Gypsy homeland.

The final scene of the drama is set a week later in Almeria where the Gypsies are about to set sail for their new African home. Silva has become a homeless wanderer, but, still fervently loving Fedalma, comes to bid her farewell. Silva has been crushed by events. Fedalma blames herself for Silva's torment and for the death of her father, who might have been the savior of her race:

> We
> With our poor petty lives have strangled one
> That ages watch for vainly.
>
> (308)

Silva tells her that he intends to go to Rome to renew the oath of Christian fidelity that he had set aside in becoming a Gypsy:

> Fedalma, think of me
> As one who will regain the only life
> Where he is other than apostate.
>
> (311)

Fedalma knows that all is finished between them despite their love, and sails off to found "the new Gypsy Carthage" in Africa. It is as a discouraged would-be Aeneas that Fedalma leaves her Dido-like Silva, as she seeks a homeland for her Gypsy Trojans in Africa—a reversal of both the sexes and continents of destination in Virgil's epic.

The Spanish Gypsy's underlying plot, like that of *Silas Marner* and *Felix Holt,* concerns "the disinherited one." Both Eppie and Esther renounce their inheritances to remain in humbler positions; moreover Esther declasses herself further to join Felix Holt in his mission to the working class. Fedalma, like Esther, chooses to follow a mission. Fedalma's acceptance of the inheritance of which she has been long deprived leaves her in a hum-

bler, yet in one sense a more glorious position. She yields her prospective
rank as Silva's duchess in response to the primal loyalty of blood, and she is
restored not merely to her Gypsy people but to her proper rank as queen
and savior of the Gypsies. In worldly terms, however, Fedalma, like Eppie
and Esther—and like Felix Holt—has permitted sentiment to win over
calculation.

Eliot believed that good tragedy "must represent irreparable collision
between the individual and the general": we sympathize with the individual but accept the "irresistible power" of the general, she observed in her
notes to *The Spanish Gypsy*. Silva represented the tragedy of "entire rebellion" against his inherited position; Fedalma, the tragedy of "grand submission" to "an hereditary lot"; Zarca, the tragedy of vain "struggle for a
great end." A woman, Eliot postulates, finds herself with an inherited
misfortune: she may be stricken with an inherited disease, or may be a
negro, "or have other marks of race repulsive in the community where she
is born, etc. etc." It would be "almost a mockery" to tell a person disadvantaged in this way to seek her individual happiness. Such happiness could be
attained only "through large resignation and acceptance of the inevitable."
Eliot concluded that individual efforts to accommodate such a burden-
some heritage, when properly motivated and operating within the limits
circumstances made necessary, might (as in Fedalma's case) become a force
for communal good.[8]

To see the Comtian strain in *The Spanish Gypsy* then, one must read the
epic drama as a conflict between private, individual concerns (and necessities) and those of all of society. When confronting this problem, Romola,
after much hesitation and inner conflict, finally follows Antigone in choosing the private over the communal; in *The Spanish Gypsy,* Creon and the
communal triumph, as national necessity overwhelms all. The passion of
Fedalma and Silva gives way to the morally overriding compulsions of
blood and race. Just as Fedalma sacrifices her petty, individual desires to
advance the greater cause of her people, so, it may be understood, in a
future Positivist era altruism would supplant egoism.

But many other passages in the epic have a decidedly anti-Positivist
cast—resembling Riehl's position, more than Comte's. This ambiguity
may account for the different reactions to the work experienced by the
English Positivists. *The Spanish Gypsy* portrays not merely the conflict between the individual and the community, but also the overwhelming authority of race. At one point, a Comtian Silva invokes reason as a guide to
action:

> Thus he called on Thought,
> On dexterous Thought, with its swift alchemy
> To change all forms, dissolve all prejudice
> Of man's long heritage, and yield him up
> A crude fused world to fashion as he would.
>
> (258–59)

But reason, Silva discovers, "seemed to wear the yoke / Of sovereign passion." What brought men together was not a society whose forms were shaped by thought, but one like that of the Gypsies and the fifteenth-century Spaniards that emerged from feeling, the "long-shared pains / Of far-off generations." Silva attempts with "the outlaw's strength" to make

> a right
> Contemning that hereditary right,
>
> (259)

But to no avail. For even while exercising reason,

> he idly played
> With rules, beliefs, charges, and ceremonies
> As arbitrary fooling,
>
> (261)

and courts disaster. For

> Such revenge
> Is wrought by the long travail of mankind
> On him who scorns it.
>
> (261)

What Eliot invoked was "that Supreme, the irreversible Past" of national history and blood, the past of the politics of inheritance, and of Riehl (264)—a victory for Burke and Coleridge over Bentham and advanced liberals.

The inherited national traditions of a race or a nation—seemingly operating through the blood—are thus, in *The Spanish Gypsy*, decisive. Eliot has the learned Jewish astrologer Sephardo say to the rational, cosmopolitan Silva:

> My lord, I will be frank; there's no such thing
> As naked manhood. If the stars look down
> On any mortal of our shape, whose strength
> Is to judge all things without preference,
> He is a monster, not a faithful man.
> While my heart beats, it shall wear livery—
> My people's livery, whose yellow badge
> Marks them for Christian scorn. I will not say
> That man is first man to me, then Jew or Gentile:
> That suits the rich *marranos;* but to me
> My father is first father and then man.
>
> (162)

Sephardo is a Jew who knows that God speaks through his people's "custom, tradition, and old sanctities" (176). On the other hand, the Gypsy

Zarca complains of his people that "our race has no great memories" (121). *The Spanish Gypsy* ends on a note of frustration: the Gypsy heroine Fedalma feels that her effort to found a homeland for her people in Africa will fail. For without "great memories," that is, an established national tradition, the task is hopeless.

Eliot sent a copy of her drama to Frederic Harrison. He sent her a note of thanks on the very day she had mailed him her book, May 25, 1868, a tribute both to his good manners and the efficiency of the Victorian postal service. He said nothing specific about the tale of *The Spanish Gypsy*, since he would hardly have had the time to read it, but a glance at the work was clearly sufficient for Harrison to know that this was no tale of the coming of Positivist sentiment to Normandy or Quebec. He reminded Eliot of his effort two years earlier to outline "a subject worthy of you, the idealisation of the Positive vision of society as a whole, especially to typify the great institution and social functions of the future." She had at that time, he recalled, thought such a subject "too abstract and wide for real art," but the idea continued to attract him. Eliot, replying, suggested that Harrison might turn his own hand to the task. Her epic, like others of the genre, was one about the past not about the future.[9]

On November 11, 1868, nearly six months later, a rather long interval given his prompt acknowledgment of the book's receipt, Harrison wrote again, this time concerning *The Spanish Gypsy* itself. After having read the drama with care, Harrison was puzzled. He had been led to believe it was *a* Positivist work—perhaps by readers like Richard Congreve—even if not *the* work he had proposed, but he himself clearly had doubts. Harrison wished to tell Eliot "fully all that I feel about it," but he could neither "gather up my ideas" nor "know very clearly what they are." He had read "your poem many many times to myself and to others, and thought over it and talked of it constantly," yet he was still uncertain as to what he might say to her. He intended to read the poem once again because he was "conscious that I have not half mastered" it. There was certainly some evidence of Positivist sentiment in the drama, he granted, but though convinced that "it is a great work," Harrison was still uncertain of its "ethos."[10]

Somewhat peremptorily, Harrison then proceeded to assume the role of Eliot's Comtian confessor and instructor, as his Positivist convictions overcame good manners. "This is far too serious a matter," the letter continued, "and one which involves social interests so far higher than any personal, for me to say anything which does not fairly represent the state of my mind." If *The Spanish Gypsy* were taken to represent the Positivist ethos, as it apparently was by some Comtists, Harrison wished to be reassured that this was properly the case. But he was not "of any clear and resolved mind about it." "On the contrary," he believed that he might "misconceive what are the real human traits of character in the principal personages." "I am not sure that either are real human types of nature." He went on, "I am not sure if the conduct of both of them, or of one of them is not treason to human life." Nor was he "at all clear what is the sum or moral of the whole."[11]

More alarming for Harrison was his fear that if he knew what Eliot's "sum or moral" was, he would disagree with her on its vital points. "For instance I hesitate, and the more I think the more I hesitate, how Zarca and Fedalma stand in true ethical judgement." Harrison described a period of mental turmoil as a consequence of his careful reading of *The Spanish Gypsy*. "I pass through revulsions of mind" on these questions "like a man in a religious crisis of scepticism and faith," he wrote; "I am ashamed of my own paralytic state of mind." Those whose judgments he trusted—he was again probably referring to Congreve—had no doubts concerning the political correctness of the drama. Only Harrison stood "like Thomas fingering the very nail prints and yet striving to believe." He begged Eliot to be kind to "this weak exhibition of a weak mind."[12]

But such generosity would have been difficult—at least immediately—for any author. We do not have any evidence of a reply from Eliot. When Harrison became engaged to a cousin some seven months later, he wrote to tell the Leweses; the letter may well have been intended to renew a lapsed correspondence and relationship.[13] Eliot's reply certainly suggests that there had been some breach. She spoke of her pleasure that "you keep me in your kind thoughts" though "space and time may keep us asunder." The Leweses clearly wished to reassure Harrison that they remained friendly; they invited him to visit and assured him that "you will find us thoroughly glad to shake hands with you."[14] There was no mention of *The Spanish Gypsy*.

Is it any wonder that Harrison was not sure of the work's ethos? Should a Positivist praise Silva's cosmopolitanism or decry his subsequent readiness to yield to national passion? Should he berate Zarca's and Sephardo's tribalism or praise their elevation of the common over the individual interest? Harrison's paralysis of mind reflected the frustration of subjecting the work to Comtian analysis. Comte had depicted the contemporary West as lacking the certitudes of an organic society—such as the feudal Middle Ages had possessed or a future Positivism would restore. The present was a period of transition in which nothing was sure and men faced a multitude of choices, all apparently valid. The consequence of this situation was profound inner struggle: men might be "locked motionless" (244) and in their despair turn to anarchy and revolution. How much sounder was a life in a well-ordered, fifteenth-century organic society, whether founded on a Spanish or a Gypsy national base. But when what Eliot seemed to praise was what Silva had decried as a law "fit for beasts of prey" not reasonable men (238), Harrison could only agree with Silva, not with Zarca, Fedalma, and Eliot.

Comte had envisioned the coming of two great solvents, science and industry, capable if not of obliterating, at least of profoundly modifying the less wholesome heritage of the past (although he saw a useful and continuing role for the nation even after the cosmopolitan Positivist society of the future had established itself). For the even more cosmopolitan English Comtists, a Positivist society would no longer speak of Gypsy or Spaniard or Jew, but of "Man." Comte had projected as an immediate goal the union of the five great nations of Europe—France, Italy, Germany, Spain, and England—in a Positivist federation. After this had been accomplished, the Orient and the Occident would eventually be united by the religion of humanity. As Silva declared, "Union is deeper than division" (238), a sentiment, in line with the opinions of English advanced liberals and the London Positivists. But for conservatives, such a program represented a wild disregard of human nature and prejudices, of the subduing larger life of the nation and "the irreversible Past" (264).

In 1902 the historian and critic Leslie Stephen would agree with Harrison in seeing *The Spanish Gypsy* as a "reductio ad absurdum" of the Comtian idea of community. The Positivists had certainly insisted on "a view of duty as corresponding to the vital instincts of the social organism." They had called on the individual to identify himself with the social body of which he is both "the product, and the constituent," and they had demanded a "consequent readiness to sacrifice life and happiness to the interest of the community into which he is born." Stephen, perceptively, recognized that such a "doctrine was already preached, though in imperfect form," by Eliot's Savonarola to Romola. In Eliot's drama, Stephen noted, this idea had become more "prominent." "Now one might accept the principle as true and valuable," Stephen concluded, but "to throw overboard all other ties on the simple ground of descent, and adopt the most preposterous schemes of the vagabonds to whom you are related, seems to be very bad morality whatever may be its affinity to positivism."[15]

John Morley felt otherwise, although he had strong reservations. In a review article in 1868 he agreed with Congreve's description of the drama as a "mass of positivism." Silva had egotistically "sacrificed the larger interests of race and nature" to his own "self-devoting passion," and consequently had brought tragedy upon himself. Fedalma, like Romola, Morley noted—without distinguishing between Romola's initial submission to Savonarola and her later revolt—had responded to the "sense of supreme obligation" we all owed to "the mighty overspreading inheritance from the past of our race, nation, family, and birthplace." This was "a destiny ready made" for men even as they were in "swaddling clothes." Morley saw in the words of Eliot's "Jew astrologer" Sephardo "the most satisfactory modern solution" to the question of free will. Yet Morley doubted that Fedalma's blood had greater influence upon her than the influence exerted by her early Spanish associations. The latter ought to have had "first claim" upon the "allegiance of her duty." Fedalma's response to the "simple sight" of Zarca was as ethically doubtful as it is "ethologically unreal." While Morley agreed with Sephardo's condemnation of "the disguised selfishness of a cosmopolitan philosopher," what authority could a father she had never known exert on Fedalma? (This, of course, was the question Eliot had already set in *Silas Marner*—although Morley did not mention this.) There

was, moreover, enough of the cosmopolitan liberal in Morley for him
to admire Silva's reliance on the "swift alchemy" of "dextrous thought"
with its ability "to change all forms, dissolve all prejudice / Of man's
long heritage, and yield him up / A crude fused world to fashion as we
would."16

Yet was not Eliot's treatment of the subject understandable, even necessary, because of the setting of her drama? In what other form could a
storyteller present such questions persuasively in a tale of a prescientific,
preindustrial fifteenth-century Spain? Moreover, the critical issue for the
drama, one might argue, was the elevation of communal interests over
private ones, as well as Eliot's insistence on the superiority of generally
accepted law and custom over the sheer delusion of an *entirely* free choice.
Such themes might, properly phrased, have contented Comte himself. Any
other handling of the themes, one might add, would, like Silva's speeches
smacking of Victorian liberalism, appear anachronistic. But in both *Daniel
Deronda* and her late essays Eliot would stand fast not by the liberal views
of Silva, but by the creed of birth and blood she had placed in the mouths
of Zarca and Sephardo. She clearly intended that creed as much or more
for nineteenth-century England as for fifteenth-century Spain. Were Eliot's
early homilies on behalf of free will undermined by her later teachings
concerning the necessities of national inheritance—as preached by, among
others, the Jewish-born Benjamin Disraeli? As we will see, she would stress
the *moral* necessity of an individual to identify himself with his nation by an
act of will.

If Frederic Harrison had reacted to *The Spanish Gypsy* with uncertainty, his
reaction to *Daniel Deronda* was entirely contemptuous. The novel was
replete with "unpleasant characters who are neither beautiful nor interesting," he wrote after Eliot's death, "terrible situations which bore rather
than terrify us, and a plot which is at once preposterous and wearisome."
Why had Eliot undertaken so uncongenial a subject? Her "insight into
modern Hebraism," Harrison speculated, was a psychological problem,
only explicable on the theory that George Henry Lewes himself was an
"unconscious, unrecognized Gentile Jew in spirit."17 This is a curious
statement whose full meaning is difficult to comprehend.

Contemporaries described both Eliot and Lewes as looking Jewish.
Her foreign looks, like those of Maggie in *The Mill on the Floss,* might in
the rural Warwickshire of her youth, where Jews were not frequently
encountered, be thought Gypsy-like. In the more sophisticated London
circles Eliot later frequented, her acquaintances may well have regarded
certain of her physical features as signs of Jewish blood. A glance at Samuel
Lawrence's portraits of George Eliot made in 1860 reveals a woman with
no single feature—oval-shaped face, long nose, deep-set eyes, or thick
lips—grandly irregular, yet comprising a far from conventionally pretty
face, giving her what some might have thought a decidedly Jewish appearance. One contemporary, James Stuart, a fellow of Trinity College, Cam-

bridge, visited her and Lewes in 1877, a year after the publication of *Daniel Deronda,* and described her "rather stately features," adding that "I think she must have had a Jewish ancestry."[18]

Eliot may herself have imagined a Jewish strain in her background, and her novels, as we have seen, put a stress in romantic fashion on blood and the effect of inheritance upon temperament, character, and appearance. Eliot studied Hebrew, and read all she could on Jewish history and traditions; together with Lewes, she visited ghettos and synagogues on the Continent, where on at least one occasion she was taken to be Jewish. She certainly was prepared to see others as being of Jewish appearance: upon meeting Calvin Stowe, husband of Harriet Beecher Stowe and author of a study of the Talmud, Eliot observed that he looked like a rabbi—Mrs. Stowe herself often referred to her husband as "my rabbi."[19] The Puritan mind, both that of England and that of New England (of Eliot as well as of the Stowes), had a certain affinity for Judaism. Eliot felt she could count on Harriet Stowe to sympathize with her disappointment that the lack of friendly feelings for Jews had spoiled the public reception of *Daniel Deronda.*[20]

Many of Eliot's views on Jews may have reminded readers of Benjamin Disraeli's early novels. In *Coningsby* Disraeli presented his own racial theories in the opinions offered by the Jewish financier Sidonia, who was modeled on Rothschild. For Sidonia, race, purity of race, was all. To be a Caucasian was sufficient cause for pride, but to be a Caucasian of "unmixed blood," as were the Hebrews, was to belong to "the aristocracy of Nature" (IV, 10). Sidonia listed, inaccurately, all the Jews who dominated European intellectual life ("who almost monopolise the professorial chairs of Germany") and, "behind the scenes," political life as well. The banker was prepared to grant, however, that Coningsby's English race was "sufficiently pure" (IV, 15). While Eliot shared the racial thinking of her time, as has been noted, she was hardly prepared to adopt such quasi-conspiratorial images or such views on racial purity.

Disraeli's *Tancred* continued these lines of speculation in a romance not unlike Scott's crusader novels, and in certain respects it constituted still another variation on *Ivanhoe.* Having been disillusioned by two English ladies with whom he had been infatuated—one turns out to be a liberal bluestocking and the other is more concerned with financial speculation than with high ideals—a devoutly Christian Tancred voyages to the East where he feels he may find the answers to the religious questions troubling him. Disraeli described Tancred's dilemma in terms that bring to mind Saint-Simon's and Comte's description of the critical era that followed the downfall of the organic state of the Middle Ages: all is uncertain, everything is in transition. Tancred believes the solution to his own spiritual confusion may be found in the Holy Land, the source of faith; Saint-Simonians had similarly undertaken a journey to the East, from which they hoped the female Messiah, a Jewess, could be brought back, to serve as the consort of the sect's *Père Suprême.* In the East Tancred finds the Jewish Eva, daughter of Besso, Sidonia's Syrian agent. She, like Sidonia an advocate of racial purity, is a believer and can sympathize with Tancred's spiritual mission, unlike Tancred's more material-minded, rationalist, and avaricious earlier loves. After a series of romantic adventures, in the course of which Eva saves Tancred's life by means of her knowledge of herbal medicine (as Rebecca had saved Ivanhoe), an adoring Tancred proposes to Eva, who also loves him. Will this Ivanhoe at last marry Rebecca, fulfilling the hopes of so many of the readers of Scott's novel? Conscious of their different races and religions, Eva urges Tancred to depart, but Tancred is determined, and Eva appears to be yielding. A shout interrupts their interview to announce the arrival of Tancred's parents, the duke and duchess of Bellamont, who Tancred knows have other marital plans for him. The novel ends with the reader uncertain whether love or filial obedience will triumph.

George Eliot's youthful opinions of Disraeli's early novels had been somewhat mixed, indeed largely negative. In a letter to Mrs. Bray in 1845 she had mocked "Mr. D'Israeli's style"; though granting that "the man hath good veins, as Bacon would say," she added that "there is not enough blood in them."[21] These remarks were written after she had read *Coningsby* and had just received *Sybil,* the second novel of Disraeli's political trilogy. But it was *Tancred,* the third novel, that provoked her full scorn. She wrote a friend in May 1847 of Disraeli's effort "to bamboozle the unfortunates who are seduced into reading his *Tancred.*"[22] In another letter written the following February, she contrasted *Tancred* unfavorably with its two predecessors, but although critical of certain of the views of Disraeli's Young England (a group of Tories who called for a revival of paternalistic and feudal traditions), she observed that Disraeli was "unquestionably an able man," and noted that she always enjoyed "his tirades against liberal principles as opposed to *popular* principles." (The italicized adjective may be seen as a foreshadowing of her essay on Riehl's populist views.) But Eliot rejected Disraeli's "theory of 'races,'" unveiled in *Coningsby* and expanded upon in *Tancred*: "It has not a leg to stand on," she declared.[23]

Eliot very strongly objected to Disraeli's insistence in *Tancred* that Europe owed her commerce, arts, and religion to the Jews. "My gentile nature kicks most resolutely against any assumption of superiority in the Jews"—indeed, she was almost ready to "echo Voltaire's vituperation"— she wrote John Sibree in early 1848. Moses was "impregnated with Egyptian philosophy," and Jesus' worth came with his transcendence of Judaism. "Everything *specifically* Jewish is of a low grade," she pronounced. Just as the European aristocracy had degenerated from too much inbreeding, so might entire races decline. "I confess," she wrote, that "the types of 'pure races,' however handsome, always impress me disagreeably." History had demonstrated that "some great revolutionary force" had generally been "called into action by which the genius of a particular nation becomes a portion of the common mind of humanity." This last sentiment was congruent with the liberal cosmopolitanism of her time—that of the Positivists, and, later, of Eliot's Silva.

Eliot then suggested that nations might be usefully kept separate "until they have sufficiently developed their idiosyncrasies"; after that they might be fused "both for physical and moral ends." The "fellowship of race," to which Disraeli attributed the "munificence of Sidonia" and the special favorable qualities of the Baronis, a Jewish theatrical family, was obviously "an inferior impulse which must ultimately be superseded"; Eliot wondered why even Disraeli, "Jew as he is, dares to boast of it."[24] While all other races were, by natural processes, "destined to extermination or fusion," she continued, the negroes were "too important physiologically and geographically" to undergo extermination—yet "the repulsion" between blacks and other races was "too strong for fusion." Jews, on the other hand, would be capable of fusing with other races.[25] In 1853, when she may have been emerging from the advanced liberalism of her *Westminster Review* period, she observed with pleasure that the Society for the Conversion of the Jews had spent £4,400 and had managed to convert but one Jew.[26] The fusion she may have envisioned here was one in which both Gentiles and Jews shared not Christianity but the religion of humanity.

By the time she wrote *Daniel Deronda* she appears not to have approved of racial fusion, and seems to have embraced the greater part of Disraeli's position. Disraeli, in *Tancred,* had rebuked the self-hatred of the semiassimilated Laurella sisters, who were persuaded that if only Jews were "well-dressed and well-mannered," the "progressive spirit of the age" would secure their acceptance. He contrasted this view with that of Tancred's beloved Eva who, proud of her race and religion, proclaimed the "splendour and superiority" of the Jews, and yearned for "the restoration of their national glory" (chap. 46). In *Daniel Deronda,* as we shall see, the narrator views, sympathetically but not approvingly, the "cosmopolitan ideas" of the Jewish musician Klesmer, who looked "forward to a fusion of the races" (chap. 22). Such an assimilationist posture would not be that of Eliot's Daniel or Mordecai. And Eliot, in what she would write about the Jews in the essays of her later years, would likewise agree with Disraeli's Eva who marveled that such a despised race could persist through the centuries "in celebrating their vintage, although they have no fruits together." Such a race would "regain their vineyards." The children of the race, Disraeli concluded, particularly of the lower classes, "born to hereditary insult, without any education . . . occupied with the meanest, if not the vilest toil, . . . an object to you of prejudice, dislike, disgust, perhaps hatred," could yet celebrate the season of the vine harvest in a fashion poets would not scorn (*Tancred,* chap. 47).

By the time Eliot wrote *The Spanish Gypsy,* her own reading, confirmed by her friend Emanuel Deutsch, had given Jews a very special position in her thinking. Deutsch, a Jew born in Silesia, served as an assistant in the Oriental department of the British Museum, and by the 1860s had become a good friend of both Eliot and Lewes. He gave Eliot lessons in Hebrew and she often referred to him as an authority on Jewish questions, address-ing him as "my dear Rabbi."[27] In October 1867 Deutsch's *Quarterly Re-view* article on the Talmud—which Eliot, who read the proofs, described in a letter to another friend as that "glorious article"[28]—aroused so much interest that this issue of the *Quarterly Review* went into six editions, an unprecedented event.[29] Christians generally regarded Jesus' preachings as very different from those of the conventional Judaism of his day. The major theme of Deutsch's article was that Jesus' moral message was in fact identical to that of the best known of the Pharisaic teachers. Deutsch's argument would have been no surprise to Eliot, who as early as 1851 had remarked that Jesus had "contributed no new element to ethics." And Eliot was convinced that Judaism was far from the loveless, legalistic religion depicted by the Gospels.[30] (Feuerbach, subscribing to the conventional view, had thought otherwise.[31])

For Eliot, I suggest, Jews came to represent conscience, moral judges who might on occasion be unpleasantly censorious: if the Gypsy and the Christian were the id, the Jew was the superego. This is how Silva sees Sephardo in *The Spanish Gypsy:*

> Ah, you denounce my sport with hawk and hound.
> I would not have the Angel Gabriel
> As hard as you in noting down my sins.

(160)

The opening scene of *Daniel Deronda* pictures Daniel, raised as an English gentleman ignorant of his Jewish origins, exercising the same moral author-ity as Sephardo had. Gwendolen Harleth, a beautiful, blonde Englishwo-man, gambling at a German spa, sees Daniel, whom she has yet to meet, "measuring her and looking down on her as an inferior," silently condemn-ing her play at roulette (chap. 1). She resents his attitude, but as the novel progresses Gwendolen increasingly feels the need to "consult Deronda that she might secure herself against any act he would disapprove": she now possesses an "outer conscience which was made for her by Deronda" (chap. 64). His manner alone, it must be presumed, endows him with this func-tion, since Daniel is not described as recognizably Jewish (to the non-Jews around him, at least). Gwendolen seeks opportunities to consult him, submits her actions and motives to his judgment, and hungers for approval.

Daniel Deronda is eventually revealed to be the son of a celebrated Jewish actress who, because of her distaste for her own people, has asked her friend Sir Hugo Mallinger to raise her son. Daniel knows nothing of this arrangement, and suspects he is Mallinger's illegitimate child. Deronda has gone to an English public school and to Cambridge, but despite his ac-cepted identity as an English gentleman feels himself to be different. The usual pastimes and aspirations of his fellows do not satisfy him; life seems dull and without meaning, though he senses that a revelation about himself might somehow alter his situation. It is at this point that the young Jewish singer Mirah enters his life. Mirah's father had taken her from England and exploited her talents on the continental stage. She has now fled from him, returning to England to find her mother and brother. Unsuccessful in her search, and without friends or resources, she attempts suicide, and is saved from drowning by Daniel and installed by him in the home of friends. Mirah, one of Eliot's faultless heroines, seeks comfort and fulfillment in her Judaism, of which she has only dim childhood memories. Daniel, much taken with Mirah, establishes her as a singing teacher and begins a search for her family.

Chance leads him to Mordecai, a mystic and scholar, later discovered to be Mirah's brother, who at their first meeting sees in Daniel the man destined to restore the Jews to a Palestinian homeland. He is disappointed to learn that Daniel is not Jewish and is therefore unfit for the mission. Because of Mirah, whom he loves, and Mordecai, whom he admires, Deronda begins a study of the Hebrew language and Judaism under Mordecai's instruction. His love for Mirah, who will only marry a Jew, and his growing involvement with Mordecai, makes Daniel wish himself Jewish, and he is delighted when he later discovers his long-estranged mother and finds that he is a Jew. Deronda now understands why he has previously been uneasy; he has a new purpose in life, may marry the girl he loves, and can take up his messianic destiny.

This is, of course, a variation on the myth of the disinherited one presented in *The Spanish Gypsy*. Fedalma, kidnapped from her father and people, regains her national inheritance and leads her people to an African homeland; Daniel Deronda, deprived of his Jewish heritage by his mother, is happily restored to it and takes up a similar mission. "Breed" has in all ways happily triumphed over "pasture," feelings over calculation. In de-classing himself, in rejecting his status as an English gentleman in favor of the status of a despised Jew, Daniel like Fedalma may become the savior of his people, the long-awaited king of Israel. A disinherited Deronda is restored to his heritage.

Scott's *Ivanhoe*—like *Daniel Deronda* and *The Spanish Gypsy*—was, readers will recall, a story of a disinherited one. When Ivanhoe returns from the wars in the Holy Land, he enters the tournament lists without revealing his identity: "[T]he device on his shield," is "a young oak-tree pulled up by the roots, with the Spanish word *Desdichado,* signifying Disin-herited" (chap. 8). He is known afterward as "the Disinherited Knight." Ivanhoe is a Saxon, a member of a despised subject race known by its Norman masters for laziness and gluttony. His father, Cedric, has plans for the redemption of the Saxons from thralldom and the restoration of their independence, plans that depend upon the marriage of the beautiful Row-ena and the oafish Athelstane, both descendants of ancient Saxon kings; for this reason, Cedric discourages the love that Ivanhoe and Rowena feel for each other. Ivanhoe, discontented with the Saxon separatism of his father, serves King Richard in the Crusades as a way of uniting Saxon and Nor-man into one people. Cedric condemns his son for following the alien ways of the Norman court and disinherits him. All ends happily enough, for Cedric relents, after the intervention of King Richard, and restores his son to his patrimony, both of property and of the heritage of a despised race. But an Anglo-Norman melting pot, not Saxon independence, is Scott's solution, not unlike Eliot's youthful hopes for racial "fusion." Still, fusion has its limits: anticipating Fedalma's quest of Africa and Daniel's of Palestine, Scott sends the beautiful Jewess Rebecca and her father off to Moorish Spain, where they can live more peacefully than in a Christian country.

Can we regard the plot of *Daniel Deronda* as that of a somewhat inverted *Ivanhoe*? After a quest common to romantic novels, the disinherited Daniel, like Ivanhoe, reclaims his family and national inheritance. In so doing, Daniel wins the dark, Jewish Mirah, while rejecting the blonde and beautiful "Saxon" Gwendolen, reversing Ivanhoe's choice of the fair Rowena over a brown-haired Rebecca (and thus fulfilling Maggie's fantasy in *The Mill on the Floss* that the dark-haired girl would, in contrast to the conventional novel plot, triumph over the light-haired one). Instead of returning from the Holy Land to England to achieve a Saxon share in the realm, as does the crusader Ivanhoe, Daniel leaves England for Palestine to establish a Jewish homeland. Mirah will not consider marriage with Daniel until he discovers that he is Jewish, just as Rebecca similarly had rejected her Knight Templar admirer because he is a Christian. (Rebecca's situation and sentiments are those of *The Spanish Gypsy*: "[N]or hold I so light of country or religious faith," she declared, "as to esteem him who is willing to barter these ties" in order "to gratify an unruly passion for the daughter of another people" (*Ivanhoe*, chap. 39). Mirah (like Fedalma) follows Rebecca in wishing to redeem her people, and is compelled, like Rebecca, to listen "to the fictions and surmises which seem to convert the tyrant into the victim" (*Ivanhoe*, chap. 37).

The myth and political programs of Fedalma and Daniel, one might suggest, mirror those of the disinherited Moses, and a disinherited Jesus. Moses, also deprived of his family and national inheritance, had been raised an Egyptian prince. Made aware that he was a Hebrew, he relinquished his superior for an inferior status, and determined to lead his enslaved people to freedom and their own land. Jesus, like Moses, in what Northrup Frye might call a displacement of the original story, is also disinherited. Of uncertain paternity and awaiting an obscure mission, until the coming of John the Baptist clarifies his purpose, Jesus, disinherited so that he might redeem men from their sins, asked, in his dying words, why his father had abandoned him. Deronda, abandoned by his mother, has his mission revealed to him by Mordecai. That mission is a terrestrial one, like that of Moses, as well as one of redemption—a national not an individual redemption.

In Eliot's novel this redemption has a sexual component. Eliot rejected the idea that sex was sinful, following her favorite philosopher, Feuerbach. In Daniel and Mirah, passion is permitted to unite with virtue even as Eliot displayed in Gwendolen an unhappy woman who, successful in securing a rich husband she does not love, lacked both virtue and passion. Gwendolen may have been intended as a respectable, nineteenth-century Magdalen who has sold herself into an unhappy marriage and sees Daniel as a possible savior. Such a view gains strength, perhaps, when we recall her family name, Harleth, so similar to "harlot."[32]

From his earliest years, we are told, Deronda had hoped to be a political leader, like Pericles or George Washington. A political career for Daniel would have pleased Sir Hugo Mallinger, a liberal Whig, who declares, "We want a little disinterested culture to make head against cotton and capital, especially in the House." But in the pursuit of such an ambition, Daniel is limited by his modesty, and by "a subdued fervour of sympathy, an activity of imagination on behalf of others . . . that struck his companions as moral eccentricity." To an English gentleman's description of the Jamaican Negro as "a beastly sort of baptist Caliban"—in 1865, as noted earlier, there had been an insurrection of Jamaican blacks that had been brutally repressed—Deronda speaks up for Caliban (chap. 29). "Unlike the great Clive," Deronda "would rather be the calf than the butcher." Though he feels himself injured because of what he at first believes to be his illegitimate birth, his "sense of injury" has bred "not the will to inflict injuries and climb over them as a ladder, but—a hatred of all injury" (chap. 16). Eliot presented Daniel as a liberal—akin, perhaps, to Will Ladislaw—not a fanatic.

But is there not at least the appearance of fanaticism in Mordecai, a fanaticism that affects first his sister and then Deronda? Mordecai's monomania, if it may be called such, is both religious and national, as that of Zarca was racial, yet Eliot, no more the friend of fanaticism than her admired Scott, appeared to approve of it. In a letter to her publisher Blackwood before *Daniel Deronda* was completed, Eliot spoke of her effort to portray Mordecai in "an outline as strong as that of Balfour of Burley," the rabid Covenanter in Scott's *Old Mortality*. Yet she wished to present her proto-Zionist not as an embodiment of fanatical intolerance, as was Scott's Balfour, but as "a much more complex character and a higher strain of ideas." (Nor would she depict Mordecai as Disraeli had Sidonia, she wrote Blackwood; the reading public might well prefer Disraeli's Jews, she observed, but "I was not born to paint Sidonia."[33])

But what was it that made the Covenanter Balfour the emblem, for Eliot as for Scott, of a despised bigotry, while Daniel, Mordecai, and Fedalma were heroic? The narrator of *Daniel Deronda* asks whether Mordecai had not fixed on Daniel his "despair of his own life," and his "irrepressible hope in the propagation of his fanatical beliefs." This desire to pass on an obsession had certainly characterized Balfour's fixation upon Harry Morton as his successor in the Covenanters' struggle. Eliot has Daniel speculate on the various kinds of fanaticism, from the person who believes he has "the mathematical key of the universe" to such "monomaniacs" as "a social reformer with coloured views of the new moral world in [Owenite] parallelograms" (chap. 41)—this last like Stephen Morley in Disraeli's *Sybil*. After greater acquaintance with Mordecai's views, Daniel concludes that a man is fanatical only when "his enthusiasm is narrow and hoodwinked, so that he has no sense of proportions, and becomes unjust and unsympathetic to men who are out of his own track." Using this measuring rod, Daniel decides that Mordecai is no fanatic. Daniel specifically dismisses a comparison made between the Jewish messianist and the Covenanters. "Mordecai is an enthusiast," he declared; "I should like to keep that word for the highest order of minds—those who care supremely for grand and general benefits to mankind" (chap. 46).

Questions of nationality come up at the meeting of "The Philosophers" club held at the Hand and Banner public house which Mordecai attends, and which he describes as "poor men given to thought." When Mordecai brings Daniel to the club, its members—four Jews, a Scotsman, an Irishman, and three Englishmen—are discussing the law of progress in terms made familiar by H. T. Buckle's then well-known *History of Civilization*, published in 1857 and highly regarded by liberals. Pash, a Jewish watchmaker, scoffs at the reactionary idea of nationality that he finds gaining influence. This amuses Deronda, who finds "a piquant incongruity between Pash's sarcasm and the strong stamp of race on his features." Pash believes the feeling of nationality to be dying an inevitable death, but Deronda is convinced that the sentiment might again "revive into strong life." "Nations have revived," he declares, adding, very much like Disraeli's Sidonia in *Tancred*, that there may soon be "a great outburst" of national feeling among Arabs, to which a delighted Mordecai says "Amen." (For Disraeli, and it would appear for Eliot as well, the term "Arab" included the Jew.) Pash grants that national feeling may be true of "backward nations," or those marked by oppression, but in Europe "the sentiment of nationality is destined to die out," for "the whole current of progress is setting against it" (chap. 42). In response to the English copying-clerk Lilly, who merges the idea of progress with that of the laws of development, as Buckle had in his *History,* Daniel denies the equation that change necessarily means progress; further, he rejects the idea of fatality that haunted Buckle's volumes in favor of a role for free will:

> There will still remain the degrees of inevitableness in relation to our own will and acts, and the degrees of wisdom in hastening or retarding; there will still remain the danger of mistaking a tendency which should be resisted for an inevitable law that we must adjust ourselves to,—which seems to me as bad a superstition or false god as any that has been set up without the ceremonies of philosophising.

Political leaders like Pericles and Washington, in other words, had an independent role to play and were not mere puppets of necessity, economic or otherwise. A so-called progressive cosmopolitanism need not inevitably triumph, nor is the sense of nationality inescapably doomed: all that is needed is for men to have the will to revive it. Mordecai agrees, and pronounces, "Woe to the men who see no place for resistance in this generation!" (chap. 42).

Mordecai despairs that so many of his race have mixed with Gentiles, regretted their Jewish inheritance, and mocked at Jewish separateness. Such people had a sorry lot. Held in contempt as Jews, and "alien in spirit" if not "in form," to Gentiles, they can not fully share "hearty kindred and fellowship" with the latter. The Jewish optical-instrument maker Gideon (modeled on the lens-grinder Spinoza, whom we know Eliot admired, and maintaining Spinoza's assimilationist views) sees himself as "a rational Jew" who believes that the granting of political equality is a sufficient justification for "getting rid of all our superstitions and exclusiveness." He calls for a gradual melting into the general population as "the order of the day in point of progress." Mordecai protests that he too is a rational Jew, but he sees the past as his parent, and points to the strength of "the hidden bonds" of kinship. He argues that it is not rational for a Jew to give up "the monuments of his law" which bear "the breath of social justice, of charity, and of household sanctities," and to forget "the fortitude of martyred generations, as mere stuff for a professorship." But Mordecai's audience, enchanted by the dicta of a liberal progress, cannot grasp his meaning (chap. 42).

Israel was "the heart of mankind," Mordecai continues, "if we mean by heart the core of affection which binds a race and its families in dutiful love." (He notes also, in the spirit of Feuerbach, "the reverence [of Judaism] for the human body which lifts the needs of our animal life into religion.") Israel was a nation that fused "religion and law and moral life," and managed to preserve the national spirit under the most harsh persecution. But only with the reestablishment of a national state might the Jewish sense of community be fully realized, Mordecai insists. There was enough learning, and talent, and wealth "to redeem the soil" of Israel and to found a "republic where there is equality of protection"; this Jewish republic could then plant "the brightness of Western freedom amid the despotisms of the East." The "outraged Jew" would then have "the dignity of a national life" and "a defence in the court of nations." Daniel, in support of Mordecai, reminds the club of how impossible Mazzini's hopes for Italian national unity had appeared before they proved victorious. All that is needed is "the leaven," "the seed of fire," Mordecai proclaims, adding that even the assimilationist Baruch Spinoza, who "had not a faithful Jewish heart, though he had sucked the life of his intellect at the breasts of Jewish tradition," had seen the possibility that Israel might "again be a chosen nation," for "ours is an inheritance" that continues to live in millions of hearts. For Mordecai, "the strongest principle of growth" is "human choice," and Jews must *will* the Messianic time into being. The "blasphemy of this time" is that men see themselves under the sway of deterministic forces and doomed to passivity. Mordecai finally adds, perhaps contrasting the Jewish pharisaic belief in free will with a Pauline predestination, that "the divine principle of our race is action, choice, resolved memory" (chap. 42).

There is clearly much of Eliot herself in Mordecai's sermon, and in Mordecai's insistence that the sense of nationality should be identified with choice, with free will. By use of free will, Mordecai seems to say, one must choose the morally necessary path of identifying oneself with the national spirit. Hegel had seen such an identification with the *Volksgeist* as ordained by a historical necessity with which an individual would be wise to make his peace. Only in this way, Hegel argued, could we fully realize ourselves, and secure true liberty. Mordecai apparently agreed that a man of virtue who sought self-realization must freely choose to take on himself the obligations of his family's and nation's inherited past.

When Daniel discovers that he is Jewish, he experiences the pleasure of being able to join his love for Mirah to "my duty—it is the impulse of my feeling—to identify myself, as far as possible, with my hereditary people" (chap. 53). All his life Daniel has "longed for some ideal task, in which I might feel myself the heart and brain of a multitude—some social captainship, which would come to me as a duty, and not be striven for as a personal prize" (chap. 63). Now he has found his mission. "The idea that I am possessed with is that of restoring a political existence to my people, making them a nation again," he announces, or at least to "awaken a movement in other minds, such as has been awakened in my own." And like Disraeli who had traveled to the East in his youth, Daniel goes "to the East to become better acquainted with the condition of my race," as he tells a despondent Gwendolen, whom he rejects in favor of Mirah, and who cannot grasp his purpose and his hopes (chap. 69).

In the 1860s and 1870s Disraeli was the most articulate political spokesman for the need to preserve the British national inheritance from both a divisive and alienating individualism and a cosmopolitanism that denied the bonds of a shared past. At this time he was speaking as an Englishman and an Anglican—having been converted at age twelve when his father joined the Church of England—and not, as in the novels of his early years, as the Jewish Sidonia. In the 1860s Disraeli defended the national church against those who wished to disestablish it, and sought to reclaim for it the Coleridgian goals he had preached in *Coningsby* and *Sybil*.[34] In April 1872, in an address delivered in Manchester, he defended the historic institutions of his country, notably the monarchy, then under attack by such radical Liberals as Sir Charles Dilke, and praised "the wisdom of your forefathers."[35] In his well-known speech at the Crystal Palace two months later, his contrast between the Tory dedication to national principle and the Liberal party's inclination to cosmopolitanism anticipated Mordecai's argument to the public-house philosophers.

In this Crystal Palace speech Disraeli charged the Liberals with having succumbed to the influence of continental philosophy when they made "war on the manners and customs of the people of this country under the pretext of Progress." He claimed to be speaking on behalf of ordinary Englishmen, and particularly on behalf of the working classes who were proudly patriotic. England would have to choose between continental, cosmopolitan principles and its own national inheritance. Because the Liberal party had failed to follow national principles, the country now looked on that party "with mistrust and repugnance." The Tory leader was convinced that Englishmen would choose the national principle that would maintain Britain as "a land of liberty, of prosperity, of power, and of glory."[36] And indeed, two years later, in 1874—after a campaign that stressed the antinational tendencies of Gladstone's Liberal government— the Tories were swept into office.

Eliot's correspondence and her later essays (confirming the message of *Daniel Deronda*) justify the conclusion that in contrasting Gladstone's liberal cosmopolitanism with Disraeli's nationalism, she preferred the views of Disraeli. She had long been a patriot, though also an opponent of Britain's imperial adventures. When in Geneva, as early as 1849, she heard a preacher place patriotism ("dévouement à la patrie") above even devotion to the church, she approved. "We never heard of it in England after we leave school," she observed at that time,[37] and she complained about this failure into her last years. In 1879 she scoffed at the modish "affectation of undervaluing everything native, and being too fine for one's own country." But she also insisted that Englishmen should see "a corresponding attachment to nationality as legitimate" in all peoples and "its absence" as "a privation of the greatest good." While England had no right to impose its political rule or culture on other nations, it ought to resist the liberal view that decried national feeling as an outgrown barbarism.[38]

Writing of a crisis within Gladstone's government in 1873, Eliot told the Tory Blackwood of her wish that "there were some, solid philosophical Conservative to take the reins—one who knows the true function of stability in human affairs."[39] After the election of 1874 put Disraeli in power, she informed a friend that she did not at all "mind the Conservative majority."[40] Later that month she wrote Blackwood that she was "rather tickled" that this first election by secret vote had gone against the Liberal believers in "Salvation by Ballot."[41] "You remember me as much less a conservative than I have now become," she wrote another correspondent. "I care as much for the interests of the people," she added, "but I believe less in the help they will get from the democrats."[42]

Perhaps even the assertions of Jewish pride in *Coningsby* and *Tancred*, which Eliot thought so objectionable in the 1840s, were bathed in a more tolerable light after she and Emanuel Deutsch became friends. A number of commentators have identified Mordecai and his views with Deutsch. Mordecai's opinions were the same as those the left-Hegelian Moses Hess put forward in his *Rome and Jerusalem* (1862). In the 1840s the Jewish Hess was a socialist journalist and assimilationist, of the type denounced by Riehl. The writings of the anti-Semitic German *völkisch* writers wounded Hess and prompted a reconsideration of his position. From a Spinozoist assimilationism, Hess turned to a kind of Jewish nationalism.[43] Deutsch may have made a similar intellectual journey. (We know that Lewes met Hess during a continental trip.[44])

The Jews, for Eliot, as for Disraeli, were a model, not of a rootless cosmopolitanism—the role assigned to them by conservatives on the Continent—but of a sound regard for the preservation of their inherited national tradition. All this had been said in *The Spanish Gypsy,* in the pronouncements of Sephardo, but in this drama Jews remained at the periphery. With a popular Jewish-born prime minister in the 1870s, Eliot may have concluded, prematurely as things turned out, that the reading public was better prepared to accept the Jewish dimension of *Daniel Deronda.*

The novel simply compounded the surprise and at times irritation that had greeted *The Spanish Gypsy.* In 1880, after Eliot's death, Frederic Harrison derided her decision to make race rather than humanity her highest goal.[45] Others noted the similarity of theme in the two works with more polite distaste. An 1876 article in the *Saturday Review* saw in both books the message that "fidelity to race stands with the author as the first of duties and of virtues," linking as it did "past and future." Nor did it matter, the reviewer added in a clear reference to the pariah status of Gypsies and Jews, "what the character of the race is."[46] In the same year the critic George Saintsbury, apparently forgetful of *Ivanhoe* and its imitators, doubted whether "the mystical enthusiasm for race and nation" had "sufficient connexion with broad human feeling to be stuff for prose fiction to handle." This subject, "the excellence of obeying the instigations of kinship and duty," Saintsbury noted, was "a fresh variation on the theme which has informed so much of George Eliot's work."[47]

After the publication of *Daniel Deronda* revealed the continuing distaste for Jewish subjects even in a liberal England, Eliot wrote an essay attacking what she saw as the persistence, in altered guise, of medieval anti-Semitism. In this 1879 piece titled "The Modern Hep! Hep! Hep!," the call that accompanied anti-Jewish rioting during the Crusades, Eliot defended the Jew on two grounds: first, for his devotion to his national history and to his sense of distinctiveness, which she saw as a model for the English, who were in danger of losing national memories necessary to a "sense of corporate existence";[48] and, second, for the Jew *qua* Jew, for his preservation of good qualities despite the persecution that might have left him bereft of them, as well as for the special role Judaism had played in the development of Christian civilization.

In this essay, Eliot examined "the preservation of national memories" (among Jews and other peoples) as "an element and a means of national greatness." It was because Mazzini's imagination had retained the memory of Italy's glorious past as a corporate entity that Italy had again become a nation, she wrote, along the lines of Daniel's and Mordecai's views. It was a patriotic sense of national community that elevated man above the level of

brute, and made us the superiors of "emigrating rats and free-loving ba-
boons." Only a people capable of remembering its past as a "bond of
obligation" could strive not merely for "material possession," but for "spiritual ends"—"the satisfaction of a great feeling that animates the collective
body as with one soul." A people capable of worthy deeds must respond
with "an answering thrill" when reminded of its heroes whose sacrifices
had helped to maintain "its national existence," and whose "past labours
and struggles" had achieved the "freedom and well-being," which, "thus
inherited," might by their efforts be "transmitted unimpaired to children
and children's children."[49]

It was this "national consciousness" that enabled nations to maintain
free institutions and to resist foreign conquest, she declared. Not merely
"the nobleness of a nation," but "the nobleness of each individual citizen"
depended on this national consciousness. For a genuine sense of "dignity
and rectitude," we must feel a tie with an entity "worthy of sacrifice, a
continual inspiration to self-repression and discipline by the presentation
of aims larger and more attractive to our generous part than the securing of
personal ease or prosperity." "The time is not come," she admonished her
readers, "for cosmopolitanism to be highly virtuous, any more than for
communism to suffice for social energy."[50]

And in these matters the Jew was a worthy example, Eliot continued.
From the study of the Bible, Jews educated themselves to "a sense of
separateness unique in its intensity," and "to identify faithfulness to its
national traditions with the highest social and religious blessings." In the
fights of the Maccabees against the Hellenists and the Zealots against
Rome, the national party among the Jews fought against a "demoralising
fusion," an assimilationism advocated by admirers of the foreign powers.
The Maccabees and the Zealots had understood that it was necessary to
tighten "the bands of conservatism" to preserve "the sacred ark." For her
part, she declared, "I share the spirit of the Zealots."[51]

Yet the English, like other Europeans, blamed the Jews for vices that
were inescapable accompaniments of the persecution they had suffered
during the long effort to compel them to renounce their "hereditary ties."
But what Christians should do instead was marvel at their virtues "under
the shadow of oppression,"[52] notably their "predominant kindliness" and
their "pity for the fatherless and the widow."[53] The Jewish sense of national separateness kept them from the cynical "cosmopolitan indifference"
which might have been the result of missing the "inward identification"
with the nationality among whom they lived in their "inherited privation."
More than any other race, the Jews suffered from the lack of the "sense of
special belonging which is the root of human virtues, both public and
private," and consequently experienced "some corresponding moral degradation." Yet, Eliot wrote, rejecting the conventional view, they had "escaped with less of abjectness and . . . hard hostility towards the nations
whose hand had been against them" than would have been the condition of

a people without "their adhesion to a separate religion founded on historic memories" and "their characteristic family affectionateness."[54]

Eliot observed that while liberals were free of the old form of anti-Semitism, with its religious basis for holding Jews guilty for the Crucifixion, nonetheless these rationalists and "philosophic thinkers," men who had won for Jews, Dissenters, and Catholics full citizenship, continued to condemn the Jews. These "anti-Judaic advocates" were disappointed that the granting of political equality to Jews had not led to their complete assimilation. They regretted that the new opportunities opened to Jews permitted too many of them to become successful in commercial and political life. These "liberal gentlemen" now shared the sentiments of those who earlier had opposed the full emancipation of the Jews, and complained of a spirit of Jewish "universal alienism (euphemistically called cosmopolitanism)."[55]

These liberals had reverted on this matter "to medieval types of thinking." They now insisted that "the Jews are made viciously cosmopolitan by holding the world's money-bag, that for them all national interests are resolved into the algebra of loans, that they have suffered an inward degradation stamping them as morally inferior, and 'serve them right,' since they rejected Christianity."[56] But did these "liberal pleaders" intend to repeal the emancipatory laws?[57] Eliot suggested that many liberal Englishmen had come to an unfavorable view of Jews because they disapproved of Disraeli, whom they dismissed as being without scruples—as if, she added, the Tory prime minister was less scrupulous than Walpole or Chatham had been.[58]

Not only the submerged peoples of Europe, like the Italians and Poles, but also the Jews deserved a national future. Yet the same men who valued evidences of "civilization" among Australian aborigines, dismissed the Jewish religion as a semibarbarous "Moloch-worship" that had better disappear. They were apparently entirely unaware of the "organised memory of a national consciousness" among the world's seven million Jews which looked toward the restoration of a Jewish state in Palestine. Why were Englishmen "so eager for the dignity" of unknown and primitive peoples while they sneered at "a renovated national dignity" for the Jews who gave them their religion?[59]

Jews ought certainly to continue to cherish their "store of inheritance." They must remain conscious of the "immortal achievements and immortal sorrows" of their ancestors who had "transmitted to them a physical and mental type" sufficiently "strong" and "eminent" to form "a new beneficent individuality" among nations and, rising above ancient scorn, to "nobly avenge the wrongs done to their Fathers." There was "a sense in which the worthy child of a nation that has brought forth illustrious prophets, high and unique among the poets of the world, is bound by their visions." The "effective bond of human action is feeling," and a "worthy" Jew must feel a "kinship" with "the glories and the sorrows" of his people. To do otherwise would be to share in the "blinding superstition" that "a theory of human well being" can disregard "the influences which have made us human."[60]

While these last words were addressed to Jews and the Jewish condition, Eliot clearly intended a more general statement, and aimed her words especially at liberal Englishmen who regarded a sense of nationality as a tribal atavism. She turned for support to Mill's *On Liberty,* which had argued that the world would be enriched by "the freedom of individual men to persist in idiosyncrasies." Why should not "the idiosyncrasy of a nation," Eliot asked, contribute to an enriching diversity?[61] Mill, in his essay on Coleridge, had also observed that a sense of nationality encapsulated much that was valuable, despite the contrary assertions of English liberals, and was not doomed to disappear in the near future. Writing in similar terms, Eliot asserted that the "spirit of separateness" which "created the varying genius of nations," and which "like the Muses, was the offspring of memory," had not yet completed "its work in the education of mankind."[62]

Englishmen ought to retain as long as possible "those national traditions and customs which are the language of national genius," Eliot argued. It was calamitous to a "great historic people" like the English to "undergo a premature fusion with immigrants of alien blood," thus endangering the survival of its "distinctive national characteristics." Its language and its speech would necessarily be corrupted by such fusion, and its political and social culture would be misunderstood. European nations must guard against "a too rapid effacement of those national traditions and customs which are the language of the national genius." It was "in this sense that the modern insistence on the idea of Nationality" was particularly valuable.[63] The cosmopolitan solidarity of humanity preached by advanced liberals and Positivists was no doubt a desirable, and more rational, final goal, but ties more immediately realizable, and more warming, were to be found in national sentiment. And for Eliot feeling was better than thought. This was the culmination of Eliot's politics of national inheritance.

Epilogue

John Morley noted in his *Recollections* that a number of critics had thought George Eliot "the most considerable literary personality since the death of Goethe." Morley himself, though admiring Eliot, was not ready to go so far.[1] The idea of progress was central to his vision, and Eliot had failed him on this score. She was capable of arousing "the nobler emotions," Morley granted, in an earlier work, but she possessed too great a "sense of the iron limitations that are set to improvement in present and future by inexorable forces of the past." Morley found George Sand more prepared to "press on to whatever improvement may chance to be within reach if we only make the attempt," and therefore Eliot's superior.[2]

Charting the stages in Eliot's ideological development, Morley noted her early start in a "fervid evangelicalism," her passage "with equal zeal" to the "rather harsh and crude negations" of freethinking radicalism, particularly during her association with the *Westminster Review*, and then to what Eliot herself had described as a "religious and moral sympathy with the historical life of man." This sympathy had become "the new seed of a positive faith," as well as of "a semi-conservative creed."[3] Morley recalled the influence of Mill's essay on Coleridge, which "first awoke in many of us, who were then youths at Oxford, that sense of truth having many mansions." Mill had stressed "the desire and power of sympathy with the past," and "the value of Permanence in States, which form the reputable side of old conservatisms." This "sentiment and conviction," Morley continued, "never took richer or more mature form than in the best work of George Eliot. . . . It was this that made her a great moral force at that epoch."[4] Morley clearly felt, however, that Eliot had learnt the value of conservatism too well.

The year preceding her death George Eliot published the *Impressions of Theophrastus Such,* virtually a compendium of the nineteenth-century conservative politics of inheritance and tradition in opposition to doctrinaire systems. The name Theophrastus was that of a disciple of Aristotle, to whom his Victorian namesake, Eliot wrote, "might have objected . . . as too much of a systematizer," preferring "the freedom of a little self-contradiction as offering more chances of truth." "My father was a Tory," Eliot's Theophrastus observes, "who had not exactly a dislike to innovators and dissenters, but a slight opinion of them as persons of ill-founded self-confidence." Theophrastus, though more of a radical than his father, as Eliot was more of a liberal than her Tory father, possessed a "historical point of view" and was pleased to share in certain conservative prejudices that were part of "my paternal inheritance." England, unique in the many-sidedness of its faith and its practice of compromise, displayed for Theophrastus both "stability" and a "susceptibility to change." Even reformers in England had come to recognize that "the perfection of society" was not immediately at hand. Theophrastus's father had viewed "the noisy teachers of revolutionary doctrine" as "a variable mixture of the fool and the scoundrel," and sought the national welfare in "a strong government which could maintain order."[5] His son, and Eliot, plainly agreed.

A prime object of Eliot's regard, at times bordering on veneration, was the national tradition—the "divine gift of a memory" of the past that "gives the sense of corporate existence"—against which she saw the liberal, individualistic, and cosmopolitan England of her time turning.[6] Such feelings did not diminish her love of humanity. For Eliot, the tension between the nation, on the one hand, and the ideal of humanity she had first learned from Feuerbach, on the other, was a real one, just as the tension between *Volk* and *Humanität* had been for Herder a century earlier. Eliot, however, believed the liberal posture of cosmopolitanism to be a self-deception, and saw in the communalism and national feeling of the Tories a more realistic, and a more warming, path to virtue.

Eliot's ideal society would unite both virtue and individual happiness in a community of sympathy. "The choice of Hercules" was "a pretty fable" (the myth depicted Hercules choosing virtue over material and sensual happiness), *Middlemarch*'s latitudinarian clergyman Farebrother observed, but it "makes it easy work for the hero," making it appear "as if the first resolves were enough." We must not only take charge of our own characters, Farebrother continued, but help others in the virtuous development of theirs. What was needed was sympathy. "I suppose," Farebrother suggested, that "one good resolve might keep a man right if everybody else's resolve helped him" (chap. 18). John Wesley (and Dinah Morris) had attempted to establish a community of sympathy in the Methodist societies, one which George Eliot had depicted with understanding in *Adam Bede.* Eliot had come to believe that only a national society, founded on family, and reinforced by a sense of a common inheritance and destiny, could prove a tenable basis for a wide-ranging fellowship of compassion in modern times.

As an alternative to the abstract, universal, ideological utopias of the doctrinaires, she offered the politics of national inheritance. Eliot viewed the national tradition as a frame of life that connected past, present, and future, making it possible to recognize duties of parents to children and children to parents. These links to past and future would enable men and women to overcome their natural egoism and to extend their sympathy, first to the individual beings with whom they had a tie of blood and responsibility, and then to the wider group with whom they shared a common heritage of language, culture, and history. The leap from love of family to love of all humanity was too great a one, she believed, to be realizable in a foreseeable future. The movement from egoism to altruism, from selfishness to compassion, was rooted in the moral bonds of family and national community.

While Comte had certainly understood the importance of the historical heritage in shaping the present, his social theory saw men as more or less homogeneous, or easily made so once they had arrived at the scientific stage of development. His was the position of Pash or Gideon in the Philosophers club. But inheritance and the national tradition became the key concepts of George Eliot's politics, as they had been those of Burke and Coleridge, and of Scott and Disraeli. For Eliot, the political legacy she was unwilling to forfeit included England's traditional institutions and beliefs, which the Comtists dismissed as relics of a metaphysical era. She believed that to stress the imperfections of parliamentary government or the futility or immorality of the English spirit of compromise (in the manner of advanced liberals, Benthamites, and Comtists) would endanger the orderly progress of society. On such questions she agreed with the sentiments of her friend Herbert Spencer. Most prominently in *Romola* and in *Middlemarch,* she displayed what might be called the liberal-conservative elements of her outlook: the upholding of liberty and individual happiness that accompanied her insistence on duty and virtue.

Of course, the plot of inheritance, which she so frequently utilized, was a stock contrivance of nineteenth-century writers of romance. And some of these, Scott and Bulwer-Lytton among them, had, like Eliot, employed inheritance as a political metaphor. The historical romance implied, even demanded, such a use, which may in part explain Eliot's attraction to the genre. She was, however, unique in the different meanings she gave to the political metaphor, liberal as well as conservative, and in the rich and interconnected context of other significances—biological, religious, philosophical, ethical—that the metaphor possessed in her hands.

Lord Acton, in his 1885 article, wrote of George Eliot's "wonderful intellect" and declared that her novels called for interpretation as much as Goethe's *Faust* and Dante's *Paradiso.*[7] A few weeks after Eliot's death, Acton, in a letter to Gladstone's daughter, elaborated on what he saw as

Eliot's unique "touch" in her fiction: she could depict the "inner point of view" of men and women who came "in the grasp" of ideological systems, "systems of religion and philosophy, and of politics," and this "without attraction, or caricature." So artful, so persuasive, was she, that the person portrayed might say that "she gave rational form to motives he [himself] had imperfectly analyzed."[8] And, indeed, we have seen that the finely-wrought texture of the ideologies described in her novels sometimes left readers uncertain of Eliot's own position. We have noted that Eliot had baffled, again and again, even so perceptive a critic as Frederic Harrison.

In June 1877 an unrelenting Harrison, despite all his hesitations concerning the genuineness of her Positivist sympathies, asked George Eliot to follow "Oh may I join the choir invisible," a hymn she had written for the Comtists, with other hymns. She might become the poet of the movement, he declared. But Harrison continued to have his doubts as to how Eliot felt about the Comtists, their ideas and projected institutions. He noted his belief that she differed from Comte, "but where you differ, wherein, how far; when you agree, how far—that is what we all want to know, those who accept Comte's ritual in different degrees." He went on, "Your readers are perpetually asking themselves the question—what is your real mind on this subject, and they answer in different ways." Harrison had long wondered why Eliot had not dealt with this question, and "not by way of poetry, but by philosophy."[9]

Eliot had in fact replied to Harrison's inquiry in a letter to him written seven years earlier. She shrank from "decided 'deliverances' on momentous subjects," she wrote at that time.[10] This was her usual response to those who sought to have her supply more definite political or moral instruction. Over the years she politely parried Harrison's efforts to make her commit herself to a less ambiguous position, explaining that the true role of the novelist was to present life in its "highest complexity," not to construct diagrams of utopias. She saw her role as "purely aesthetic."[11] More explicitly, in 1878 she told Mrs. Peter Taylor, an active campaigner for advanced liberal social and political causes, that her "function is that of the *aesthetic,* not the doctrinal teacher." It was appropriate for an artist "to feel keenly for one's fellow-beings," and to rouse the "nobler emotions" that made men desire to attain the "social right," but not to preach specific remedies for "particular calamities."[12]

In a letter to a Positivist physician from Leeds in 1868, while disowning much of what, moved by "considerations of momentary expediency," she might have said in her conversation (and, one might add, her correspondence), George Eliot described her highest moments as occurring in her novels, where her "dearest beliefs" were "deliberately, carefully" set down. She clearly saw herself as a moral teacher, not simply an impartial painter of life's complexities. The "inspiring principle" that "alone gives me courage to write," she said, is "that of so presenting our human life" as to achieve "a clearer conception and a more active admiration of those vital elements which bind men together and give a higher worthiness to their existence." She wished to assist her readers in distinguishing these essentials from "more transient forms on which an outworn teaching tends to make them dependent."[13] She hoped to inculcate a sense of duty, "peremptory and absolute," with a closely linked sense of mission, without which life could have neither significance nor genuine happiness. These would replace the no-longer-tenable ideas of God and immortality.[14]

For Carlyle and for Mill, as later for Eliot, happiness must be sought by indirect means: a person had to follow some grand interest or some cause apart from himself. To seek a personal and individual happiness as a prime object could only bring failure and distress. Gwendolen Harleth discovers this. Adam Bede and Caleb Garth are builders, more concerned with leaving their mark as contributors to the happiness of their fellows than with becoming rich. Mary helps Fred Vincy to avoid the snares of a meaningless existence as an unbelieving clergyman and to find where his talents and duty lie. Felix Holt has undertaken a political mission, as has Will Ladislaw, and their wives find happiness in sharing these self-imposed duties. Romola anticipates Dorothea's search for her special duty, and finds it, for a period at least, where a nineteenth-century English Saint Theresa cannot. The ideal of sympathy leading to service to others unites these characters.

In 1895 Frederic Harrison observed of Eliot's novels that "romance had never before in England been written with such a sense of responsibility, with such eager subtlety of form, and with such high ethical purpose."[15] Harrison might have been startled to learn that Eliot's "high ethical purpose" led her, over the years, to praise the moral and political uses of war. Eliot saw war as instilling a sense of duty and as serving to reinforce feelings of national solidarity. The romances of Sir Walter Scott, with their emphasis on heroism, honor, loyalty, and chivalric duty, the most traditional and conservative of virtues, had touched her heart in girlhood, and continued to influence her later years. In 1840 when she was just twenty-one and reading a work on Louis XIV, she wrote of becoming "quite martial in my spirit," and of so sympathizing with Louis's generals as "losing my hatred of war." Though war might be a scourge, she observed at this time, it might also be a necessary release for aggressive passions, and a war against a foreign enemy might be an effective counter "to our national humours that are growing to so alarming a head."[16] She would persist in such an outlook. In 1875, when she was fifty-six, she found herself in the "anomalous condition of hating war and loving its discipline," which she said, "has been an incalculable contribution to the sentiment of duty."[17] George Eliot's romances were rather different from Scott's, but they had similar roots and a similar political direction.

We may compare Eliot's attachment to the national tradition and her view of war to the similar readiness of the twentieth-century socialist novelist and journalist George Orwell (admired in his lifetime and afterward for maintaining a high ethical ideal) to call himself a patriot, to the surprise and annoyance of the liberal and socialist intellectuals who respected him so much. Orwell thought and wrote much on tradition, patriotism, nationalism, and what seemed an inescapable adjunct of such issues, for him as for Eliot, of the Jews and anti-Semitism. Dismissing the antinational attitudes of people on the left who were so "'enlightened' that they cannot understand the most ordinary emotion," he described (in terms resembling those of Eliot) "the spiritual need for patriotism and the military virtues, for which, however little the boiled rabbits of the Left may like them, no substitute has yet been found."[18] In 1940, the first full year of Britain's war with Nazi Germany, Orwell wrote of the allegiance men experienced to an "organism" within which "they feel themselves to be immortal."[19] He noted that English civilization was "continuous, it stretches into the future and the past, there is something in it that persists, as in a living creature."[20] He himself felt a strong loyalty to what was distinctively and characteristically English, even including flaws and foibles. Five years later, in his "Notes on Nationalism," Orwell distinguished between nationalism and his own patriotism: "By 'patriotism,'" he wrote, "I mean devotion to a particular place and a particular way of life, which one believes the best in the world but has no wish to force on other people." It was "defensive, both militarily and culturally." The nationalist, on the other hand, wished to acquire more power and prestige for the nation into which he has chosen "to sink his own individuality."[21] Orwell associated anti-Semitism with nationalist doctrine.[22]

In *Civilization and Its Discontents* (1930) Sigmund Freud wrote of man's innate inclination to aggression and—as had the young George Eliot—of a community that sought to convert aggressive feelings into a libidinal tie joining its members. For Freud, the effort to expand the bonds of community to wider and wider circles—from family, to clan, to locality, to nation, and, finally, to all of mankind—was, no doubt, commendable, but such an effort was fraught with danger. It was not easy, perhaps it was impossible to fulfil the commandment of loving your neighbors as yourself. The wider the range of those one was asked to love, the more intense would become the natural aggressive inclinations of men to oppose such a program. In a variation of George Eliot's frequently proclaimed dictum, Freud pronounced that "instinctual passions are stronger than reasonable interests."[23] Freud added, somewhat ruefully, that, as a target of the hostility, "The Jewish people, scattered everywhere, have rendered most useful services to the civilizations of the countries that have been their hosts."[24]

A widespread European anti-Semitism was, one might suggest, why Eliot chose to focus her final novel on the Jews, on the threshold of making a decision between assimilation and the cultivation of their national inheritance. In the century since Eliot's death Jews have served as an emblem for many, often contradictory, creeds. They have been praised and denounced as capitalists and socialists, rootless cosmopolitans and clannish nationalists, even as racists. But Eliot saw Jews as a model of devotion to their national and religious inheritance. Unlike liberals like Bulwer-Lytton who decried the Jewish sense of separateness as a form of hatred of mankind, Eliot, like Disraeli and like Scott, admired those qualities that enabled Jews not only to retain their identity under repression but also to produce living moral exemplars comparable to the fictional Rebecca of York, Eva, Mirah, Mordecai, and Deronda. And unlike the liberals who bemoaned the failure of Jews to assimilate fully, Eliot stressed the advantages to humanity of diversity, and proclaimed herself akin to the Zealot separatists. More specifically, she urged Jews to be conscious of their separate national identity and, not merely as self-defense but as an essential element of a positive cultural and political program, to establish a national homeland in Palestine.

In 1948, two years before his death, George Orwell suggested in a review of the French Marxist and existentialist Jean-Paul Sartre's *Portrait of the Antisemite* that Sartre's view of the Jew was "dangerously close to antisemitism." Sartre, Orwell complained, appeared to have substituted different categories of men—"all classifiable in much the same way as insects"—instead of seeing them as human beings. At this "stage of history," Sartre had argued, Jews were wrong if they attempted to assimilate, and Gentiles were wrong if they ignored Jewish separateness. Sartre wished Jews to be seen as Jews in the national community, and not as ordinary Frenchmen or Englishmen. The result of views such as Sartre's, Orwell declared, would make anti-Semitism "more prevalent."[25]

Had Eliot anticipated Sartre's position? If Daniel and Mordecai represented her views, as her other writings give us some grounds for believing, she disapproved of assimilationist Jews such as Klesmer and Pash, preferring what Sartre called "authentic Jews," who proudly acknowledged their heritage. In her approval of Deronda's new nationalist awareness, then, was she suggesting that Jews had no real place in the national societies of western Europe? One may easily argue that this was the logic of Daniel's position. But was this sense of separateness to be freely willed (as in the case of Deronda's choice not to follow Klesmer's or Pash's path of assimilation) or made necessary by some form of racial inheritance? It was because "progress" had decreed (and was bringing about) assimilation, that Eliot— far from prescribing that Gentiles not recognize Jews as fellow citizens— urged that it would be unworthy, if not immoral, for Jews to yield their precious national and religious heritage. Of course, as I have suggested, her chief purpose was to turn Englishmen from the cosmopolitan tendencies of global interests to a greater dedication to their own national heritage and traditions.

In late 1989 the writer and critic Cynthia Ozick detailed the anti-Semitism of T. S. Eliot, in his later years perhaps the most admired literary figure in the English-speaking world,[26] and some eighteen months later Irving Howe, another distinguished critic, confessed how shaken he had been as a young man to discover Eliot's strong, sometimes venomous, dislike for

Jews. Howe described Eliot's anti-Semitism as a moral defect in a man who had long been one of his cultural heroes. He was particularly troubled by a paragraph in T. S. Eliot's 1934 lectures at the University of Virginia which declared:

> The population should be homogeneous; where two or more cultures exist in the same place they are likely either to be fiercely self-conscious or both to become adulterate. What is still more important is unity of religious background; and reasons of race and religion combine to make any large number of free-thinking Jews undesirable.

"A spirit of excessive tolerance," Eliot concluded, "is to be deprecated."[27] Howe now wrote that he had previously pardoned Eliot with a "resigned shrug," recognizing that "anti-Semitism is so deeply ingrained in Western culture, even the best writers may succumb to it." But other writers had avoided this pitfall, and Howe noted two, James Joyce and George Eliot.[28]

T. S. Eliot's enemy, like Riehl's almost a century earlier, was a society "worm-eaten with Liberalism" and a cosmopolitanism that deprecated the national tradition.[29] Eliot's lecture extolled "tradition," which he defined, as had Riehl, as "habitual actions, habits and customs" which represented "the blood kinship of 'the same people living in the same place.'"[30] Like Riehl as well, T. S. Eliot saw tradition, properly understood, as "of the blood, so to speak, rather than of the brain: it is the means by which the vitality of the past enriches the life of the present." Tradition represented "the reconciliation of thought and feeling."[31]

In his final Virginia lecture T. S. Eliot described what he saw as the special position of George Eliot. Unlike such predecessors as Jane Austen, Dickens, and Thackeray, who had criticized the world by traditional (and therefore praiseworthy) standards, and who were consequently "orthodox," with George Eliot "the first suspicion of heresy creeps in." She had "unfortunately" combined her "profounder moral insight and passion" with "the dreary rationalism of the epoch of which she is one of the most colossal monuments." Her morals were "individualistic," the product of the "aggrandisement and exploitation of *personality*," and not "a matter of tradition and orthodoxy—that is, of the habits of the community formulated, corrected, and elevated by the continuous thought and direction of the Church."[32]

Although George Eliot had certainly cut herself off from the church, her twentieth-century namesake failed to see that, though a freethinker, Eliot was, no less than himself, an enemy to "the dreary rationalism of the epoch." Moreover, also like himself, she was a Coleridgian, a disciple of the Burkean politics of tradition. Although she at times masked her views for personal reasons, she abjured the abstract, utopian politics of the Positivists and advanced liberals of the middle Victorian decades, with which T. S. Eliot and other writers, her contemporaries as well as ours, have identified her, in favor of the traditional English politics of compromise. If he had not uncritically accepted the more stereotypical view of George

Eliot, T. S. Eliot might have recognized the strong evidence that her world outlook was in many respects similar to his own, and also to that of the pantheon of British conservatism (Burke, Coleridge, and Disraeli) whom he would discuss in a 1955 address on "the Literature of Politics." She would have denounced, as he did in this talk, historical determinism and the puerility of "the Jacobinism of the obstinate doctrinaire." In searching for "literary influence, not only philosophical, but imaginative, upon politics," T. S. Eliot stressed, as, in part, George Eliot had also, the influence of the novelists Sir Walter Scott and Disraeli.[33]

But George Eliot was not, as T. S. Eliot proclaimed himself to be, a monarchist, an Anglo-Catholic, and a classicist. Nor was she an anti-Semite, formed (as T. S. Eliot had been) in the school of Charles Maurras, the anti-Dreyfusard editor of the *Action Française,* the writer from whose threefold motto and war cry (monarchism, Catholicism, classicism) his Anglo-American admirer would adopt his own.[34] In her political posture, George Eliot was English, not, like T. S. Eliot, no matter what he thought himself, continental. In a manner frequently encountered among British thinkers of the past two centuries, George Eliot adapted what she learned from European thinkers (in her case, Herder, Feuerbach, Comte, and Riehl) to suit the English palate, which was her own taste as well. The British political tradition found continental political anti-Semitism as unacceptable as it did systematic ideologies in general, of which anti-Semitism has formed so prominent a part in the past century. The British Fascist Sir Oswald Moseley would discover this to be true in the 1930s.

Perhaps the most perceptive exponent of Herder's (and Eliot's) nonaggressive cultural nationalism at present is Sir Isaiah Berlin, one of our day's most respected liberal men of letters. As a Jew (and a Zionist), Berlin envisions a Deity who seeks variety among his creatures. A cultural group for Berlin is not necessarily one of race or blood, but one of shared common historical experiences, customs, and life-style. Individuals within such a group feel most themselves and consequently most capable of making a contribution to civilization within the framework of their own national heritage. Herder's view that world conquerors like Alexander, Caesar, and Charlemagne were "the villains of history" because they worked to extirpate national cultures, gains Berlin's approval. The efforts of these conquerors to secure an aggressive uniformity was destined to failure because of the strength of the national idea. Nationalism had similarly triumphed over the men of the French Enlightenment who persuaded themselves that all men were at bottom the same and shared the same values, the natural scientists who in their stress on general laws appeared to confirm this universalism, and the Marxists who dismissed national culture and constructed uniform regulations to govern the political and cultural lives of disparate communities. Berlin concludes:

> Like Herder I regard cosmopolitanism as empty. People can't develop unless they belong to a culture. . . . Where men and women are not products of a

culture, where they don't have kith and kin and feel closer to some people than to others, where there is no native language—that would lead to a dessication of everything that is human. . . . If you think that all this will one day give way to one universal language—not just for learned purposes or politics or business, but to convey emotional nuances, to express inner lives . . . this would not be one universal culture, but the death of culture.

In Russia, he notes, such men had imposed "the despotism of the Soviet Tower of Babel."[35]

It was similar feelings about "kith and kin," as we have seen, that moved George Eliot. Following Herder, Eliot regarded the liberal cosmopolitanism of the Positivists (the successors of the Enlightenment philosophies and the forerunners of the Marxists) as premature, convinced that attempts at imposing such a uniformity would be futile. She praised cultural variety, and urged even such pariah peoples as the widely dispersed Gypsies and Jews not to abandon their national inheritances. She believed, as would Berlin, that social science, developed by Comte and expounded by his followers, with its general laws, would not produce truth, but, rather, that its faith in such laws would result in the imposition of a despotic republic of virtue. She offered a third alternative to liberals of her time—neither Savonarola's nor Comte's oppressive utopias nor the *völkisch* racism of a Riehl—but a liberal-conservative love for the national tradition as one among many in a world of cultural pluralism. This was the path charted by such liberal nationalists as Herder and Mazzini, who enlisted the cultural and political traditions of their countries to uphold the ideals of both humanity and nationality.

George Eliot did not seem to have understood that in summoning "national tradition" as a defense against her previous attractions to systematic religious, social, and political doctrine, she had yielded to still another ideology. For the facts of any nation's past are so numerous and, without some deliberate effort at patterning, so lacking in inherent purpose, that one may construct more than one "tradition." Eliot might have opted for a British radical tradition, or a liberal one, or a socialist or a cosmopolitan tradition—all recoverable, with respectable intellectual credentials, and, at core, ideological. Her choice stemmed from the peculiar circumstances of the time in which she lived, the alternatives offered to her by her milieu as well as her own life experiences.

Just as (in the fashion described by Aristotle's *Politics*), monarchy might degenerate into autocracy, aristocracy into oligarchy, and democracy into anarchy, so might loyalty to the cultural heritage and patriotism be transformed into an aggressive nationalism. This has, tragically, all too often been the experience of the twentieth century. Events have too frequently appeared to justify Franz Grillparzer, the nineteenth-century Austrian dramatist, in his description of the decline of the Enlightenment's cosmopolitan ideal as one from humanity, to nationality, to bestiality.[36] What began as the fruitful pursuit of the national heritage and of cultural pluralism could, and in many instances, has, become a demonic, xeno-phobic savagery. We have recently seen the atrocities stemming from the breakup of Yugoslavia.

In the 1930s the French writer Julien Benda accused intellectuals who subscribed to nationalist sentiments of "la trahison des clercs," of having betrayed the ideals of their calling.[37] But we cannot expect George Eliot (whom both Feuerbach and Comte had prepared for a recognition of her duty to humanity) to have foreseen our century's nightmarish experience when she advanced the case for the national tradition and for pluralism. For we have also seen the ugly consequences of doctrinaire systems—however well-meaning—which discounted and disowned the past in pursuit of utopian dreams.

In the England of Eliot's day, a current of antinational cosmopolitanism had established itself in liberal circles to counteract the smug sense of British superiority to be found among the Tories. George Eliot, as well as some liberals such as Mill and Spencer, was prepared to see great value in the inherited national tradition that many liberals, no less than the Positivists, were willing to discard. For many reasons, as we have seen—personal, intellectual, and political—she sought to escape from the pain of disinheritance that an alienating modern *Gesellschaft* had made more intense, and which threatened to rob her and her countrymen of their past. She favored an invigorating cultural diversity over the regimented uniformity that characterized the utopias of the nineteenth-century's political prophets. And consequently she chose to stress that part of her beliefs that was most overlooked by her circle and the liberal reading public that constituted her principal audience. In doing so she became one of the more sensitive and articulate exponents of the social-conservative politics of tradition—and of the politics of national inheritance.

Notes

Prologue

1. Justin McCarthy, *Reminiscences,* 2 vols. (New York: Harper, 1899), 1:310.

2. Lord Acton, "George Eliot's Life," *Nineteenth Century* 17 (1885):485.

3. G. M. Young, *Victorian England; Portrait of An Age* (1936; rpt. Garden City, N.Y.: Doubleday-Anchor, 1954), 15–17.

4. Discussion of Eliot's achievement, stressing her views on subjects of feminist concern, may be found in such works as S. M. Gilbert and Susan Gubar, *The Madwoman in the Attic: The Woman Writer and the Nineteenth-Century Literary Imagination* (New Haven, Conn.: Yale University Press, 1979), and Deirdre David, *Intellectual Women and Victorian Patriarchy: Harriet Martineau, Elizabeth Barrett Browning, George Eliot* (Ithaca, N.Y.: Cornell University Press, 1987). See also Elaine Showalter, *A Literature of Their Own: British Women Novelists from Brontë to Lessing* (Princeton, N.J.: Princeton University Press, 1977); and Gillian Beer, *George Eliot* (Brighton, Eng.: Harvester Press, 1986).

5. George Eliot to Mrs. Charles Bray, 25 July 1871, *The George Eliot Letters,* 9 vols., ed. Gordon S. Haight (New Haven, Conn.: Yale University Press, 1954–55; 1978), 5:170. Subsequent textual references to these letters appear as *GEL.*

6. G. H. Lewes to Alexander Macmillan, 26 August 1878, *GEL,* 7:65.

7. Such distinctions between traditional and modern society became the common currency of sociological analysis in the nineteenth century. The positions of the leading social thinkers, sketched in the text, were essential to their most systematic writings, to certain of which I will have occasion to refer in greater detail subsequently. See Auguste Comte, *The Positive Philosophy of Auguste Comte,* 2 vols.; trans. and ed. Harriet Martineau (1853; London: Trübner, 1875; orig. in 6 vols., 1830–32); Herbert Spencer, *Principles of Sociology,* 3 vols. (1876–85; New York: Appleton, 1887–97); Sir Henry Maine, *Ancient Law* (London: John Murray,

1861); and Ferdinand Tönnies, *Community and Society,* trans. and ed. C. P. Loomis (1887; New York: Harper Torchbooks, 1963).

Suzanne Graver has made good use of Tönnies's insights in her *George Eliot and Community: A Study in Social Theory and Fictional Form* (Berkeley and Los Angeles: University of California Press, 1984). See also D. R. Carroll, *"Felix Holt*: Society as Protagonist," *Nineteenth-Century Fiction* 17 (1962):237–52, and Ian Milner, "The Quest for Community in *The Mill on the Floss," Prague Studies in English* 12 (1967):77–92. The links between Eliot's religious views and her stress on community are explored in Martin J. Svaglic, "Religion in the Novels of George Eliot," *Journal of English and Germanic Philology* 53 (1954):145–59.

8. H. T. Buckle, *History of Civilization in England,* 3 vols. (1857; London: Longmans, Green, 1871), 1:190–93, 198. See also Bernard Semmel, "H. T. Buckle: The Liberal Faith and the Science of History," *British Journal of Sociology* 27, no. 3 (September 1976):370–86.

9. One can find good treatments of nineteenth-century ideological systems in George Lichtheim, *The Concept of Ideology and Other Essays* (New York: Random House, 1967), esp. 3–46; and J. L. Talmon, *Political Messianism: The Romantic Phase* (New York: Praeger, 1960), esp. 15–124, 229–92.

10. George Eliot, "The Progress of the Intellect" (1851), in Thomas Pinney, ed., *Essays of George Eliot* (New York: Columbia University Press, 1963), esp. 28–29, 31. Subsequent textual references to this collection of essays appears as *Essays.*

11. R. K. Webb, *Harriet Martineau: A Radical Victorian* (New York: Columbia University Press, 1960), 303–4.

12. Quoted in G. S. Haight, *George Eliot: A Biography* (New York: Oxford University Press, 1968), 302, 405.

13. W. M. Simon, *European Positivism in the Nineteenth Century* (Ithaca, N.Y.: Cornell University Press, 1963), 195–98, 211.

14. Basil Willey, *Nineteenth Century Studies* (1949; rpt. New York: Columbia University Press, 1964), 207.

15. John Viscount Morley, *Recollections,* 2 vols. (London: Macmillan, 1917), 1:68–72.

16. McCarthy, *Reminiscences,* 2:176, 178.

17. Josiah Royce, "George Eliot as a Religious Teacher" (1881), in *Fugitive Essays* (Cambridge, Mass.: Harvard University Press, 1925), 271–72.

18. Acton, "George Eliot's Life," 483–84.

19. Ibid., 476, 479.

20. Herbert Spencer, *An Autobiography,* 2 vols. (New York: Appleton, 1904), 2:430. W. H. Simon has also observed that the religious side of positivism appealed to her "most strongly," but the precise meaning Simon attaches to Positivist religion—whether Comtian rituals or a veneration of humanity—is uncertain; see Simon, *European Positivism,* 208.

21. Quoted in Simon, *European Positivism,* 212.

22. Beatrice Webb, *My Apprenticeship* (London: Longmans, Green, 1926), 98, 28–30, 138–40.

23. This is a conclusion much like that of Martha S. Vogeler, in her "George Eliot and the Positivists," *Nineteenth-Century Fiction* 35 (Fall 1980):406–31; also see M. S. Vogeler, "The Choir Invisible: The Poetics of Humanist Piety," in G. S. Haight and R. T. Van Arsdel, eds., *George Eliot: A Centenary Tribute* (Totawa, N.J.: Barnes and Noble, 1982), 76–79. T. R. Wright argues, effectively if not always persuasively, that Eliot owed more to Comte than present-day writers have

been willing to grant; see T. R. Wright, "George Eliot and Positivism: A Reassessment," *Modern Language Review* 76, pt. 2 (April 1981):257–72. Also see Bernard J. Paris, "George Eliot's Religion of Humanity," *English Literary History* 29 (1962):418–43; Paris has discussed other aspects of Eliot's intellectual development in his *Experiments in Life: George Eliot's Quest for Values* (Detroit, Mich.: Wayne State University Press, 1965). An earlier effort to sketch the intellectual background of Eliot's thinking, notably the influence of Spinoza and Feuerbach as well as Comte, may be found in Paul Bourl'homme, *Essai de biographie intellectuelle et morale* (Paris: Librairie Ancienne Honoré Champion, 1933); see also William Myers, *The Teachings of George Eliot* (Leicester, Eng.: Leicester University Press, 1984). Myers presents Eliot as a teacher—stressing her debts to Comte, Feuerbach, Spencer, and the physiologist Alexander Bain—thus modifying "the 'anti-didactic' or "anti-ideological' asumptions of mainstream George Eliot criticism" (9).

24. Auguste Comte, *A General View of Positivism*, trans. J. H. Bridges (1848; London: Trübner, 1865), 18–20.

25. Adam Smith, *The Theory of Moral Sentiments* (1759; New York: August Kelley, 1966) esp. 3–30, 44–59.

26. Herbert Spencer, *The Data of Ethics* (1879; New York: Appleton, 1890), 134, 215–20, 224–29, 237–44, 251, 255–56.

27. Martha S. Vogeler, *Frederic Harrison: The Vocation of a Positivist* (Oxford: Clarendon Press, 1984), 223–24.

28. George Eliot, "Worldliness and Other-Worldliness: The Poet Young" (1859), *Essays*, 375.

29. J. W. Cross, *George Eliot's Life*, 3 vols. (Boston: Houghton Mifflin, 1908), 3:316–17; the three volumes of the *Life* form vols. 23–25 of the Warwickshire edition of *The Writings of George Eliot*.

30. Eliot is depicted as Burkean, in certain of her writings, in Philip Fisher, *Making Up Society: The Novels of George Eliot* (Pittsburgh, Pa.: University of Pittsburgh Press, 1981), 14–15. A nineteenth-century literary critic dealt perceptively with a number of these themes; see Edward Dowden, "George Eliot," *Contemporary Review* (August 1872), an article included in John Holmstrom and Lawrence Lerner, eds., *George Eliot and Her Readers; A Selection of Contemporary Reviews* (London: Bodley Head, 1966), 164–70. See also Thomas Pinney, "The Authority of the Past in George Eliot's Novels," *Nineteenth-Century Fiction* 21 (1966):131–47.

31. George Eliot to Mr. and Mrs. Charles Bray and Sara Hennell, 5 August [1849], in *GEL*, 1:293. This reference to Herder was occasioned by her encounter with a grandson of the German writer in a Swiss hotel. See also Eliot, "Three Months in Weimar" (1855), in *Essays*, 90–91, in which Eliot noted that Herder was "the only one of its great men" to whom Weimar had erected an open-air statue.

32. Herder's position on these issues appears in J. G. von Herder, *Reflections on the Philosophy of the History of Mankind*, ed. F. E. Manuel (1784–91; Chicago: University of Chicago Press, 1968), 3–78. See also F. E. Manuel, "Editor's Introduction," in Herder, *Reflections*, ix–xxv; and more particularly, Isaiah Berlin, *Vico and Herder: Two Studies in the History of Ideas* (New York: Viking, 1976), 143–216.

33. Herder, *Reflections*, 144.

34. There is a brief discussion of Eliot's involvement with a nationalist "ideology" in *Daniel Deronda* in Alexander Welsh, *George Eliot and Blackmail* (Cambridge, Mass.: Harvard University Press, 1985), 309, 312–13n.

Chapter 1

1. George Eliot to Mme. E. Bodichon, 21 December 1869, *GEL*, 5:74.

2. George Eliot to Mrs. A. H. Pears, 28 January 1842, *GEL*, 1:125.

3. George Eliot to Sara Hennell, 9 October 1843, *GEL*, 1:162.

4. Ibid., 1:162–63. Unless otherwise noted, all emphasis in quoted matter is in the original.

5. George Eliot to Alexander Main, 9 August 1871, *GEL*, 5:175; see also George Eliot to Charles Bray, 13 September 1855, *GEL*, 2:215.

6. Though what I have called "the myth of the disinherited one" does not enter the discussion, Eliot's use of myth is addressed in Joseph Wiesenfarth, *George Eliot's Mythmaking* (Heidelberg, Germany: Carl Winter, 1977).

7. Northrop Frye, *Fables of Identity: Studies in Poetic Mythology* (New York: Harbinger, 1963), 1, 23, 36, 38.

8. A. N. Wilson, "Introduction" to *Ivanhoe*, by Sir Walter Scott (London: Penguin, 1984), xv.

9. Quoted in Wilson, "Introduction," xv. Frye has observed that "in every age the ruling social and intellectual class tends to project its ideals in some form of romance"; these are frequently stories "where the virtuous heroes and beautiful heroines represent the ideals and the villains the threats to their ascendancy." See Northrop Frye, *Anatomy of Criticism: Four Essays* (Princeton, N.J.: Princeton University Press, 1957), 186.

10. Northrop Frye, *The Secular Scripture: A Study of the Structure of Romance* (Cambridge, Mass.: Harvard University Press, 1976), 101.

11. Ibid., 102.

12. This theme of Eliot has been briefly discussed in Thomas Pinney, "Another Note on the Forgotten Past of Will Ladislaw," *Nineteenth-Century Fiction* 17 (June 1962): 72.

13. Emily Davies to Jane Crowe, 21 August [1869], *GEL*, 8:465–66.

14. Ibid., 8:465.

15. George Eliot to Sara Hennell, 9 October 1843, 1:162–63.

16. G. H. Lewes, "Spinoza," *Fortnightly Review* 4 (1 April 1866): 400–01.

17. See Frye, *Secular Scripture*, 161. On this question, see Raymond Williams, *Culture and Society, 1780–1950* (New York: Columbia University Press, 1958), 103.

18. Talcott Parsons and E. A. Shils, *Toward a General Theory of Action* (Cambridge, Mass.: Harvard University Press, 1962), 77–91.

19. This question has aroused considerable controversy. See, for example, the discussion in W. J. Harvey, "The Intellectual Background of the Novel: Casaubon and Lydgate," in *Middlemarch: Critical Approaches to the Novel,* ed. Barbara Hardy (New York: Oxford University Press, 1967), 25–26.

20. A perceptive treatment of this issue in Eliot's writings may be found in George L. Levine, "Determinism and Responsibility in the Works of George Eliot," *PMLA* 77 (1962):268–79.

21. J. S. Mill, *A System of Logic, Ratiocinative and Inductive* (1843), in *Collected Works,* 33 vols., ed. J. M. Robson (Toronto: University of Toronto Press, 1974), 8:839–42.

22. J. S. Mill, *Autobiography of John Stuart Mill,* ed. J. J. Coss (New York: Columbia University Press, 1960), 93–100, 76–77, 118–19. See also the discussion in Bernard Semmel, *John Stuart Mill and the Pursuit of Virtue* (New Haven, Conn.: Yale University Press, 1984), 45–47.

23. Henry Senior's strict Calvinist father (the novelist's grandfather) had punished him in his will by leaving him considerably less than what was bequeathed to his less rebellious siblings. The courts broke the will, providing Henry Senior with a bequest equal to that of his brothers and sisters. A confused and resentful Henry Senior struggled to bring his ambivalent sentiments regarding his father—and God—into some harmony. One day he was seized by fear and panicked at the thought of an invisible squatting figure in his room whom he believed to be diabolical; this brought on a nervous collapse which a friend described as a "vastation," a stage in the regeneration of man described by the Swedish mystic Emanuel Swedenborg. Reading Swedenborg convinced Henry Senior that this vastation would reconcile him to God and to his father. "I had no doubt that this being or self of mine . . . came originally as a gift from the hand of God; but I had just as little doubt that the moment the gift had left God's hand . . . it became as essentially independent of him in all spiritual or subjective regards as the soul of a child is of its earthly father." In this way, by a compromise analogous to that made by Mill, Henry Senior had achieved his measure of free will and his therapeutic independence from his father. As the novelist's biographer has observed, "He could be his [own] father." Leon Edel, *Henry James: A Life* (New York: Harper & Row, 1985), 1–11.

Chapter 2

1. H. A. Taine, *History of English Literature,* 4 vols., trans. H. Van Laun (1883; New York: Ungar, 1965), 4:107–09, 109n.

2. Acton, "George Eliot's Life," 485.

3. F. R. Leavis, *The Great Tradition* (1948; New York: New York University Press, 1967), 1–27.

4. Though only glancing attention is given to Eliot, others who shared her role, most prominently Mill, are discussed in Stefan Collini, *Public Moralists: Political Thought and Intellectual Life in Britain 1850–1930* (Oxford: Clarendon Press, 1991); for Eliot, see p. 89.

5. See Levine, "Determinism and Responsibility"; for a discussion of the mix of Eliot's "intuitional morality and her deterministic sense of the world," see J. B. Schneewind, "Moral Problems and Moral Philosophy in the Victorian Period," *Victorian Studies* 9 (1965, Suppl.): 43–46.

6. Lewis S. Feuer, *Ideology and the Ideologists* (Oxford: Basil Blackwell, 1975), 5–6.

7. See Cross, *George Eliot's Life,* 1:78.

8. Ibid., 1:92–93.

9. George Eliot to Charles Bray, 16 July [1855], *GEL,* 2:210. The ambivalences in George Eliot's view of phrenology are explored in N. N. Feltes, "Phrenology from Lewes to George Eliot," *Studies in the Literary Imagination* 1 (1968): 13–22; and in T. R. Wright, "From Bumps to Morals: The Phrenological Background to George Eliot's Moral Framework," *Review of English Studies* 38 (1982):35–96.

10. For the correspondence of Mill and Comte on phrenology, see *Lettres inédites de J. S. Mill à Auguste Comte,* ed. L. Lévy-Bruhl (Paris: Alcan, 1899), 31–32, 38–39, 56, 66–68, 73–78, and 85.

11. George Eliot to Sara Hennell, 9 November 1857, *GEL,* 2:402.

12. George Eliot to Charles Bray, 15 November 1857, *GEL,* 2:403–04.

13. Ibid., 2:403.

14. See, for example, *GEL,* 1:144n; also see George Eliot to Sara Hennell, 9

June 1852, *GEL,* 2:33–34. For Martineau on free will, see J. Drummmond and C. B. Upton, *The Life and Letters of James Martineau,* 2 vols. (London: Nisbet, 1902), 2:272–73. For Martineau's position within Unitarianism, see Robert K. Webb, "A Crisis of Authority: Early Nineteenth-Century British Thought," *Albion* 24, no. 1 (Spring 1992):4–7; and Robert K. Webb, "Transplanting the Vine: Manchester College in London and Oxford," *Faith and Freedom* 44, pt. 3, no. 132 78–91.

15. See George Eliot to Mr. and Mrs. Charles Bray, 20 September [1849], *GEL,* 1:310; and George Eliot to Mrs. Charles Bray, [3 October 1851], *GEL,* 1:363. For Mill and free will, see Semmel, *John Stuart Mill,* esp. chap. 1.

16. Quoted in Cross, *George Eliot's Life,* 1:101.

17. David F. Strauss, *Life of Jesus,* 3 vols., trans. Marian Evans (1835; London: Chapman & Hall, 1846), 1:ix–xii.

18. Ibid., 1:35.

19. Ibid., 1:80–84.

20. Ibid., 3:397.

21. Ibid., 3:398–402.

22. Ibid., 3:437–39; see also 441–42, 445–46.

23. George Eliot to Sara Hennell, 29 April 1854, *GEL,* 2:153.

24. George Eliot to Mrs. Henry Houghton, 4 February (?) 1849, *GEL,* 1:276.

25. Ludwig Feuerbach, *The Essence of Christianity,* trans. George Eliot (1841; trans. 1854; New York: Harper Torchbooks, 1957), 46–49.

26. Ibid., 47–49.

27. Ibid., 263.

28. Ibid., 165.

29. Ibid., 167.

30. Ibid., 156.

31. Ibid., 251–55, 260.

32. Ibid., 266–69.

33. See Karl Marx, "Theses on Feuerbach" (1845), in *The Marx–Engels Reader,* ed. R. C. Tucker (New York: Norton, 1972), 107–09; and "The German Ideology [1845–46]," Part 1, in *Reader,* 111–64.

34. *GEL,* 1:21n.

35. George Eliot to Maria Lewis, 30 March 1840, *GEL,* 1:45. The same complaint would be made against Eliot by contemporary religious commentators. One such writer, probably a Calvinist Evangelical, saw in a number of writers a "systematic effort" to attempt to "exaggerate the moral qualities that are supposed by them to underly our fallen nature." He was particularly disturbed that Felix Holt's morality ("not the offspring of grace, but our own manufacture") secured Esther's "conversion" and not "the regeneration of the Holy Spirit." See George McCrie, *The Religion of Our Literature* (London: Hodder and Stoughton, 1875), 290–94. A more recent French Catholic writer suggested that Eliot's repudiation of religion was due to her having overly identified Christianity with Calvinism, and consequently to her not finding "the inner light of a grace that supports the good instincts and the free will [*la liberté*] of man." See Placide-Gustave Maheu, *La Pensée religieuse et morale de George Eliot: Essai d'interprétation* (Paris: Maurice Didier, 1958), 11.

36. Cross, *George Eliot's Life,* 1:75–77.

37. Ibid., 1:91.

38. George Eliot to Martha Jackson, 16 December 1841, *GEL,* 1:122–23.

39. Haight, *George Eliot,* 65.

40. George Eliot to Sara Hennell, 7 October 1859, *GEL,* 3:174–77. For a discussion of the role the free-will theology of Methodist Arminianism played in British social and political life in the eighteenth and nineteenth centuries, see Bernard Semmel, *The Methodist Revolution* (New York: Basic Books, 1973).

41. George Eliot, "The Influence of Rationalism: Lecky's History" (1865), *Essays,* 404, 409.

42. George Eliot, "Evangelical Teaching: Dr. Cumming" (1855), *Essays,* 185, 187–88.

43. George Eliot to John Blackwood, 11 June 1857, *GEL,* 2:347–48.

44. George Eliot to Sara Hennell, 18 November 1870, *GEL,* 5:121–22.

45. See excerpt in *GEL,* 6:97n3.

46. George Eliot to Mrs. H. F. Ponsonby, 10 December 1874, *GEL,* 6:98–100.

47. George Eliot to Mrs. H. F. Ponsonby, 19 August 1875, *GEL,* 6:166–67.

48. John Morley, "The Life of George Eliot," in *Critical Miscellanies,* 3 vols. (1886; London: Macmillan, 1904), 3:131–32.

49. J. S. Mill, "Bentham" (1838), in *Essays on Ethics, Religion, and Society,* ed. J. M. Robson, in *Collected Works,* 10:77.

50. Ibid., 10:79, 91, 94–98.

51. J. S. Mill, "Coleridge" (1840), in *Collected Works,* 10:117, 133.

52. Ibid., 138–41.

53. Mill, "Bentham," *Collected Works,* 10:99.

54. Mill, "Coleridge," *Collected Works,* 10:135.

55. Ibid., 10:137–39.

56. S. T. Coleridge, *On the Constitution of the Church and State,* ed. John Colmer, in *The Collected Works of Samuel Taylor Coleridge,* 16 vols. (Princeton, N.J.: Princeton University Press, 1976), 10:24–25.

57. Ibid., 10:71–72, 53.

58. Edmund Burke, *Reflections on the Revolution in France,* ed. T.H.D. Mahoney (1790; Indianapolis, Ind.: Liberal Arts Press, 1955), 24–25, 28–29.

59. Ibid., 35–38.

60. Ibid., 38–39.

61. Edmund Burke, *An Appeal from the New to the Old Whigs* (1791; Indianapolis, Ind.: Bobbs-Merrill, 1962), 19.

62. Ibid., 119–20.

63. Ibid., 130–31.

64. Auguste Comte, *A General View of Positivism* (1865, trans.; New York: Robert Speller, 1956), 178, 168–78.

65. Ibid., 403.

66. Ibid., 400–401, 403–04.

67. Auguste Comte, *System of Positive Polity,* 4 vols. (1852–1854; 1875, trans.; New York: Burt Franklin, 1968), 3:305–10.

68. Ibid., 4:402–03.

69. George Eliot to Charles Bray, 23 December 1857, in *GEL,* 2:415. Comte's views on race were somewhat uncertain. While prepared to see differences existing among what he termed the white, black, and yellow races, he saw such differences as possessing a declining significance as progress made men more prepared "to do justice to the qualities of the despised races"; see Comte, *System,* 2:378.

70. George Eliot, "Woman in France: Madame de Sablé" (1854), *Essays,* 55–59.

71. George Eliot, "Three Months in Weimar" (June 1855), *Essays,* 83, 89.

72. George Eliot, "Liszt, Wagner, and Weimar" (July 1855), *Essays,* 100–02.

73. George Eliot, "German Wit: Heinrich Heine" (1856), *Essays,* 223–27.

74. George Eliot, "A Word for the Germans" (1865), *Essays,* 388.

75. Acton, "George Eliot's Life," 481.

76. G. P. Gooch, *History and Historians in the Nineteenth Century* (1913; London: Longmans, Green, 1955), 523–26.

77. See, for example, George L. Mosse, *The Crisis of German Ideology: Intellectual Origins of the Third Reich* (New York: Grosset and Dunlap, 1964), 19–24, 155.

78. George Eliot, "The Natural History of German Life: Riehl" (1856), *Essays,* 289–90.

79. Ibid., 272.

80. Ibid., 268.

81. Ibid., 270–73.

82. Ibid., 279.

83. Ibid., 214, 282, 284–85.

84. Ibid., 288–89.

85. Ibid., 287.

86. Ibid., 286–87.

87. Ibid., 289–90.

88. Ibid., 298–99.

89. Wilhelm Heinrich Riehl, *Die Naturgeschichte des deutschen Volkes,* ed. H. Naumann and R. Haller (1854; Leipzig, Germany: Philipp Reclam, 1934), 297.

90. Ibid., 299.

91. Ibid., 311–12.

92. See the essay by Thomas Pinney, "The Authority of the Past in George Eliot's Novels," *Nineteenth-Century Fiction,* 21 (1966):131–47.

Chapter 3

1. The best work on Saint-Simon remains Frank E. Manuel, *The New World of Henri Saint-Simon* (Cambridge, Mass.: Harvard University Press, 1956). For the Saint-Simonians, see George G. Iggers, *The Cult of Authority: The Political Philosophy of the Saint-Simonians* (The Hague: Martinus Nijhoff, 1990), and Frank E. Manuel, *The Prophets of Paris* (New York: Harper Torchbooks, 1965), 151–93. For Comte, see Manuel, *Prophets,* 251–96; E. Littré, *Auguste Comte et la philosophie positive* (Paris: Hachette, 1863); and Henri Gouhier, *La Jeunesse d'Auguste Comte et la formation du positivisme,* 3 vols. (Paris: J. Vrin, 1933–41).

2. See R.K.P. Pankhurst, *The Saint-Simonians, Mill and Carlyle* (London: Sidgwick and Jackson, 1957); and Semmel, *John Stuart Mill,* 56–57, 61–77, 124–29, 161–66, 178–81.

3. See Lévy-Bruhl, ed., *Lettres inédites,* 208–9, 246–51, 275–80, 115.

4. Comte, *System of Positive Polity, passim.*

5. For Mill's high regard for Comte's philosophy and his philosophy of history, see J. S. Mill, "Auguste Comte and Positivism," in *Essays on Ethics,* in *Collected Works,* 10:263–327.

6. Ibid., 10:328–68.

7. Comte, *System of Positive Polity,* 4:296–97.

8. Ibid., 4:324–25.

9. Ibid., 4:419–21.

10. Jacques Barzun, *Darwin, Marx, Wagner: Critique of a Heritage* (1941; New York: Doubleday Anchor, 1958), 36n.

11. Frederic Harrison to George Eliot, 19 July 1866, *GEL,* 4:284–85. (For Harrison's counsel on the law of inheritance, see his letters to Eliot in January 1866, *GEL,* 4:216–19, 222–31.)

12. Ibid., 4:286–87.

13. Ibid., 4:287.

14. Ibid., 4:287–88.

15. Ibid., 4:288–89. That Harrison's advice helped to shape Eliot's *Middlemarch* has been argued by J. F. Scott, in his "George Eliot, Positivism, and the Social Vision of *Middlemarch,*" *Victorian Studies* 16 (1972–73): 59–76. Scott notes that Eliot's attitude toward Comte and positivism was "compounded of pronounced respect and persistent reservations" (59).

16. George Eliot to Frederic Harrison, 15 August 1866, *GEL,* 4:300–301.

17. John Blackwood to George Eliot, 7 November 1867, *GEL,* 4:395. A number of writers have expressed unhappiness with the relative conservatism of Felix Holt's politics—most notably, perhaps, Raymond Williams. Williams contrasts the English radical William Cobbett's honesty in seeking reform and his sympathy for the working class with Felix's timidity and fear of the proletarian mob. Williams describes Eliot's mood in this novel as that of Thomas Carlyle's antidemocratic *Shooting Niagara* and Matthew Arnold's *Culture and Anarchy.* See Williams, *Culture and Society,* 105, 107. See also George Levine, "Introduction" to *Felix Holt, the Radical* (New York: W. W. Norton, 1970), who notes that "Felix Holt is no more a radical . . . than Barry Goldwater" (ix) A similar view of Eliot's "social-political conservatism" may be found in John Goode, "Adam Bede," in *Critical Essays on George Eliot,* ed. Barbara Hardy (New York: Barnes and Noble, 1970), in which Goode attributes the conservatism of Adam Bede to Riehl's *Natural History;* see 20–21.

Also of interest is Arnold Kettle's contrast between Transome's aristocratic manner and Holt's plebeian radicalism in his "'Felix Holt, the Radical,'" in *Critical Essays on George Eliot,* ed. Hardy, 102, 109. Less persuasive is Norman Vance's effort to attribute Eliot's view of landholding in *Felix Holt* to what was a genuinely radical chapter on that subject in Herbert Spencer's 1851 *Social Statics.* See Norman Vance, "Law, Religion, and the Unity of Felix Holt," in *George Eliot: Centennial Essays and an Unpublished Fragment,* ed. Anne Smith (Totowa, N.J.: Barnes and Noble, 1980), 106–07.

18. George Eliot, "Address to Workingmen, by Felix Holt" (1868), in *Essays,* 417.

19. Ibid., 418–21.

20. Ibid., 421–22.

21. Ibid., 422–24.

22. Ibid., 425–27.

23. Ibid., 425–29.

24. Ibid., 426, 429.

25. Quoted in *GEL,* 4:395n. Arnold was critical not only of Harrison, but (in Mill's case unfairly) of "men like Comte or the late Mr. Buckle, or Mr. Mill" as

enemies of culture and advocates of moral anarchy. See Matthew Arnold, *Culture and Anarchy* (1867; New York: Bobbs Merrill, 1971), 53–54.

26. George Eliot to Frederic Harrison, 7 November 1867, *GEL,* 4:395.

27. Hugh Witemeyer has written on the theory of the historical novel as practiced by Scott, Bulwer-Lytton, and Eliot in "George Eliot's *Romola* and Bulwer-Lytton's *Rienzi,*" *Studies in the Novel* 15, no. 1 (Spring 1983):62–71.

28. Quoted in G. H. Lewes, *Robespierre* (London: 1849), viii.

29. Ibid., 55, 190.

30. Ibid., 394–95.

31. Ibid., 313.

32. Ibid., 349. Given this derogatory portrait, it is difficult to comprehend James Scully's conclusion in his biographical article on Lewes in the eleventh edition of the *Encyclopaedia Britannica* (1910) that Lewes had made "an ingenious attempt to rehabilitate Robespierre" (16:520).

33. See Gordon S. Haight, *George Eliot: A Biography* (New York: Oxford University Press, 1968), 326. Avrom Fleishman sees the role of positivism in *Romola* rather differently in his *The English Historical Novel* (Baltimore: Johns Hopkins University Press, 1971), 155–63. So do J. B. Bullen in "George Eliot's *Romola* as Positivist Allegory," *Review of English Studies* 26 (1975):425–35; Myers, *Teaching of George Eliot,* 58–64; and Nancy L. Paxton, "Feminism and Positivism in George Eliot's *Romola,*" in *Nineteenth-Century Women Writers of the English-Speaking World,* ed. R. B. Nathan (New York: Greenwood Press, 1986), 143–150.

34. J. S. Mill, "On Liberty," in *Essays on Politics and Society,* in the *Collected Works,* ed. J. M. Robson (Toronto: University of Toronto Press, 1977), 18:238. A contemporary critic, R. H. Hutton, in an 1863 review in the *Spectator,* saw Eliot's "artistic purpose" not as depicting a pre-Reformation struggle for liberty but as an attempt "to trace out the conflict between liberal culture and the more passionate form of the Christian faith in that strange era which has so many points of resemblance with the present"; see Holmstrom and Lerner, eds., *George Eliot and Her Readers,* 57. (Eliot wrote Hutton that there was "nothing fanciful" in his view; see George Eliot to R. H. Hutton, 8 August 1863, *GEL,* 4:96–97.) In an 1879 essay in the *Edinburgh Review,* on the other hand, the conservative publicist W. H. Mallock noted that in Savonarola's efforts to convert Romola there was "hardly one appeal to Christianity on its supernatural side"; Mallock also noted that "Savonarola is the spokesman of Humanity made divine, not of Deity made human." See W. H. Mallock, "George Eliot," in *George Eliot: The Critical Heritage,* ed. David Carroll (New York: Barnes and Noble, 1971), 455.

George Levine has seen the confrontation between Romola and Savonarola as one "between public and personal ethics"; see George Levine, "'Romola' as Fable," in *Critical Essays on George Eliot,* ed. Hardy, 94. And a similar position has been presented in Laurence Poston III, "Setting and Theme in Romola," *Nineteenth-Century Fiction* 20 (1966):362.

35. George Henry Lewes to John Blackwood, 28 May 1861, *GEL,* 3:420.

36. Quoted in Haight, *George Eliot,* 351.

37. George Eliot to John Blackwood, 30 January 1877, *GEL,* 6:335–36.

38. J. S. Mill to Harriet Mill, 15 January 1855, in *The Later Letters of John Stuart Mill, 1849–1873,* ed. F. E. Mineka and D. N. Lindley, in *Collected Works,* 14:294.

39. J. S. Mill, "Utilitarianism," in *Essays on Ethics,* in *Collected Works,* 10:235, 238–39; see also Mill's "Auguste Comte and Positivism," 10:335–36.

40. Frederic Harrison, *George Eliot's Place in Literature* (London: Edward Arnold, 1895), 73.

41. George Eliot, "The Antigone and Its Moral" (1856), *Essays*, 262–63.

42. Ibid., 263–65.

43. Ibid., 265. Eliot is presented as a brilliant portrayer of the Creons of the ancien régime but a failure in dealing with Antigones (like Felix Holt, Ladislaw, and Deronda) in Linda Bamber, "Self Defeating Politics in George Eliot's *Felix Holt*," *Victorian Studies* 18 (1975):420–21. Bamber does not discuss Romola as an Antigone figure, but this does form part of the argument in Gerhard Joseph, "The *Antigone* as Cultural Touchstone: Matthew Arnold, Hegel, George Eliot, Virginia Woolf, and Margaret Drabble," *PMLA* 96 (1981):22–35.

44. George Eliot, "The Antigone and Its Moral," 265.

Chapter 4

1. Quoted in F. W. Hirst, *Early Life and Letters of John Morley*, 2 vols. (London: Macmillan, 1927), 1:177.

2. Ibid., 1:178.

3. Ibid., 1:187.

4. Ibid., 1:199.

5. Ibid., 1:178.

6. G. H. Lewes, "Comte," *Fortnightly Review* 4 (1 January 1866):404.

7. George Eliot to Mrs. Richard Congreve, 16 January 1867, *GEL*, 4:333.

8. See the exchange of letters between George Eliot and Herbert Spencer during this period, especially *GEL*, 8:42–45, 50–51, 56.

9. See Spencer, *Autobiography*, 2:123–30, 565–72. See also Sydney Eisen, "Herbert Spencer and the Spectre of Comte," *Journal of British Studies* 7, no. 1 (1967):48–67.

10. Spencer, *Autobiography*, 2:430–31. Nancy L. Paxton sees much of Eliot's writings and thinking as a reaction to Herbert Spencer's ideas—at times of submission to Spencer's views, at other times of confrontation with them. She describes (at times persuasively, though often in exaggerated terms) Spencer as a racist and male chauvinist. See Nancy L. Paxton, *George Eliot and Herbert Spencer; Feminism, Evolutionism, and the Reconstruction of Gender* (Princeton, N.J.: Princeton University Press, 1991), 118–21, 141–43, 210, 220. Another writer has described Spencer as "a powerful influence on that ideology which George Eliot transmuted into art"; see W. J. Harvey, "Idea and Image in the Novels of George Eliot," in *Critical Essays*, ed. Hardy, 155; see also 157–59. For a scattered but substantial treatment, see Myers, *The Teaching of George Eliot*, 4, 39, 56–57. None of these accounts deals with the influence of Spencer's politics.

11. Spencer, *Autobiography*, 1:458–59.

12. George Eliot to Mr. and Mrs. Charles Bray, 4 December 1849, *GEL*, 1:322.

13. G. H. Lewes, *Comte's Philosophy of the Sciences* (London: 1853), 1–2.

14. Ibid., 343.

15. Ibid., 11–12.

16. G. H. Lewes to H. D. Seymour, 13 January 1865, *GEL*, 8:330–32. The paper's prospectus, published in March, spoke of the *Fortnightly*'s intention of "aiding Progress in all directions as "one of tendency, not of doctrine," but curiously omitted a call to order; See *GEL*, 8:335–36.

17. Lewes, "Comte" (1866), 402.

18. Ibid., 404–05.

19. Ibid., 405.

20. Ibid., 410.

21. Ibid., 403.

22. G. H. Lewes, "Comte and Mill," *Fortnightly Review,* no. 34 (1 October 1866):385.

23. Ibid., 397–402.

24. Ibid., 403–04.

25. McCarthy, *Reminiscences,* 178–82; see also W. M. Simon, "Auguste Comte's English Disciples," *Victorian Studies* 7 (1964–65):161–72.

26. McCarthy, *Reminiscences,* 181–82.

27. Henry Collins and Chimen Abramsky, *Karl Marx and the British Labour Movement: Years of the First International* (London: Macmillan, 1965), 125.

28. Quoted in Collins and Abramsky, *Karl Marx,* 187.

29. E. S. Beesly, *Catiline, Clodius, and Tiberius* (London: Chapman and Hall, 1878), 2–3, 7, 16–17, 30, 35–37.

30. Ibid., 41–42, 82–83.

31. G. H. Lewes to E. S. Beesly, [9(?) May 1865], *GEL,* 8:338.

32. Anthony Trollope to G. H. Lewes, 1 June 1865, *GEL,* 8:342.

33. Richard Congreve, *Essays Political, Social, and Religious* (London: Longmans, Green, 1874), 110.

34. See E. S. Beesly, *The Sheffield Outrages and the Meeting at Exeter Hall: Two Letters* (London: E. Truelove, 1867), esp. 5–6, 11–12. For a discussion of the Sheffield outrages, see Sidney Webb and Beatrice Webb, *The History of Trade Unionism* (1894; London: Longmans Green, 1950), 259–61, 268–69; and Bernard Semmel, *Jamaican Blood and Victorian Conscience* (Boston: Houghton, Mifflin, 1963), 138–39. Also see George Eliot's letter (sympathetic to Beesly's defense of Broadhead though not to Broadhead's actions): George Eliot to Mrs. Charles Bray, 16 July 1867, *GEL,* 4:374 and n.

35. Congreve, "Mr. Broadhead and the Anonymous Press," in *Essays,* 165–75; esp. 165, 167, 169–70, 173.

36. George Eliot to Mrs. Richard Congreve, 28 July 1867, *GEL,* 4:378.

37. George Eliot to John Blackwood, 8 January 1868, *GEL,* 4:414.

38. Frederic Harrison, *The Political Function of the Working Classes: a Lecture Delivered at the Cleveland Street Institution, on March 25, 1868* (London: J. Kenny, 1868), 11.

39. Ibid., 5–7, 9–10.

40. Ibid., 15, 17.

41. E. S. Beesly to Karl Marx, 13 June 1871, in Royden Harrison, ed., *The English Defence of the Commune 1871* (London: Merlin Press, 1971), 16–17.

42. Frederic Harrison to John Morley, March 1871, in Harrison, ed., *English Defence,* 17–18.

43. Harrison's articles of May 1871 appears in Harrison, ed., *English Defence;* see esp. 169, 171.

44. Ibid., 187–89.

45. Ibid., 196–99.

46. Harrison, "The Fall of the Commune," August 1871, in Harrison, ed., *English Defence,* 202–25.

47. Ibid., 229–30.

48. Ibid., 232, 234–35.

49. Ibid., 121–30.

50. Herbert Spencer, *The Study of Sociology* (1873; New York: Appleton, 1886), 396–97.

51. Ibid., 397–99.

52. Viscount Samuel, *Memoirs* (London: Cresset Press, 1945), 18.

53. Morley, *Recollections,* 1:82.

54. John Morley, "Joseph de Maistre," in *Critical Miscellanies,* 2:329.

55. John Morley, *On Compromise* (1874; London: Macmillan, 1928), 185–86.

56. Ibid., 188–89.

57. Ibid., chap. 3.

58. Ibid., 4.

59. Ibid., 13–15.

60. Ibid., 30–35, 81–84.

61. George Eliot to John Sibree, 8 March 1848, *GEL,* 1:253–55. On Eliot's view that the nature of society made compromise necessary, see Thomas Pinney, "The Authority of the Past in George Eliot's Novels," *Nineteenth-Century Fiction* 21 (1966):131–47. A conception of *Middlemarch* as in good part a political novel may be found in B. G. Hornback, *Middlemarch: A Novel of Reform* (Boston: Twayne, 1988), 86–98. And, of course, I must refer again to J. F. Scott's argument about the influence of Frederic Harrison and positivism on *Middlemarch* in Scott, "George Eliot, Positivism, and the Social Vision of *Middlemarch.*" See also Jerome Beaty, "History by Indirection: The Era of Reform in *Middlemarch,*" *Victorian Studies* 1 (1957):173–79.

62. Gordon Haight has taken issue with Henry James's view of Lydgate as the "true hero" of *Middlemarch;* for Haight, the difference in social standing between a medical man like Lydgate, despite his aristocratic connections, and a lady in county society like Dorothea was not easily bridged, while Ladislaw, whom he sees as the true hero, was a gentleman despite certain shadows in his family's past. See Gordon S. Haight, "George Eliot's 'Eminent Failure,' Will Ladislaw," in *This Particular Web,* ed. Ian Adam (Toronto: University of Toronto Press, 1975), 36–37.

63. An unpersuasive view that an agnostic Eliot employed the figure of Saint Theresa ironically is made by F. E. Court, in "The Image of St. Theresa in *Middlemarch* and Positive Ethics," *Victorian Newsletter,* no. 63 (Spring 1983):21–25.

64. That Ladislaw is at least partially Jewish has been argued by Jerome Beaty, "The Forgotten Past of Will Ladislaw," *Nineteenth-Century Fiction* 13 (1958):159–63. R. A. Greenberg rejects this view in "The Heritage of Will Ladislaw," *Nineteenth-Century Fiction* 15 (1961):355–58. Greenberg's argument that public gossip rather than the true state of affairs has labeled Ladislaw a Jew is seconded by Pinney, "Another Note on the Forgotten Past of Will Ladislaw," 69–73.

65. George Eliot to Mrs. Nassau John Senior, May 1874, *GEL,* 4:46–47.

66. George Eliot to Charles Lee Lewes, 28 May 1880, *GEL,* 7:289.

67. Frederic Harrison to J. W. Cross, 6 May 1880, *GEL,* 7:271–72.

68. Frederic Harrison, *Memories and Thoughts* (London: Macmillan, 1906), 184; see also 293.

69. See George Eliot to Mrs. Richard Congreve, 10 June 1880, *GEL,* 7:296.

70. Cross, *George Eliot's Life,* 3:310–12.

71. Ibid., 3:316–19.

72. Ibid., 3:311–12.

73. George Eliot to Sara Hennell, 4 December 1880, *GEL,* 7:344.
74. Spencer, *Autobiography,* 2:429–30.

Chapter 5

1. George Eliot to Frederic Harrison, 15 August 1866, *GEL,* 4:301.
2. George Eliot to Mrs. Richard Congreve, 16 December 1868, *GEL,* 4:496.
3. Haight, *George Eliot,* 376n.
4. Quoted by D. N. Wilson, "Introduction," *Ivanhoe,* xix.
5. Victor Hugo, *Littérature et philosophie mêlées,* in *Oeuvres Complètes* (Paris: Albin Michel, 1934), 319; see also 320.
6. Eliot, "Three Novels" (1856), *Essays,* 326–28.
7. Cross, *George Eliot's Life,* 3:9–10. Eliot divided her drama into five books rather than into acts and scenes; the numbers after the quotations from *The Spanish Gypsy* refer to pages of the Warwickshire edition of *The Writings of George Eliot* (Boston: Houghton Mifflin, 1908), vol. 18.
8. Cross, *George Eliot's Life,* 3:11–14.
9. Frederic Harrison to George Eliot, 25 May [1868], *GEL,* 4:447–48.; and George Eliot to Frederic Harrison, [25 May 1868], *GEL,* 4:448.
10. Frederic Harrison to George Eliot, 11 November 1868, *GEL,* 4:483–84.
11. Ibid., 4:484–85.
12. Ibid., 4:485.
13. Frederic Harrison to George Eliot, 5 June 1869, *GEL,* 5:42.
14. George Eliot to Frederic Harrison, 6 June 1869, *GEL,* 5:43.
15. Leslie Stephen, *George Eliot* (London: Macmillan, 1902), 165–66.
16. John Morley, "The Spanish Gypsy," *Macmillan's Magazine* 18 (July 1868):281–87.
17. Frederic Harrison, *George Eliot's Place in Literature* (London: Edward Arnold, 1895), 73. William Baker notes that a philo-Semitic Lewes chose the part of Shylock for his first considerable theatrical performance; see William Baker, "George Eliot and Zionism," in *Daniel Deronda: A Centenary Symposium,* ed. Alice Shalvi (Jerusalem: Jerusalem Academic Press, 1976), 53.
18. Quoted in *GEL,* 6:413n.
19. See Edmund Wilson, *Patriotic Gore: Studies in the Literature of the American Civil War* (New York: Oxford University Press, 1966), 64.
20. For a discussion of Eliot's relationship with Judaism, see William Baker, *George Eliot and Judaism* (Salzburg, Germany: Institut für Englische Sprache und Literatur, Universität Salzburg, 1975).
21. George Eliot to Mrs. Charles Bray, 25 May 1845, *GEL,* 1:192–93.
22. George Eliot to Mary Sibree, 10 May 1847, *GEL,* 1:234–35.
23. George Eliot to John Sibree, 11 February 1848, *GEL,* 1:245–46.
24. Ibid., 1:246–47.
25. Ibid., 1:246.
26. George Eliot to Sara Hennell, 28 May 1853, *GEL,* 2:102.
27. See George Eliot to [Emanuel Deutsch], 7 July 1871, *GEL,* 5:160–61.
28. George Eliot to Mme. Eugène Bodichon, 16(?) November 1867, GEL, 4:399.
29. George Eliot to Emanuel Deutsch, 16 December 1867, *GEL,* 4:409; see also Morley, *Recollections,* 1:90.

30. George Eliot's Draft for John Chapman to James Martineau, 29 August 1851, *GEL*, 8:26–27.

31. Feuerbach described Judaism as "the most narrow-hearted egoism," and Jehovah as "nothing but the personified selfishness" of the Israelites; see Feuerbach, *Essence of Christianity*, 298, 113–14.

32. That Gwendolen's marriage is a form of prostitution is noted in Catherine Gallagher, "George Eliot and *Daniel Deronda*: The Prostitute and the Jewish Question," in *Sex, Politics, and Science in the Nineteenth-Century Novel* (Baltimore: Johns Hopkins University Press, 1986), 51–52.

33. George Eliot to John Blackwood, 25 February 1876, *GEL*, 6:223.

34. T. E. Kebbel, ed., *Selected Speeches of the Late Right Honourable The Earl of Beaconsfield*, 2 vols. (London: Longmans, Green, 1882), 2:555–617.

35. Ibid., 2:492, 512.

36. Ibid., 2:524, 527–29, 534–35.

37. George Eliot to Mr. and Mrs. Charles Bray, and Sara Hennell, 5 August 1849, *GEL*, 1:294.

38. George Eliot, *Impressions of Theophrastus Such* (1879; New York: Thomas Nelson, 1925), 265–66.

39. George Eliot to John Blackwood, 14 March 1873, *GEL*, 5:387.

40. George Eliot to Mme. Eugène Bodichon, [9] February 1874, *GEL*, 6:14.

41. George Eliot to John Blackwood, 20 February 1874, *GEL*, 6:21–22. I must note that J. S. Mill was also an opponent of the secret ballot as subversive of the moral responsibility of the voter; see Semmel, *John Stuart Mill*, 99–102. The Reverend Rufus Lyon, in *Felix Holt*, was an opponent of the ballot for these reasons.

42. George Eliot to François d'Albert-Durade, 1 August 1878, *GEL*, 7:47.

43. Moses Hess, "Rome and Jerusalem" (1862), in *The Zionist Idea: A Historical Analysis and Reader,* ed. A. Hertzberg (New York: Meridian Books, 1960), 117–34. See also Isaiah Berlin, *Against the Current: Essays in the History of Ideas* (London: Hogarth Press, 1979), 213–51. For the depiction of Deronda as "a prophet and a potentially world-historical hero" (in the Hegelian mode), see Sara M. Putzell-Korab, "The Role of the Prophet: The Rationality of Daniel Deronda's Idealist Mission," *Nineteenth-Century Fiction* 37, no. 2 (September 1982):170–87.

44. See Berlin, *Against the Current,* 246. Baker observes that there is no evidence that Eliot read Hess, but notes that another scholar, Harold Fisch, has pointed out the similarity of language betweeen Hess's Zionist work and Eliot's; see Baker, "George Eliot and Zionism," 58, and n30.

45. See Vogeler, *Frederic Harrison,* 62.

46. "Daniel Deronda," *Saturday Review* (16 September 1876), in Holmstrom and Lerner, eds., *George Eliot and Her Readers,* 145–46.

47. George Saintsbury, "Daniel Deronda," *Academy* (9 September 1876), in Holmstrom and Lerner, eds., *George Eliot,* 145–46.

48. Eliot, *Theophrastus Such,* 261.

49. Ibid., 260, 263–67.

50. Ibid., 265–68.

51. Ibid., 268–69.

52. Ibid., 274–75.

53. Ibid., 280–81.

54. Ibid., 278–79.

55. Ibid., 282.

56. Ibid., 276–78.

57. Ibid., 282.

58. Ibid., 289.

59. Ibid., 286, 288–90.

60. Ibid., 290, 292–93.

61. Ibid., 292.

62. Ibid., 283–86.

63. Ibid., 283–86.

Epilogue

1. Morley, *Recollections,* 16–17.

2. Morley, "George Eliot," in *Miscellanies,* 3:126–27, 130.

3. Ibid., 3:118.

4. Ibid., 130–32.

5. George Eliot, *Theophrastus Such,* 26, 33–34, 30, 39, 37.

6. Ibid., 261.

7. Acton, "George Eliot's Life," 464.

8. Herbert Paul, ed., *Letters of Lord Acton to Mary, Daughter of the Right Hon. W. E. Gladstone* (London: 1902), 60–61.

9. Frederic Harrison to George Eliot, 12 June 1877, *GEL,* 9: 194; see also Eliot's possible—and equivocal—reply: George Eliot to Frederic Harrison, 14 June 1877, *GEL,* 6:387–88.

10. George Eliot to Frederic Harrison, 15 January 1870, *GEL,* 5:76.

11. George Eliot to Frederic Harrison, 15 August [1866], *GEL,* 4:300.

12. George Eliot to Mrs. Peter Taylor, 18 July 1878, *GEL,* 7:44.

13. George Eliot to Clifford Allbutt, August 1868, *GEL,* 4:472.

14. F.W.H. Myers, *Essays—Modern* (London: Macmillan, 1883), 268–69.

15. Harrison, *George Eliot's Place in Literature,* 77–78.

16. George Eliot to Maria Lewis, [13 February 1840], *GEL,* 1:37.

17. George Eliot to John Blackwood, 7 February 1875, *GEL,* 6:123.

18. George Orwell, "My Country Right or Left" (1940), *The Collected Essays, Journalism and Letters of George Orwell,* 4 vols., ed. Sonia Orwell and Ian Angus (New York: Harcourt, Brace, 1968), 1:539–40. See also Peter Stansky and William Abrahams, *Orwell, the Transformation* (New York: Knopf, 1980); and W. J. West, ed., *Orwell, the War Broadcasts* (London: BBC/Duckworth, 1985).

19. Orwell, "Notes on the Way" (1940), *Collected Essays,* 2:17–18.

20. Orwell, "The Lion and the Unicorn: Socialism and the English Genius" (1940), *Collected Essays,* 2:57.

21. Orwell, "Notes on Nationalism" (1945), *Collected Essays,* 3:362.

22. Ibid., 3:375–76.

23. Sigmund Freud, *Civilization and Its Discontents* (1930; New York: Norton, 1962), 59; also see 49, 56–62.

24. Ibid., 61.

25. Orwell, "Review of J-P. Sartre's *Portrait of the Antisemite*" (1948), *Collected Essays,* 4:452–53.

26. Cynthia Ozick, "T. S. Eliot at 101," *New Yorker* (20 November 1989), pp. 119–28.

27. See Irving Howe, "An Exercise in Memory; Eliot and the Jews: A Per-

sonal Confession," *The New Republic,* 11 March 1991, p. 30; for the passage from the Virginia lectures, quoted by Howe, see T. S. Eliot, *After Strange Gods: A Primer of Modern Heresy* (New York: Harcourt, Brace, 1939), 20.

28. See Howe, "An Exercise in Memory," 29; see also Edward Alexander, "Correspondence," *The New Republic,* 8 April 1991, p. 6; and Edward Alexander, "George Eliot's Rabbi," *Commentary* 92 (July 1991):28–31.

29. T. S. Eliot, *After Strange Gods,* 12, 42, 44, 53.

30. Ibid., 17–18.

31. Ibid., 32.

32. Ibid., 57–58. In 1939 T. S. Eliot's *The Idea of a Christian Society* (1939; London: Faber, 1946) extended the arguments of his Virginia lectures, without specifically discussing the position of the Jews. Once again "Liberalism," and here also "Democracy," were the enemy, as are the views of the *"doctrinaire."* From liberalism, he wrote, there had come its opposite, an "authoritarian democracy" akin to such totalitarian states as Nazi Germany and Stalin's Russia. (Eliot even employed in this essay, and may have coined, the term "totalitarian democracy.") Once again he broached, although somewhat more critically, the ideal of a traditional local and/or national community. In this tract he invoked Coleridge and the Coleridgean idea of clerisy; indeed, the book itself may be seen as an updating of Coleridge's *Church and State.* At times Eliot seemed sympathetic to "the corporative state," not so much that of Mussolini but that of the program set forth in the Vatican's 1931 encyclical, *Quadrigesimo Anno,* as a model for a Christian Society (11–18, 21, 29–30, 35–36, 70). But the style is vague and elusive.

33. See T. S. Eliot, "The Literature of Politics," in *To Criticize the Critic* (New York: Farrar, Strauss & Giroux, 1965), 137–40, 142–44.

34. For Maurras's influence on T. S. Eliot, see *To Criticize the Critic,* 142–43; and Russell Kirk, *Eliot and His Age: T. S. Eliot's Moral Imagination in the Twentieth Century* (New York: Random House, 1971), 106, 161–62, 190, 317.

35. Nathan Gardels, "Two Concepts of Nationalism: An Interview with Isaiah Berlin," *New York Review of Books* 38, no. 19 (21 November 1991):19–20, 22–23.

36. Quoted in Friedrich Meinecke, *The German Catastrophe: Reflections and Recollections* (Boston: Beacon Press, 1950), 53; also see 75.

37. Julien Benda, *The Treason of the Intellectuals* (1928; New York: Norton, 1969). Benda, of Jewish background himself, made a special target of what he described as "a certain *Jewish nationalism*" (11–12).

Index